The Bible on Culture

FAITH AND CULTURES SERIES

An Orbis Series on Contextualizing Gospel and Church
General Editor: Robert J. Schreiter, C.PP.S.

The *Faith and Cultures Series* deals with questions that arise as Christian faith attempts to respond to its new global reality. For centuries Christianity and the church were identified with European cultures. Although the roots of Christian tradition lie deep in Semitic cultures and Africa, and although Asian influences on it are well documented, that original diversity was widely forgotten as the church took shape in the West.

Today, as the churches of the Americas, Asia, and Africa take their place alongside older churches of Mediterranean and North Atlantic cultures, they claim the right to express Christian faith in their own idioms, thought patterns, and cultures. To provide a forum for better understanding this process, the Orbis *Faith and Cultures Series* publishes books that illuminate the range of questions that arise from this global challenge.

Orbis and the *Faith and Cultures Series* General Editor invite the submission of manuscripts on relevant topics.

Also in the Series

FAITH AND CULTURES SERIES

The Bible on Culture

Belonging or Dissenting?

Lucien Legrand

ORBIS BOOKS

Maryknoll, New York 10545

The Catholic Foreign Mission Society of America (Maryknoll) recruits and trains people for overseas missionary service. Through Orbis Books, Maryknoll aims to foster the international dialogue that is essential to mission. The books published, however, reflect the opinions of their authors and are not meant to represent the official position of the Society. To obtain more information about Maryknoll and Orbis Books, please visit our website at www.maryknoll.org.

Published by Orbis Books, Maryknoll, New York, U.S.A.

Biblical citations in this volume are often Father Legrand's own translations from and paraphrases of texts in original biblical languages. Others are taken from standard modern language translations in European and Indian language editions. In general, Catholic systems of divisions into chapters and verses are used, and this will explain some few differences between Scripture references in this volume and standard Protestant critical editions and translations.

Abbreviations in notes and the bibliography follow the system of the Society of Biblical Literature. References to journals and reference works not found in the SBL list are given in full, except that *TOB* is used to abbreviate *Traduction Œcuménique de la Bible,* which was published in Paris by Éditions du Cerf-Société Biblique Française in 1988.

Manufactured in the United States of America.

Library of Congress Cataloging in Publication Data

Legrand, Lucien, 1927–
    The Bible on culture : belonging or dissenting / Lucien Legrand.
        p. cm. — (Faith and cultures series)
    Includes bibliographical references and indexes.
    ISBN 1-57075-330-X (pbk.)
        1. Bible—Social scientific criticism.   2. Religion and culture—Mediterranean Region—History.   I. Title.   II. Series.

    BS521.88.L44 2000
    220.9'5—dc21

                                                            00-058452

Contents

Foreword

Robert J. Schreiter, C.PP.S.

One can approach the question of the Bible and culture from a number of different vantage points. One can look at the Bible as a cultural document itself—or better, a series of cultural documents. Exegetes have traced the patterns of borrowing from other literatures, of the emendation and reshaping of texts in light of new circumstances, and the interpreting of old traditions in new ways. The Bible embraces a whole series of different cultures over several millennia, and one can see within those diverse times and places a whole range of possible cultural interactions.

Further, one can view the Bible as a producer of culture as well as a product of it. The New Testament itself is already a product of the cultural development in Israel over fifteen hundred years of history. The Jewish and Christian Scriptures went on to have a powerful influence on the developing cultures of Europe and the Mediterranean rim. In the nineteenth and twentieth centuries, missionary movements touched cultures beyond this geographic region in a dramatic way.

By the latter half of the twentieth century, Christians began to reflect much more directly on the meaning of culture in the formation of human persons and of the process of believing itself. The awareness of the importance of culture as mirrored in the Second Vatican Council's Pastoral Constitution *Gaudium et spes* (1965) is indicative of this. But it was the diversity of cultures in which Christianity found itself, together with the realization that it had become a world faith, a world church, that raised more pointedly the questions of the relation of faith and culture. Just how faith affected culture, and how culture affected faith, needed closer scrutiny than had been the case up to that time. The study of this complex interaction also needed a more profound theology of culture, that is, a way of understanding the scope and action of culture from a Christian perspective. Just how was a Christian to go about understanding and interacting with culture? How does one understand Christian identity in light of culture?

It was in the 1970s that the language of "inculturation" and "contextualization" came into being, prompted especially by the phenomenon of the world church, that is, the shapes Christian identity was taking in cultures that did not have a long history of Christianity. The categories of culture developed within the social sciences were still relatively unknown in theological and church circles. A great deal of activity was undertaken to meet these new challenges.

We are now a quarter of a century beyond those first soundings of the theme. We are considerably more aware of the complexities involved. It is also apparent that inculturation is not simply a task for the churches outside Europe and North America. The decline of Christianity, especially in Europe, can be seen as a failure to inculturate the Christian message in changing social and cultural circumstances. Even within the time of a quarter of a century, there is still no thoroughgoing theology of culture.

This book by Lucien Legrand addresses two of the major challenges that the understanding of faith and culture faces as we move into the twenty-first century. First, it gives a nuanced and sophisticated view of how key movements and figures within the Bible were enmeshed in the culture-making process. At times, movements reflected a kind of emergence out of a cultural complex. At other times, movements and figures within movements consciously set themselves apart from the surrounding culture in order to indict the culture or to produce something new. At still other points, cultures were absorbed into movements, either on a selective or a wholesale basis. What all of this points to is an extremely complex picture that does not admit of simple description. There is no biblical "culture," only an array of cultures in constant interaction. The voice of the Creator can be heard in the king and in the prophet, in the making of culture and in the critique of it. By looking at this range of possibilities, Legrand offers us a palette from which to paint a polychrome version of the world, yet also at times to draw stark contrasts. As Israel and then the church oscillated between tranquillity and crisis, this panoply of possibilities would be needed. By describing the variety to be found in the Bible, Legrand offers the resources for building a theology of culture that goes beyond dichotomies of either/or, for/against, or the only slightly more nuanced approaches found in H. Richard Niebuhr's much-read classic *Christ and Culture.* The title of the book is well chosen: it is about the Bible *on* culture. Although it is neither an exhaustive treatise on the subject chosen nor a completely developed theological reflection on culture, this book provides an indispensable resource for any future theology of culture.

A second contribution that Legrand makes to the larger discussion is most evident in the opening and the conclusion of the book, although there are references scattered throughout, especially relating his own experience as a missionary in India. This contribution is to the language of inculturation itself. He is quick to point up the shortcomings of this neologism, which sits well neither in theology nor in the social sciences. Although this has been known for a long time, what is especially helpful here is pointing out the poverty of the language of inculturation to describe the complex cultural interactions that Christians experience in their day-to-day living. At times these interactions are not taken seriously enough in the interest of protecting already existent forms of faith. Moreover, as Legrand repeatedly notes, this concern for culture is not just something for foreign missionaries or members of the so-called younger churches. By pointing to the interactions within the Bible, Legrand calls once again to mind that both culture and faith need to be understood in all their complexities.

Legrand's book will contribute significantly both to a theology of culture and to the continuing refining of the language of inculturation. For both of these things we need to be truly grateful.

Preface

This study started with a series of lectures I was invited to give in the Dioceses of Mananjary and Mahajunga, Madagascar, on the topic of "Inculturation in the Bible." They were further developed in postgraduate courses conducted by the Departments of Missiology and Biblical Studies in the Theology Faculties of Bangalore, India, and of Antananarivo, Madagascar.

The setting is not irrelevant. In the so-called mission countries, "inculturation" is an important concern. In those parts of the world, the gospel has been proclaimed, accepted, and is lived authentically. Yet there remains a certain uneasiness insofar as Christianity is perceived as foreign to the local culture. Attempts at "adaptation" were well meant, but they still looked like attempts to foist a foreign body into a reluctant organism. By giving its credentials to the local church, Vatican II put the question on the proper track. Faith in Jesus Christ is to be appropriated by each human group in its own way. Faith is not an extraneous element that has somehow to force or sneak its way into the soul and course of life of various people. It is a light poured by the Spirit in the hearts of individuals and societies. Its radiance comes from within and must be reflected in the various aspects of the mentality, life, manners, thought, arts, and culture of the local people.

The term "inculturation" has been a way to formulate the responsibility of each local church to give shape to the faith it lived. It has now become a topical subject. The word, originally coined by theologians,[1] entered the official ecclesiastical circles when it came into repeated use in the discussions of the 1977 Roman Synod on catechesis[2] and was proposed as a topic for special

---

[1] On the origins of the term "inculturation," see L. E. Espinosa, "Los primeros pasos de la Inculturación: De Lovaina a Roma," *Voces* 10 (1997): 133-151; N. Standaert, "L'histoire d'un néologisme: Le terme 'inculturation' dans les documents romains," *NRT* 110 (1988): 555-570; A. Quack, "Inculturation: An Anthropologist's Perspective," *Verbum SVD* 34 (1993): 3-17. P. Charles seems to have been the first to use the term in an article; see "Missiologie et Acculturation," *NRT* 75 (1953): 15-32, with reference to the anthropological study of Melville Herskovits. It was then adopted in the discussions of the twenty-ninth *Semaine de Missiologie* of Louvain in 1959 (published in *Mission et Cultures non-chrétiennes: Rapports et Compte-rendu de la XXIXe Semaine de Missiologie. Louvain 1959* [Bruges: Desclée de Brouwer, 1959]).

[2] "Notably by Cardinal Jaime Sin of Manila and by Jesuit superior general, Pedro Arrupe . . . Father Arrupe gave further currency to the term when he used it in his 1978 letter to Jesuits throughout the world" (E. Hillman, "Inculturation," in *The New Dictionary of Theology,* ed. J. A. Komonchak, M. Collins, and D. A. Lane [New York: M. Glazier, 1987], 512-513).

study to the Pontifical Biblical Commission.[3] It received the papal accolade in the encyclicals of Pope John Paul II *Catechesi Tradendae* on catechesis (Oct. 16, 1979) and *Redemptoris Missio* on the mission (Dec. 7, 1990), which devoted three lengthy paragraphs to the subject (§§52-54). Recently, it loomed large in the deliberations and in the documents of the Federation of Asian Bishops' Conference (FABC),[4] of the African Synod of 1994, and of the Asian Synod of 1998.

It was certainly an improvement on the previous terms "adaptation," "accommodation," and "indigenization." Built on the pattern of the word "incarnation," "inculturation" gave the missiological term a solid christological background. Yet, as I proceeded in my study, I found that the word could hardly fit with all the aspects of the biblical data. To start with, linguistics itself betrayed a certain inadequacy.[5] "Inculturation" refers to "culture," a term that belongs to anthropology. But anthropology knows of "acculturation" and "enculturation"; "inculturation" is not part of its word stock. We have therefore a pseudo-technical term, not recognized by the discipline it refers to. Theological language remains isolated in an area where it has taken the risk to venture. The failure of the grafting seems to point out to some latent incompatibility.

Actually each of the three semantic components of the word (in-culturation) is fraught with ambiguity.

1. The *in-* of *in-*culturation seems to imply a pure, disincarnated faith that would have to enter the concrete world of various cultures. But the message has never existed as pure *logos*. From the very beginning it has been word made material reality in creation and human flesh in incarnation. It has always taken culturally conditioned forms of expression in the course of history. This is why now the terms "interculturation" or "transculturation" have been proposed, but they too present their own difficulties. They evoke an external faith forcing its way into a certain culture and compelling it to accept the intrusion. This is no mere theoretical objection. Representatives of the great religions have actually objected to Christian attempts at "inculturation" and have denounced them as other forms of missionary aggressiveness. As guardians of

---

[3] "La session plénière tenue par la Commission Biblique Pontificale en Avril 1979, avait pour thème 'L'inculturation de la foi à la lumière de l'Ecriture'" (*Foi et Culture à la lumière de la Bible* [Turin: LDC, 1980], 9). On "inculturation" in the Bible, see the general bibliography following the preface.

[4] L. Nemet, "Inculturation in the FABC Documents," *East Asian Pastoral Review* 31 (1994): 77-94; S. Bevans, "Twenty Five Years of Inculturation in Asia: The Federation of Asian Bishops' Conference, 1970-1995," *FABC Papers* 78 (1997): 20-36.

[5] The *Oxford Dictionary* does not know the word "inculturation." "Inculture," rare and obsolete, has the sense of "want of culture or cultivation." The *Supplement* has "acculturation" in the sense of "adoption and assimilation of an alien culture" (I,13), "enculturation" ("culture inculcating its own values") (I,941), and "intercultural" (II,331).

their traditions, they are not happy to witness what they consider to be an encroachment by uninvited outsiders.[6]

2. *Culture,* the second component of the word "in-*cultur*-ation raises a double problem. There is first a problem of *definition*. What is culture? The word "culture" is heavily loaded with world visions conditioned by historical experiences and geographical settings. In my native Western world, culture took overtones of artistic refinement: a "cultured person" was expected to be "enlightened, polished, refined, urbane."[7] When I came to India, I entered a milieu in which culture was closely connected with religion and where the intercultural exchange often took the shape of interreligious dialogue. During a sabbatical stay in Africa, I found the question of "inculturation" put in terms of attitude toward traditional customs, including possibly polygamy[8] and even other ancestral practices, which non-Africans would have—maybe too easily—labeled as witchcraft.

As shown by K. Tanner, in the Western world itself, "culture" has had different connotations. In France it was "intimately connected from the first with issues of social control in an increasingly centralized state": culture was an ideal that unified an originally heterogeneous society but tended to do away with its plurality. In Germany, it had nationalistic overtones, being "what made the German people . . . a unified social body capable of contrast with other nation states": culture was what made Germany truly German. In Britain, it was a "principle of self-criticism" meant to make "something human out of the raw capacity, animal passions, and natural self will that modern life had unleashed": culture was what turned an uncouth boor into a gentleman.[9]

Presently culture is seen as a part of the anthropological field. No longer viewed as an ideal proposed by or enforced on a given society, it is taken as a "non evaluative, and context relative notion."[10] In other words, all human societies have cultures, but they vary from group to group. "The fact of 'culture'

---

[6] The Chinese theologian Kwok Pui-Lan speaks of "hermeneutical vandalism" and adds: "Out of respect for the integrality of other people's religious traditions, I do not wish to interpret their images from my own Christian perspectives" ("Gospel and Culture," in *Christianity and Crisis* 51 [1991]: 224, quoted by R. S. Sugirtharajah, "Introduction, and Some Thoughts on Asian Biblical Hermeneutics," *BibInt* 2 [1994]: 257).

[7] So says the Thesaurus of my computer!

[8] "Le thème-vedette (du Synode Africain) a été incontestablement celui de l'inculturation auquel se rattache notamment la proposition de l'institution d'une commission interdisciplinaire pour la réforme du modèle canonique du mariage afin qu'il prenne en considération les coutumes africaines en la matière . . ." (A. Vanneste, "Chronica," *ETL* 70 [1994]: 535). Cf. E. Hillman, *Polygamy Reconsidered* (Maryknoll, N.Y.: Orbis Books, 1975).

[9] K. Tanner, *Theories of Culture: A New Agenda for Theology* (Minneapolis: Fortress Press, 1997), 6-16 (quotations taken respectively from pp. 6, 9, 13).

[10] Ibid., 24.

is common to all; the *particular pattern* of culture differs among all."[11] However, anthropologists themselves are not quite clear about what constitutes culture. A standard explanation considers "culture" to be what is acquired in opposition to "nature," which would denote what is genetically innate. But this definition is less rigorous than it looks, since the borderline between genetic and acquired traits remains a moot scientific problem. Explaining culture as the product of life in society is equally ambiguous since "forms of social structure are as much the result of varying cultural influences as are the particular forms of economies, technologies, ideologies, arts, manners, and morals at different places. In short, specific human societies are more determined by culture than the reverse, even though some form of social life is a precondition of culture."[12] It is the problem of which is first, the chicken or the egg. With the anthropologists we can be satisfied with a descriptive definition comprising all kinds of learned behavior, "that complex whole which includes knowledge, belief, art, morals, law, custom, and any other capabilities and habits acquired by man as a member of society."[13] Put in terms of symbols, culture is "an historically transmitted pattern of meanings, embodied in symbols, a system of inherited conceptions expressed in symbolic forms by means of which men communicate, perpetuate, and develop their knowledge about and attitudes towards life."[14]

Another problem is that the "culture" implied in "in-*cultur*-ation" seems to be implicitly taken in the singular. In the present context of "globalization," cultures crisscross each other in any given place. This is not a new phenomenon. The Mediterranean world of the early church was already a "global village." Paul, the Jew from Tarsus in Cilicia, is a typical but not isolated case. The broad term *Hellenism* is an umbrella that covers a great variety of subcultures.

This pluralism includes conflicting forces. Cultures are not consistent wholes. The apparent consensus of a given culture hides internal struggles for power and domination. A dominant culture is too often the privilege of the dominating classes of a society. Vast sections of the population are left deprived of the benefits of this "culture." Either they remain voiceless and marginalized or they give expression to their protest through subcultures and countercultures which the dominant "culture" will try to silence by open or covert violence. The point has been developed in the context of "conflict soci-

---

[11] J. Bennett and M. Tumin, *Social Life* (New York: Knopf, 1948), 209.

[12] A. L. Kroeber, *Anthropology* (New York: Harcourt, Brace & World, 1948), 10.

[13] E. B. Tylor, *Primitive Culture* (London, 1913), 1:1, quoted by M. Dhavamony, "The Christian Theology of Inculturation," *StMis* 44 (1995): 5.

[14] Clifford Geerts, *The Interpretation of Cultures* (New York: Basic Books, 1973), 89 (also quoted by Dhavamony, "Christian Theology," 6). Jules Gritti distinguishes two levels of "culture": the practical, tangible, and observable level of customs, techniques, forms of initiation and the symbolic level of traditions, rites, myths, and languages (*L'Expression de la Foi dans les Cultures Humaines* [Paris: Centurion, 1975], 13). A third level might be added, that of the values, of what is considered to be important.

ologies" inspired by Max Weber and Karl Marx. Culture and "inculturation" may not always be as noble as they seem.[15]

3. The third semantic element implied in inculturation is the ending -*ation,* which, says the *Oxford Dictionary* "forms nouns of action." This ending supposes a deliberate activity. Now, in most cases and at the deepest level, cultural influence will be more imbibed than deliberately induced. Cultural forms are rarely produced artificially. They more commonly emerge from the soil, from society, and from history and come to existence without deliberate human intent.

Aware of those problems, theologians have gone in search of other categories. They speak of "contextualization" or "incarnation." But those words also have their shortcomings.[16]

Contextualization follows the model of hermeneutic theology and substitutes an inductive for a deductive method. Concretely, it keeps the discussion open to liberation perspectives since they belong very much to the "context." Will the new term meet with lasting assent? It is not sure. Heavy and abstract, it will repel those who dream of poetical or narrative theology. In the wake of hermeneutics, "contextualization" views reality as a "text" to be deciphered. This can be a satisfactory construction to the intellect, but it is rather dry fare to chew. Life can hardly be reduced to script.

The word "incarnation" has also been proposed. It is flawless, consecrated by tradition and sanctified by its application to the central mystery of Jesus Christ. But therein lies an ambiguity. It is true that the Christian economy is entirely marked by God's manifestation in the Word made flesh. But this does not mean that the word "incarnation" can apply to every facet of Christian existence. This would make theological precision impossible. The incarnation of the Word is unique, and there can arise only confusion if the same term is applied indiscriminately to other aspects of Christian life.

It is the noble but arduous task of systematic theologians to conceptualize the faith message of the Bible. While recognizing the validity of their endeavor, we can but sympathize with their frustrations as they keep on

---

[15] Cf. J. Dupuis, "Méthode théologique et théologies locales: adaptation, inculturation, contextualisation," *Seminarium* 32/1 (1992): 68-69. A typical instance is the *Dalit* problem in India. The *Dalit,* or outcastes, cannot identify with the Hindu culture that marginalizes them. Similarly, the Dravidian south opposes the "sanskritization" coming from the north. Inculturation in India cannot be reduced to "brahminization."

[16] On theological investigations concerning inculturation, see L. J. Luzbetak, *The Church and Cultures* (Maryknoll, N.Y.: Orbis Books 1988); David J. Bosch, *Transforming Mission: Paradigm Shifts in Theology of Mission* (Maryknoll, N.Y.: Orbis Books 1991), 420-431, 447-456. As noted by G. Gispert-Sauch in his appreciative review of Bosch's book in *Vidyajyoti* 56 (1992): 623-625, a "rich missiological tradition in India . . . is not sufficiently reflected" in foreign surveys. See Felix Wilfred, *Sunset in the East?* (Madras: University of Madras, 1993) and the various papers of the great Indian exegete G. M. Soares-Prabhu, collected in the edition of his complete writings, vol. 1, *Biblical Themes for a Contextual Theology Today* (Pune: Jnana-Deepa Vidyapeeth, 1999).

- Biblical theological approach
- Inculturation

searching for conceptual precision in a world of fast-changing speculative paradigms.

The task of biblical theology is different. It is more analytic. It takes into account the rich variety of the biblical text at different times, in different circumstances. It is not merely descriptive or it would not be theology. As theology, it attempts to make sense of the baffling variety of facts. But, before it tries to organize its faith perception, it takes time to go slowly through the evidence without having immediately to pin its observations on leading key concepts. As much as possible we must allow the biblical history to speak for itself and tell us of the different ways in which the people of the Bible adjusted and reacted to their surroundings, in the light of their faith, in various ways, at different times and in diverse settings and circumstances.

The Biblical Commission sensed the difficulty of steering the biblical message through the hazards of systematic conceptualization. Though the topic assigned to its members was "The inculturation of faith in the light of the Scriptures," they preferred to entitle their report "Faith and Culture in the Light of the Bible."[17] Such will be also the approach of the present study. It will keep free from too narrow a focus on "inculturation," the better to take into account the various forms of interrelationship that can exist between the biblical message and the surrounding cultures. It may seem presumptuous to compete with a work done by such a scholarly and authoritative Areopagus. The only excuse is that the Biblical Commission worked as a commission and produced a set of papers which, though linked by a converging interest, remained a loosely connected collection. A more unified survey remains possible.

Covering the entire biblical field would be an enormous task: we can only propose soundings. Hopefully they will show enough variety to be sufficiently representative. For the Old Testament, we shall examine the times of beginnings of Israel in Canaan, the royal period, and the important encounter with Hellenism in the last centuries B.C.E. New Testament times are shorter. Yet they present the contrast of two very different incarnations of the message, those of Jesus the Galilean and of the Church of the Nations.

A double observation to conclude. When looking at the attitude of the Bible toward culture, it should not be in view of finding models that could be copied and applied directly to the different situations of today's churches. The Bible is not a book of recipes but the record of the trajectories of the Spirit, a Spirit that remains always completely free and unpredictable. "Those who believe in me will do greater things still" (John 14:12): we cannot foresee where the Spirit will lead us. But the Bible will at least put us on the right track.

The last point goes without saying. And yet . . . for too long a time, the problem of "inculturation" has been considered a problem of the "young

---

[17] *Foi et Culture* (see n. 3 above).

churches" belonging to the "Third World." It was viewed therefore as a rather secondary subsection of that hybrid theological discipline called missiology. This is a strange perception. Culture belongs to all humankind. Cultural mutations and crises are not proper to Asia and Africa. By giving more attention to the problem, Third World theologies are ahead of what is still considered mainstream theology. Let this mainstream theology take note of what is happening elsewhere if it is not to become a backwater left behind by the fast flow of today's developments. It has begun to pay attention to liberation theology, coming from South America. Africa and Asia have some other pages to proffer to the world theological agenda. Western theology may have to take a leaf out of this agenda and learn from it to face its own acute problems of cultural crisis.[18] This is not just a "missiological" task but the plain duty of any theology in the momentous upheavals that we witness at the turn of the millennium.

---

[18] It has begun to do so; see the survey presented by Tanner, *Theories of Culture,* 61-69.

Part One

Israel and the Nations

The attitude of biblical Israel toward surrounding cultures presents a rich field of observation. Its history covers a long period of time, going back to the second millennium B.C.E. Its geographical range extends over a good part of the Eurasian continent, from Greece and Rome in the west to Iran and even India in the east (Est. 1:1; 3:13; 8:9, 12). In Africa it comprises Egypt and Sudan down to Ethiopia. In this vast span of time and space, it meets with a great variety of anthropological, socioeconomic, and political situations. Its interaction with native and alien cultures was manifold.

The field is vast. To cover it in its entirety would amount to a general introduction to the Old Testament. The few soundings proposed here may be sufficiently representative at least to provide a few basic orientations.

1

Israel and Canaan

*Your origin and your birth were in the land of the Canaanites; your
father was an Amorite and your mother a Hittite. (Ezek. 16:3)*

*You shall annihilate them, the Hittites, the Amorites, the Canaanites, the
Perizzites, the Hivites and the Jebusites . . . so that they may not teach
you the abhorrent things that they do for their gods. (Deut. 20:16-18)*

These two antithetic texts expose the ambivalent attitude of the Israelites
toward the land in which they lived. On the one hand, the text of Deuteronomy 20:16ff. describes an attitude of radical confrontation in the context of
a chapter dedicated to the "Holy War." On the other hand, the Israelites are
reminded of their deep roots in the land, even if those roots may not have
always been glorious.

It is not easy to account historically for the complex relationship that
linked Israel with the native population globally designated as "Canaanites."
Their civilization is well known through both ancient writers[1] and modern
archeological discoveries (Byblos, Ugarit, Ebla, etc.). Yet it cannot be said
that certainty has been reached as regards the encounter of the Hebrews with
the Canaanites.

The settlement of the tribes of Israel in Canaan is certainly one of the
most difficult questions of historical research in biblical matters. During
the last few years, quite a number of studies have been devoted to that
question. But it can hardly be said that a consensus has been reached.[2]

The biblical data themselves are complex and open to several interpretations. In their attempts to reconstitute the historical beginnings of Israel as a

---

[1] See the long list of ancient (Egyptian, Mesopotamian, biblical, Greek, and Phoenician)
sources in B. Peckham, "Phoenicia, History of," *ABD,* 5:349-355.

[2] J. Briend, "Israel et les Gabaonites," in *La Protohistoire d'Israel,* ed. E. M. Laperrousaz
(Paris: Cerf, 1990), 121.

people, scholars follow different models.[3] The standard explanation based on Joshua 1-12 supposes a *conquest* of Canaan by tribes coming from the Sinai peninsula via Transjordan. Giving more importance to Judges 1-2, other authors have proposed *a gradual process of immigration* of poor desert tribes lured by the rich farmlands of Canaan. More recently, a sociological model has been proposed by G. E. Mendenhall and N. K. Gottwald.[4] The Hebrew movement would have been essentially a *peasants' revolt*, the rising of a landless proletariate against the landowners and their sociopolitical and religious system. Still more radical is the recent reconstruction of N. P. Lemche.[5] According to this hypothesis, the Israelites would be Yahwistic Canaanites. More precisely, "Canaanites" would be the term used in late Yahwistic literature to express the opposite of what Israel stood for. The term "Canaan" would serve as a foil, symbolizing what the Israelites rejected in the culture of the world from which they issued and to which they belonged.

The debate goes on and this is not the place to go into the merits and demerits of the various positions. Insofar as relation with culture is concerned, it should be noted that the first two models view Israel as a foreign body entering Canaan and suppose an encounter between two alien cultures. The other two models view the emergence of Israel from within the native Palestinian population and give more emphasis to the continuity within a Northwest Semitic cultural entity.

While emphasizing one or the other aspect, any model has to take into account the opposite pole of the cultural interrelationship. Those who think of a penetration of Israel as an outside group have to reckon with reciprocal ethnic and cultural Canaanite infiltrations. Vice versa, models of internal evolution or revolution acknowledge disruptions in the process. They speak of "displaced Canaanites, both geographically and ideologically."[6] They often concede the external input of a "Moses or Exodus group" that did come from Egypt and "provided the key catalytic ingredients for the creation of Israel."[7]

Present-day scholarship is now better equipped to situate the emergence of Israel in Canaan in the "exceedingly complex set of socio-economic, cultural, and political changes on the LB-Iron I horizon in the Levant, with many regional variations."[8] This general perspective and the archaeological

---

[3] See a summary of the main positions in A. R. Ceresko, *The Old Testament: A Liberation Perspective* (Maryknoll, N.Y.: Orbis Books, 1992), 118-128.

[4] G. E. Mendenhall, *The Tenth Generation: The Origins of the Biblical Tradition* (Baltimore: Johns Hopkins University Press, 1973); N. K. Gottwald, *The Tribes of Yahweh. A Sociology of the Religion of Liberated Israel 1250–1050 B.C.E.* (Maryknoll, N.Y.: Orbis Books, 1979).

[5] N. P. Lemche, *Early Israel: Anthropological and Historical Studies on the Israelite Society before the Monarchy,* VTSup 7 (Leiden: Brill, 1985).

[6] W. G. Dever, "Ceramics, Ethnicity, and the Question of Israel's Origins," *BA* 58 (1995): 207.

[7] Ceresko, *Old Testament: A Liberation Perspective,* 125.

[8] See W. G. Dever, "Israel, History of (Archeology and the Conquest)," in *ABD* 3:549-553, who insists: "It cannot be stated too categorically: the emergence of Israel in Canaan was not

data point to a strong continuity between the presumably Israelite villages of the First Iron Age and the material culture of Canaanite Late Bronze Age. Yet there was newness in "the combination and adaptation of existing cultural elements—such as the courtyard houses, silos, and terrace agriculture—with a few novel elements."[9]

The emergence of Israel is to be situated in the context of the cultural crisis that marked the transition from the Late Bronze Age to the Iron Age in Canaan, toward the thirteenth century B.C.E. The Amarna Letters testify to the weakening of the Egyptian shield over the Palestinian city-states, which entered a period of decadence.

> The end of the Late Bronze Age in Canaan came less with a bang than with a whimper . . . The archeological record is often uncertain . . . but we get the impression that the lessening of Egyptian control was a slow and gradual one . . . Life became markedly different. Previous affluent Canaanite merchants were unable to maintain the high standard of living they had come to enjoy. No longer could they barter for the exotic products of distant lands or commission craftsmen . . . A much different flavor began to pervade the cities and towns. Roadways were empty of the pharaoh's messengers, tinkers from Hatti, and Cretan artisans enjoying the travels of their trade . . . The once prosperous seaports ceased to ring with the cacophony of bantering Canaanite longshoremen, Cypriot sailors, and Aegean seamen.[10]

---

an isolated, 'unique' event, but rather an integral (albeit small) part of a gradual, exceedingly complex set of socio-economic, cultural, and political changes on the LB-Iron I horizon of Palestine and cannot be understood apart from the larger context of that history" (p. 551). In addition to the complexity of the textual and archaeological data, there is also the intricate question of the anthropological model implicitly or explicitly adopted in retracing proto-Israelite society. The term "tribe" is exceedingly ambiguous, being applied to such different realities as the nomads of the Arabian or Sahara deserts, little Amazonian groups living in prehistoric conditions and the well-organized and highly developed states of northeast India. The recent conflicts in Central Africa, not to speak of Kosovo, Timor, and Chechnya, have projected a tragic image of the complex socioeconomic, ethnic, and religious factors covered by the catchall term "tribe." They raise also the question of why some of those conflicts get the qualification of "tribal" while others do not. See a critical study of the usual anthropological models in Gottwald, *Tribes of Yahweh*, 294-298, 355-367; and especially N. P. Lemche, "Israel, History of (Premonarchical Period)," *ABD* 3:531-533.

[9] "There is nothing in the material remains to suggest that these are 'pastoral nomads settling down'—on the contrary, they appear to be skilled and well-adapted peasant farmers, long familiar with local conditions in Canaan. What is 'new' is simply the combination and adaptation of existing cultural elements—such as the courtyard houses, silos, and terrace agriculture—with a few novel elements. This distinctive 'hybrid' material culture served as the basis for the agricultural settlement of the hill country and the emergence of a distinctive new social order, as well as, in all probability, a new ethnic identity and solidarity. Nevertheless, the overall cultural traditions of these Iron I villages show rather strong continuity with LB Age Canaan, especially in the pottery" (Dever, "Israel," 551). The article proceeds with a more elaborate description of the elements of continuity (p. 551) and discontinuity (p. 552) between the two periods.

[10] A. Leonard, Jr., "The Late Bronze Age," *BA* 52, no. 1 (1989): 34-35.

At the same time, coinciding with the decline or destruction of urban centers, a number of unwalled villages appear in the hills of central Canaan.

Whatever the cause or causes of the breakdown of Late Bronze Age culture, the archeological record is clear: a major shift of population, or "in"-migration, and the settlement of the Central Highlands.[11]

The neologism of *"in"-migration* is interesting. It expresses the dual antithetic aspects of belonging ("in-") and otherness ("migration") found in the new rural settlements and their emerging culture.

Confrontation and connaturality are indeed two complementary facets of the Israelite cultural stance. If Israel expressed its identity in terms of opposition to the "Canaanites," they did it from within a common stock of shared cultural environment.

CULTURAL CONFRONTATION

Whichever scenario we adopt, whether the Israelites came from within or without Canaanite society, they developed their self-awareness in opposition to the dominant culture. This opposition found its most violent expression in the theme of the Holy War (Deut. 7:1-5; cf. 13:16-18; 20:12-15).[12] The *herem*, or interdict, vowed the conquered cities to total destruction "lest they teach you the abhorrent things that they do for their gods" (Deut. 20:18). This brutality is illustrated by the destruction of Jericho (Josh. 6:24, 26), of Ai (Josh. 8:24-25, 28), of the southern (Josh. 10:28, 30, 32, 34, 37, 39f.) and northern cities (11:11-15).

At first sight, the violence of Israel's hostility is shocking and its uncompromising indictment of Baalism seems to verge on fanaticism. Apologetic considerations can legitimately be brought to bear on the issue. It is true, for instance, that it would be anachronistic to apply to such statements and

---

[11] A. R. Ceresko, "Potsherds and Pioneers: Recent Research on the Origins of Israel," *Indian Theological Studies* 34 (1997): 11. Following a clue given by J. A. Callaway ("A Visit with Ahilud: A Revealing Look at Village Life when Israel First Settled the Promised Land," *BAR* 9 [1983]: 43-44), and along the lines of the internal migration model, Ceresko goes on to give a lively description of the life of a certain Ahilud, whose name has in fact appeared on the handle of a jar excavated at Raddana, twenty kilometers north of Jerusalem. He had inherited the agricultural skills of his native Canaan (pp. 9, 13). He shared also in its "traditional beliefs and practices" especially those connected with the survival of the family (p. 13). Yet the new socioeconomic setting and the influence of the Moses group to which the "in-migrants" associated themselves led them to a new social organization and new religious symbols and perceptions.

[12] From the seminal works of G. Von Rad, *Der Heilige Krieg im alten Israel,* AThANT 20 (Zurich: Theologischer Verlag, 1951) and R. Smend, *Jahwehkrieg und Stämmebund,* FRLANT 94 (Göttingen: Vandenhoeck & Ruprecht, 1972) to the recent monograph of A. Van der Lingen, *Les Guerres de Yahvé,* LD 139 (Paris: Cerf, 1990).

actions modern norms of political ethics, themselves so very fragile that every recent conflict has seen their collapse. Also and mainly, as mentioned earlier, scholars are quite skeptical about the scenario of an Israelite conquest of Canaan by a military campaign. Commentators notice also the standardized formulation of the narratives concerning the *herem* of Jericho in Joshua 10 and their disagreement with the data of archaeology. They conclude that those accounts belong to a later layer of redaction. The background is no longer the settlement in Canaan but the crisis that went along with the Assyrian invasions of the eighth and seventh centuries and the fall of Samaria. By that time, the remnants of Israel had shriveled to the dimensions of the diminutive kingdom of Judah. The rhythmic incantations of the deuteronomistic accounts reflect more the mood of defiance of a later prophetic movement than the actual practice of earlier days. Prophets could be all the more radical in their statements, since there was no human prospect that their vision would ever be translated into real policy and that they would have to face the human shape of their oracles.

What those texts did express is that Israel came to realize the specificity and incompatibility of their religious perspectives with those of the "Amorites and the Canaanites." This religious vision was no abstract theology. The opposition of Israel to Canaan was no mere "war of religion." It was not simply one religion facing another. The conflict was cultural; it implied all the economic, social, political, and religious dimensions of a culture. Another civilization faced the city-states. This political conflict implied a clash of totally opposite conceptions of society, of clan egalitarianism versus a hierarchical establishment, of mutual justice against royal absolutism, of covenant solidarity instead of a tight administrative structure, of concern for the poor rather than the imperatives of production and the preservation of social stability.

Religious opposition belonged to that context. The God of the Hebrews was very different from the Canaanite deities. It was "a God of the people rather than the god of a city or the god of a holy place or the god of natural processes."[13] He stood not for the rich variety of the forces of nature but for a people's desperate struggle for freedom. As against the deification of the royal power, the recognition of a unique, transcendent, and just God constituted a claim of autonomy against unlimited absolutism. Even if a king were to come, he would have to recognize his vassalage to God and "to read the law of the Lord every day of his life that he might learn to fear the Lord . . . and not become estranged from his countrymen through pride, nor turn aside . . . from these commandments" (Deut. 17:19f.). As against the deification of the forces of nature and the fertility cults, acknowledging the one God as Lord of the universe amounted to claiming an area of freedom from those forces of nature and from the false absolutes of fertility and economic pro-

---

[13] Gottwald, *Tribes of Yahweh,* 685.

ductivity. This was also the signification of the Sabbath: it was meant to recall the liberation from the old slavery (Deut. 5:15). If there is a God who is above the forces of nature, there is more to human existence than drudging enslavement to the soil and its owners. If earthly powers and cosmic forces are not the ultimate realities and if there is a God that transcends socioeconomic and political forces, there is an area of freedom left to humankind. The poor have a recourse beyond kings and economic necessities; the oppressed and marginalized can look beyond the heels that crush them. When the heavens are kept open, it is hoped also that it is left open. The so-called Ten Commandments are rather the ten points of the charter of freedom given to the covenanted people. They begin with a reminder of the liberation from Egypt: "I am the Lord thy God who has brought thee out of Egypt, the place of slavery" (Exod. 20:2; Deut. 5:6). The rest is given as guidelines to keep open the area of freedom and solidarity thus granted to the former slaves.

All this would call for more elaborate analyses, which have already been made in the abundant exegetical literature concerning the Holy War and its various aspects. What is clear is that Israel found and expressed its identity by rejecting the world and religious vision of the surrounding world, its conception of society and economic structures. "Canaan" played the role of "foil, that is (of) a model embodying those things which they especially wished to avoid."[14] This struggle cannot be explained away by lenient apologetic considerations. But neither can it be reduced to "fanaticism" or to "Semitic exclusivism." It was neither a purely ideological conflict nor a matter of temperamental "Semitic" aggressiveness somehow concealed in the genes of a particular race. The violence of the conflict reveals its depth, and it is to the credit of liberational exegesis to have shown the rich complexity of the situation. The Hebrew slaves fought not only for their existence or for their "religion" but for their identity. This does not make them a model to be imitated in any circumstances, but it does give them an abiding significance for all the human struggles for freedom, dignity, and authenticity. Not as an example to be reduplicated but as "a powerful, evocative religious symbol,"[15] the struggle of Israel stands as a lesson for the ages to come.

CULTURAL CONNATURALITY

Scholars who think that the Israelites issued from the Canaanite world have to explain the disruption that alienated them from their origins. Reciprocally, those who opt for an extraneous origin must reckon with the deep and far-reaching affinities of Israel with Canaan. Even if Israel came from

---

[14] Ceresko, "Potsherds and Pioneers," 19-20.
[15] Gottwald, *Tribes of Yahweh,* 705.

outside, it did not settle as a foreign implant as, say, the International Concessions of Shanghai and other "cantonments" in the colonial ages. By acculturation if they came from outside, or simply by the very fact that they were "sons of the soil," the Israelites shared with the Canaanites the basic realities of land and language.

THE LAND

The realities of the soil were those of the eastern Mediterranean world, of its geography between sea and desert, of its geology, climate, orography, and hydrography. The outcome is a certain type of agriculture, of flora and fauna. The typical stereotype of "every one living in security under his vine or under his fig tree from Dan to Beer Sheba" (1 Kgs. 4:25), "eating of his own vine and of his own fig tree, and drinking the water of his own cistern" (2 Kgs. 18:31; cf. Micah 4:4; Zech. 3:10; 1 Macc. 14:12) is as "Canaanite" as "biblical." The geographical setting determined also a succession of seasons and of seasonal activities, a calendar of feasts of harvest, vintage, and New Year that imposed its rhythm to collective, familial, and individual life.

LANGUAGE

Of particular importance in this process of interaction is the question of *language* and the fact that "Hebrew was (just) another significant dialect of Canaanite."[16] For all their divergences, Hebrews and Canaanites partook together of a common stock of language and world vision. Language is no mere indifferent labeling of abstract realities. It is the fruit of a culture. It carries the sap of the culture from which it stems. It is the vehicle of a world vision, of an implicit system of values, of a latent but living memory giving words their intensity and metaphorical potency. Sharing in a common language means sharing in the very same soul of a culture and of a people.

SOCIAL LIFE

It was in the area of social life that Israel presented the most radical departure from the surrounding societies. Yet the contrast should not be reduced to a caricature. Israel belonged to a world that had developed an elaborate jurisprudence. Archaeology has brought out an impressive collection of ancient law codes of western Asia, Sumerian laws of Ur-Nammu (ca. 2050 B.C.E.), of Eshnunna and Lipit-Ishtar (towards 1950 B.C.E.), the Babylonian Code of Hammurapi (CH) (eighteenth century), Hittite Laws (HL) and Assyrian laws (AL) of the fifteenth century. Legal codes are highly significant. They represent a concern for justice and constitute a barrier against

---

[16] M. Noth, *The Old Testament World* (London: Adam & Charles Black, 1966), 226.

both anarchy and arbitrary absolutism. The Hebrew laws are part of this attempt to bring equity in human dealings and relationships. Commentators have noted the many parallels between the ancient laws and the Hebrew codes of the Pentateuch (Book of the Covenant in Exod. 20:22-23:19; Deuteronomic Code in Deut. 12-26; Holiness Code of Lev. 17-26). Ancient codes and Hebrew laws show a similar concern for the same problems often treated in identical terms: family problems (firstborn rights, dowries, incest, adultery), questions of sorcery (Exod. 22:17 = CH 2), of false weights (Lev. 19:36; Deut. 25:13-15 = CH 108), of boundary stones (Deut. 19:14; 27:17 = AL B 7-9; HL 168f.). Problems of cattle are frequent: cattle can be lost (Deut. 2:1 = HL 45) or stolen (Exod. 22:10 = HL 57-70); they trespass in others' land (Exod. 22:4f. = HL 98f.; 105ff.), injure passers-by (Exod. 21:28-32, 35f. = CH 250ff.). Both sides imposed the limits of equal retaliation on ferocious vendettas (Exod. 21:23ff. = HL 196f., 200, 214), etc.[17]

Differences are not lacking. For instance, the Hebrew codes do not have the elaborate Mesopotamian legislation on craftsmen, professions, merchants, adoptions . . . and wet nurses (Eshnunna 32; HL 194). Hebrew society might not yet have known such specialization and its consequent societal cleavage. The Covenant Code does not know of physical mutilation as a form of punishment, such as the cutting of the tongue (CH 192), of the ear (CH 205), of the hand (CH 218, 226, 253), the plucking of the eye (CH 193), forms of castigation which seem to have been generously distributed in Mesopotamia. Still more significantly, the Hebrew codes do not go by the hierarchical treatment attributing graded forms of penalty according to the social rank of the offender and of the victim. Thus, an injury to the eye was worth the eye of the offender if the victim was a member of the aristocracy, but just one mina of silver if the victim belonged to the commoners. If it was a slave who had lost his eye, it was the master of the slave who was to get the compensation of half the commercial value of the victim (CH 196, 198f.). By contrast, the Bible did not see any difference between nobility and commoners. If a slave had been the victim of an injury, he was to be set free, even if he had just lost a tooth (Exod. 21:28f.).[18] In Mesopotamia the slave was considered to be chattel; the loss was his master's. In Israel, the slave was a person; he had personal rights.

Perhaps the most striking difference between these (Mesopotamian) laws and those of Israel is the preponderance of laws dealing with prop-

---

[17] An elaborate list of parallels can be found in S. Greengus, "Law," *ABD* 4:245-251; idem, "Law in the Old Testament," *IDBSup,* 533-534.

[18] See L. Epsztein, *Social Justice in the Ancient Near East and the People of the Bible* (London: SCM Press, 1986), 104-134; V. P. Hamilton, *Handbook on the Pentateuch* (Grand Rapids: Baker Book House, 1982), 218-221. On the specific point of the position of women, see Phyllis A. Bird, "Images of Women in the Old Testament," in *The Bible and Liberation. Political and Social Hermeneutics,* ed. N. K. Gottwald (Maryknoll, N.Y.: Orbis Books, 1983), 258-263.

erty over those dealing with persons. In the Old Testament, the opposite is so.[19]

The laws of Israel present therefore a complex and interesting picture. The dependence from the juridical tradition of western Asia is obvious but not slavish. The term "inculturation" would be inadequate to express the relationship. Mesopotamian and other law codes antedate the formation of Israel, and the parallels are so widely scattered, from Asia Minor to the Persian Gulf, that direct borrowing is excluded: we cannot imagine the Hebrews sending study commissions all over the East to prepare their legislation! The only area where a direct borrowing could be conceived, the Canaanite world, did not have law codes.[20] The Israelite legal culture participated in the concern for justice of the surrounding world in general, emerged out of it, and continued to develop in symbiosis with that environment. Rather than *in-* or *en-*culturation, we have a double process of *emergence* and ongoing *osmosis* that goes deeper than any "inculturation" or "incarnation" or "contextualization," which all suppose an a posteriori effort. It was rather a matter of shared life and common regard for justice. While giving it the specific stamp of its faith vision, Israel took part in the noble quest for justice, which characterized the culture of western Asia.

RELIGION

Religion itself could not escape this general interaction with the surrounding world. The common folk could not be expected to dissociate the practice of agriculture and viticulture from the celebration of the fertility festivals associated with the rhythms of the seasons. From the time of Elijah onwards, this syncretism drew the ire of the prophets. References to this baalization recur like a leitmotif in the book of Judges (2:11-23; 3:7, 12; 4:1; 6:1; 10:6; 13:1) which, toward the end (Judg. 17-18), gives a lurid description of this kind of goings-on.

But the influence of Canaan was not restricted to marginal aberrations. The most official layers of Yahwistic religion imbibed the atmosphere. The *Hebrew calendar* integrated the needs of an agrarian civilization. The feasts came to embody agricultural elements (firstfruits of the barley harvest at Passover, of wheat harvest at Pentecost; booths for Sukkot). *Temples*[21] were

---

[19] W. J. Harrelson, "Law in OT," *IDB* 3:80.

[20] See the criticism of the "Canaanite hypothesis" of Albrecht Alt in H. Cazelles, *Études sur le Code de l'Alliance* (Paris: Letouzey, 1946), 166-168. The criticism remains valid: law codes have not been found in Rash Shamra, Mari, and Ebla. This does not mean that they had no law, but it does indicate that the Hebrews did not get the form of their law code from the Syro-Phoenician cultural area.

[21] In the plural before the deuteronomistic reformation and the centralization of the cult in Jerusalem.

built and, since there was no other technique available, they were built according to the pattern of the Canaanite sanctuaries. Archaeology has shown the structural similarity of the Jerusalem temple with those of earlier periods found at Megiddo, Lachish, Beth-Shan, Arad.[22] The biblical texts themselves make complacent reports of the Tyrian connection in the architecture of the temple (1 Kgs. 5:5-18). Special mention is made of Huram-abi or Master Huram, "a skilled and experienced technician," responsible for all the major and minor fittings of Solomon's temple (2 Chr. 2:13; 4:11-22; 1 Kgs. 7:13-50). A Canaanite visitor would have been quite at home in Jerusalem but for a detail that he would have considered as rather baffling: the Yahwist sanctuary was devoid of idols. It sheltered only the Ark of the Covenant in the total darkness of the Holy of Holies.

Apart from the absence of idols, the *cult* performed in the Yahwist temple(s) had also much in common with the Canaanite ritual. H. H. Rowley may venture rather too far when he asserts that "there is no evidence that the forms of the ritual of the Temple, other than the royal rites, were peculiar to Yahwism."[23] R. de Vaux is more specific:

> If we set aside sacrifices of babies, . . . then, according to the biblical evidence, Canaanite sacrifices do not seem to be materially different from those which were offered to Yahweh . . . The description of the sacrifice on Carmel (1 K 18) tells how the prophets of Baal and Elias himself prepared their holocausts in the same way, and the point of the story is lost if this was not the normal way of offering sacrifice to Baal . . . For the Deuteronomic redactor of the books of Kings, the words sacrifice and perfume-offerings sum up that cult of the "high places" which he condemns in the reign of almost every king of Judah (1 K 22:44; 2 K 12:4; 14:4 etc.). These were offerings meant for Yahweh, but Jeremias speaks in the same terms of the sacrifices and incense offered to Baal (Jer 7:9; 11:12, 13, 17; 32:29) . . . According to the Bible, then, there was a fundamental similarity between Canaanite sacrifice and Israelite sacrifice.

De Vaux continues with an elaborate study of the Canaanite terminology found in Phoenician and Punic inscriptions to "conclude that the Canaanite system of sacrifice was similar to the Israelite system: they offered at least holocausts and communion-sacrifices, vegetable produce and perfumes."

---

[22] "In its structure there was nothing peculiarly Yahwistic about the Temple . . . The Temple was not conformed to a pre-existing plan of what a Yahweh shrine should be" (H. H. Rowley, *Worship in Ancient Israel: Its Forms and Meaning* [London: SPCK, 1967], 78). Cf. Noth, *Old Testament World*, 173-177; R. de Vaux, *Ancient Israel* (London: Darton, Longman & Todd, 1961), 282-288, and plans of excavated Canaanite sanctuaries in *ANEP*, 229-232; *ANETSup*, 24f.

[23] Rowley, *Worship in Ancient Israel*, 79.

Differences do exist; for instance, "the Rash Shamra texts, like the Phoenician and Punic inscriptions, do not seem to attach any ritual importance to
the blood of the victim." Ultimately the evidence "does not justify the conclusion that Israel took all its ritual for sacrifices from Canaan, but it does
indicate that Israelite ritual is far closer to the ritual of Canaan than to that
of Mesopotamia or Arabia."[24] There again our hypothetical Canaanite visitor to the Jerusalem temple would not have been disconcerted by what he
would have witnessed in the Yahwistic cult—and by what he would have
heard also. Israelite music owed much, if not everything to Canaan, "land of
election of music, which for a long time supplied Egypt and Assyria with
artists and musical instruments."[25] As for the Hebrew poetry, it "marked a
transformation and not a disruption in the Canaanite continuum."[26] Our
Canaanite tourist might even have recognized one or the other psalm, as one
of his familiar temple hymns. Psalm 29, for instance, would have sounded to
him like a transposition of a hymn to Hadad, the Canaanite god of the
storm.[27]

Even the ways of the ancient prophets would have been familiar to him.
The "sons of the prophets" grouped around Samuel and working themselves
into an ecstatic frenzy (1 Sam. 10:5-13; 19:18-24) did not differ from the
"prophets of Baal" confronting Elijah on Mt. Carmel. Court prophets were
equally consulted by David (1 Sam. 23:2-12; 2 Sam. 5:19; 7:1-5), the
Philistines (1 Sam. 6:2-9) and Mesha, king of Moab.[28] As in the case of the
cult, this does not mean that there was nothing original in Israelite
prophetism. But it does point to an extensive common cultural and religious
background.

SENSE OF GOD

We have to go deeper into the heart of Israelite religiosity. It is the
Israelite sense of God itself that is characterized by its deep Canaanite roots.
The God of Israel is often viewed in antithetic contrast with the "pagan"
deities. The God of the Bible is viewed as a God of history, manifesting himself in acts of liberation in favor of his people, whereas "pagan" deities are

---

[24] De Vaux, *Ancient Israel,* 438-440.

[25] R. Tournay, *Les Psaumes,* BJ (Paris: Cerf, 1950), 47.

[26] A. R. Ceresko, "Recent Study of Hebrew Poetry: Implications for Theology and Wor-
ship," in *Psalmists and Sages: Studies in Old Testament Poetry and Religion,* ITS Supplements
Series 2 (Bangalore: St Peter's Institute, 1994), 131 (originally published in *Toronto Journal of
Theology* 1 [1985]: 98-112).

[27] See F. M. Cross, *Canaanite Myth and Hebrew Epic: Essays in the History of the Religion
of Israel* (Cambridge, Mass.: Harvard University Press, 1973), 151-162; M. Dahood, *Psalms I
1-50,* AB 16 (New York: Doubleday, 1965), 174-180: "virtually every word of the psalm can
now be duplicated in older Canaanite texts" (p. 175).

[28] See Mesha stone in *ANET,* 320: "Chemosh—the local god—said to me: 'Go, take Nebo
from Israel' . . . and Chemosh said to me, 'Go down, fight against Hauronen.'"

considered to be "mythical gods," more or less elaborated forms of nature or state worship. This is a very superficial perception.[29] In fact, Yahweh may have been the God of the "Moses group" that came from Egypt and, as such, he was perceived and worshiped in terms of the exodus liberating event. But he was identified with *'El*, the expression of the divine principle all over the Semitic world. In Canaan particularly, *'El* was the God of the ancestors and of the roots in the land. The standard phrase *Yahweh-Elohim* is not a tautology. It is the expression of the synthesis between the liberative perception of God and the Semitic religious sensitivity.

Special attention is to be given to the basic linguistic fact that *'El* and *'Elohim* are two of the main biblical names for God.[30] Under different dialectal differences (Akkadian *'ilu, 'ilum,* Ugaritic and Phoenician *'el,* Arabic *'ilah, 'allah*), this name is found all over the Semitic world as the name of the supreme Father and Creator, eternal and merciful.[31] By making use of this name, Israel shared in the fundamental religious experience of the Semitic world. Israel did not invent a new God. Revealing himself as *'elohim,* Yahweh, did not propose to his people a religious horizon that was foreign to that of the surrounding world, even if he enlarged and converted it.[32] On this point also, the connaturality is so deep that the word "dialogue" or "inculturation" cannot express it adequately. These words imply a situation in which the two parties face each other before coming into contact. In the case of Israel, there is no such situation in which a ready-made mental structure faces another. Israel's faith in its God emerges out of the common stock of belief in *'el.* The God of the Fathers is not alien to the *'el* of the surrounding peoples. The biblical God is the *'el* of Abraham, Isaac, and Jacob. He will manifest himself in a unique revelation through their history and that of their descendants, but the process will develop from within a shared experience of the Semitic sense of the divine.

CONCLUSIONS

We could pursue this study and go into the Canaanite mythic background of the Old Testament, the knowledge of which has been much enriched by the discoveries of Rash Shamra and Ebla. The material is so rich that this

---

[29] See J. Barr, *Old and New in Interpretation: A Study of the Two Testaments* (London: SCM Press, 1966), 65-82.

[30] Yahweh occurs about six thousand times in the Hebrew Bible and *'Elohim* about two thousand times, to which can be added some 230 uses of *'el.*

[31] See Cross, *Canaanite Myth and Hebrew Epic,* 3-75; idem, "*'el,*" *TWAT* 1:262-265.

[32] This basic linguistic consonance will be better appreciated if we realize the difficulties found by translators to express the idea of God in cultures in which the relationship with the Beyond is lived, thought, and expressed without the categories of transcendence and alterity. This is the case in most of southern and eastern Asia and wherever the religious linguistic substratum has been shaped by Buddhism, Confucianism, Shintoism, or animism.

inquiry would take us too far. The rapid survey of some of the most obvious or most significant aspects of the mutual interaction between Israelite and Canaanite cultures may suffice to draw a few conclusions.

Avoiding venturing onto the slippery slope of historical reconstructions, we tried rather to see the mutual relationship between the two opposite cultural pulls represented by "Canaan" and "Israel." In the biblical text, Canaan stands as a symbol of what Israel rejected with regard to the Semitic cultural background in which it originated. This statement can be taken both ways. Canaan stands, on the one hand, for what Israel *rejected,* but, on the other hand, for the milieu that *nurtured* its growth.

1. The biblical text bears ample evidence that Israel developed a sense of identity in opposition to the surrounding world. Israel perceives itself as Israel in a revolt against its surroundings—Egypt or Canaan. Hebrew thoughts and attitudes are marked by a deep-seated antagonism toward those dominant cultures, their value system, societal structures, and religion. The emergence of their self-awareness as people is marked by *a thorough cultural rupture.* The opposition was not only religious. It was more than a case of monotheism versus polytheism, of fight against idolatry. The antagonism covered all the aspects of human life, from family life to social and political organization, from structures of ownership to faith and rituals. It extended even to culinary matters in the case of food taboos, which are also important forms of cultural assertion. It was the confrontation of two cultures, or rather the encounter between a *counterculture* and an established culture. The religious hostility evident in the polemic against idolatry and idolaters is the crystallization of a global societal conflict equally well attested by the biblical data.

A more subdued yet equally convincing form of opposition to the Canaanite neighborhood appears in the interesting case of the Hebrew laws. Canaan had no code of laws. The codes of Israel show more distant Mesopotamian and Hittite influences. Law codes are sociologically significant since they encapsulate a group's paradigm of a just society. The departure from the Canaanite ethos and the rapprochement with more distant neighbors are unlikely to have been deliberate. Yet it does reflect a sense of kinship with societies that were groping for a legal protection of human rights against the royal absolutism of the Canaanite or Egyptian type. It would be interesting to study with more precision the strategy adopted (would it be unconsciously?) by the Hebrews, while shifting their cultural ties from Canaan to the Mesopotamian or the Hittites.

2. Yet Israel did not come to be in an isolated island. Its cultural roots are cast deeply in the world and culture of western Asia and more specifically in the western Semitic Syro-Phoenician or Canaanite area. Israel partook of the various aspects of this culture in all its various forms, such as technology, ways of life, social and political structures, language, art, poetry, religion. The dependence on this culture took different forms.

There was a process of *emergence.* This was indeed the most important factor in shaping Israelite culture. This culture was born from the realities of the soil and of its products, in dependence on the climatic, agricultural, and religious rhythms of life. It covered the area of techniques, arts, poetry, and music. It extended particularly to the area of language, symbolism, and ritual. Language is especially significant, since it provided the matrix in which the Israelite mind grew.

Deliberate *enculturation* would have been the case when Israel, having already developed a sense of identity, borrowed deliberately or unconsciously from the surrounding world. This was typically the case with the adoption of kingship. Later on, the same trend continued when Tyrian expertise was enlisted for the construction of the Jerusalem temple. This process does not correspond exactly to what we call "inculturation." It was not an attempt to project Israel's faith vision outside. It was rather a matter of taking advantage of the "riches of Canaan."

3. We have, therefore, a puzzling tangle of intercultural dependence and counterculture, of osmosis and protest, of a shared common stock carrying an inborn conflict, of a community of life permeated with the acute tension of ongoing confrontation.

Sociologically, the question is to be situated in the context of the love-hate relationship frequently to be found among people living in the same area. Intercultural relationships are complex.[33] There is a kind of social Oedipus complex that both links and opposes people living together differently. The Indian *Mahabharata* relates the battle of Kurukshetra between the Pandavas and their close relatives, the Kauravas. Greek literature has dramatized the cruel conflicts between the brothers Orestes, Aigisthos, and Agamamemnon in the House of Atreus. It is not only in Rwanda and Burundi that those somber myths continue to surface in history.

Theologically, the intertwining of protest and cultural kinship, the fact that the anti-Canaanite stand was voiced from the midst of a cultural continuum, is to be connected with the ongoing biblical paradox of incarnation and prophetic protest. The Holy and totally Other One[34] is also the one who is

---

[33] In India, for instance, the caste system induces a double antithetic type of reaction among the lower castes. On the one hand, the *dalit* movement and other forms of mobilization of the lower castes oppose the domination of the upper castes actively and sometimes violently. But in a parallel development, through a process of "sanskritization," the *dalits* and other lower castes adopt the way of life and imbibe the culture of the upper castes. See M. N. Srinivas, *Social Change in Modern India* (Delhi: Orient Longman, 1972); idem, *The Cohesive Role of Sanskritization and Other Essays* (Delhi: Oxford University Press, 1989).

[34] The primary meaning of the Hebrew root *qdš* is "apartness, sacredness" (BDB, 875). "To speak of God as 'the Holy One' is to emphasize God's separateness, God's otherness, God's mystery. This idea is expressed in Hos 11:9 when Yahweh says, 'I am God and not man, the Holy One in your midst.' Likewise, Deutero-Isaiah reports the words of 'Yahweh your God, and of the Holy One of Israel,' who says, 'My thoughts are not your thoughts, neither are your ways my ways' (Isa 55:8)" (M. G. Reddish, "Holy One," *ABD* 3:258).

closer to his people than any other god (Deut. 4:7; 5:32-34). The transcendent God is also immanent. Incarnation and judgment cannot be dissociated. A witness to that God and fidelity to him imply that the prophetic protest against the unholiness of the world be expressed from within a total communion with this world.

2

Kings and Prophets

Israelite identity expressed itself in protest against the sociopolitical system, religious symbols, and underlying values of the surrounding cultures. Yet this was not a fight between extraneous forces. Israel itself belonged to the geographical setting of the eastern Mediterranean world and to its West Semitic culture. The conflict *with* surrounding cultures was also a conflict *within* Israel's own cultural identity.

These two opposite polar trends of rejection and integration are typified by the two Israelite institutions of kingship and prophetism. Kings in general represented the accommodation to the administrative necessities and to the set patterns of political life in western Asia. This accommodation carried with it the temptation of assimilation. It was the task of the prophets to denounce the danger of losing the Yahwist identity and to voice the protest against abusive royal despotism. Now the borderline was not always clearcut. There were different types of kings and there were prophets other than Amos. Yet, on the whole, the royal and prophetic figures confronting each other in the history of Israel represent the opposite tendencies of political acculturation and countercultural protest.

POLITICAL ACCULTURATION: KINGSHIP

"A KING LIKE ALL THE NATIONS"

According to 1 Samuel, kingship originated in a tense atmosphere of crisis. The book of Judges describes a situation of perilous anarchy for the people of Israel. Caught in various tribal wars, the nascent Hebrew nation depended on occasional charismatic leaders to face the various emerging nations that occupied the Palestinian scene toward the beginning of the Iron Age. A short notice in 1 Samuel 13:19-22 shows the Israelites in a Third World position vis-à-vis the monopolizing practices of the Philistine dominating power. Having introduced the use of iron in Palestine, the Philistines intended to claim exclusive usage of the new techniques. The Hebrews were not allowed to learn and practice smithery. Socially, this situation held them in bondage. Economically, it kept them in poverty. Politically, it denied them access to more effective weapons and tactics, making revolt impossible.

If Israel was to be freed from these fetters, a coordinating authority was called for. Humiliated Israel had only to look at the surrounding people to see the advantages of a central power. It was good political wisdom that prompted the elders of the people to request Samuel to give them a king "like the other nations" (1 Sam. 8:5, 19).

But there was another side to the picture, which the redactor of 1 Samuel could expose with the advantage of hindsight. Having a king "like the other nations" exposed Israel to the "ways of the kings" (1 Sam. 8:11): taxes, enrollment of youth in the royal armies, unpaid corvées, requisition of crops and cattle, seizure of land, enslavement (1 Sam. 8:11-18). In political terms, it meant that Israel became one of the Syro-Phoenician city-states. Theologically, at least to the eyes of the deuteronomistic redactor, the appointment of a king amounted to a practical rejection of God: "It is not you they reject; it is myself" says God (1 Sam. 8:7). By opting for kingship "like the other nations," Israel ran the risk of total assimilation to the surrounding cultures and of losing its authenticity.

Israel found itself on the horns of a dilemma. Living in the midst of other countries, it could not do without set structures: in those days this meant a monarchical system. But the monarchical establishment could hardly resist the temptation of absolutism and of making an absolute of political-economic convenience. This ambiguity was to mark the entire further course of Israel life and faith.

DAVID HEIR TO CANAAN?

"Jerusalem, city of David." The phrase is fairly frequent in the Old Testament (about fifty times). It is accurate from the point of view of the faith of later Israel. It is David who made of Jerusalem the political and religious center of the newly unified Israel. But this does not mean that David is the founder of the town. Actually the city contributed as much to David and to his new religious setup as David did to the future and glory of the town.

Some seventy-five years ago, Albrecht Alt published a study on "the rise of Jerusalem."[1] According to his reconstruction, the city of Jebus conquered by David would have been a fairly insignificant settlement. Stretching in a wasp-waisted shape three hundred meters in length by sixty to eighty meters in breadth, it would have hardly covered six acres.[2] Moreover, it was situated

---

[1] A. Alt, "Jerusalems Aufstieg," *ZMDG* 79 (1925): 1-19. Our quotations follow the reprint in *Grundfragen der Geschichte des Volkes Israel* (Munich: Beck, 1970), 323-337.

[2] Ibid., 329.

in the hills, away from the main ways of communication and could not even claim to be the center of Palestine, which would have been Shiloh, nor even of Judah.[3] To the arguments of Alt, M. Noth added the observation that Jerusalem is absent from the Pentateuch and plays no role in the old Israelite traditions.[4] Alt could conclude: "It is not to Nature that Jerusalem owes its preeminence in present Palestine; it is history that forced Nature to bring about what Jerusalem came to be."[5] In short, Jerusalem would be the genial creation of David, indeed a "miraculous" happening.[6]

This supernaturalistic construction is now questioned. The town was far from being insignificant. The excavations of Kathleen Kenyon and Roland de Vaux have shown that the city extended halfway down the slope of the hill of Ophel.[7] The surface thus covered was double that supposed formerly. It could shelter a population of some 2,500 inhabitants, which made it a middle-size power amidst surrounding "cities" counting no more than fifty to five hundred souls.[8] Set on the central Judean ridge, halfway between the Mediterranean Sea and the Jordan Valley, overlooking the "way of the sea" as well as the routes of the desert, firmly established on a spur that could easily be blocked, it constituted a solid redoubt against the onslaughts coming from both the "peoples of the sea" and the lands beyond the Jordan. The existence of the town is witnessed in ancient documents. Under the name of Urusalim, it takes its due place among the twenty-five Palestinian cities referred to in the Amarna Letters, the correspondence exchanged between the Canaanite princes and their Egyptian suzerain. Six of those letters come from ʾAbdu Heba, prince of Jerusalem,[9] while the same ʾAbdu Heba is successively mentioned as an ally[10] and denounced as a troublemaker[11] by the neighboring ruler of Hebron. "These letters show the town as the center of a city state that extended from Beth Horon to Keila."[12] Until the days of David, Jebus, as it was now called, managed to keep clear of the surrounding conflicts, playing the role of a mini-Switzerland among the various powers clashing together on the eastern shores of the Mediterranean Sea.

---

[3] Ibid., 326-327.

[4] M. Noth, "Jerusalem und die Israelitische Tradition," *OTS* 8 (1950): 28-46, reprinted in *Gesammelte Studien zum Alten Testament* (Munich: Kaiser Verlag, 1957); see pp. 173-174.

[5] Alt, "Jerusalems Aufstieg," 327.

[6] "Then happened the great Marvel (*Wunder*) in the history of the city . . . Suddenly, overnight so to say, a shriveled town turned into the center of a kingdom, indeed of entire Palestine" (Alt, "Jerusalems Aufstieg," 333).

[7] Kathleen Kenyon, *Jerusalem: Excavating 3000 Years of History* (London: Thames & Hudson, 1967), 31-50; eadem, *Archeology in the Holy Land*, 3rd ed. (London: Ernest Benn, 1969), 343-344.

[8] O. Keel, "L'héritage cananéen de Jérusalem," *Monde de la Bible* 122 (1999): 15.

[9] *ANET*, 487-488, letters 285-290.

[10] Ibid., 487.

[11] Ibid., letter 280.

[12] P. Welter, "Jerusalem I," *TRE* 16:595.

There is no doubt that targeting Jebus was a masterstroke of David. But the biblical texts show that the stroke was not one-sided. Having conquered the city, David found a local administration with which he had to deal. "He did not hesitate to engage the service of the Canaanite elite. In Jerusalem he reigned with two groups, on one side, his old companions from Bethlehem, on the other side the old local aristocracy. There were two high priests, two generals, two heirs to the throne."[13] To a large extent the conquest of Jerusalem turned David, the tribal chieftain and guerilla leader, into a Canaanite king and his people into a Canaanite city-state.

One of the heirs to the throne was Solomon, born from one of the wives he took in Jerusalem. The dynastic struggle that marked the succession of David saw the victory of the "Jebusite" urban element over the rural Bethlehemite clan. The high priest Abiathar was sent in exile to Anathoth (1 Kgs. 2:26). The pretender Adoniah, son of Haggith, a Judean wife (2 Sam. 3:4) was murdered (1 Kgs. 2:25) as well as Joab (1 Kgs. 2:28-34), David's nephew (1 Chron. 2:16) and the faithful companion of all his battles. With the help of Bathsheba, the Jerusalem favorite, Solomon was enthroned and, with him, the Jebusite clan took over.

With David and Solomon, Jerusalem did not become a Judean tribal city; it is Juda which turned into a Canaanite city state. The influence of the Judean countryside dwindled progressively. On the contrary, the city grew in importance so that Juda became a kind of city state around Jerusalem.[14]

SOLOMON AS A CANAANITE MONARCH

During the years when Israel developed its identity, the concrete model of centralized authority they had before their eyes was that of the Canaanite monarchs. Actually history does not seem to have been very much impressed by Canaanite kingship. It does not know in Canaan of such mighty figures as the Pharaohs of Egypt or the potentates of Mesopotamia and Persia. Nor does it record the equivalent of the Greek or Roman struggle for democracy against tyranny. Canaanite rulers were only "small kings" (*sarru sihru* in Ugaritic terminology), vassals of the "great kings (*sarru rabû*) of Egypt, Hattus or Assyria.[15] They owed this subordinate position to their divisions. Canaan and Phoenicia were never united until the Persian times and then under foreign rule. Akko, Tyre, Sidon, Berytus, Byblos, Ugarit, and Ebla were too small to stand before the mighty empires of Egypt and Mesopotamia. Those "kingdoms" were also too small and their rulers

---

[13] Keel, "L'héritage cananéen," 16.

[14] Ibid., 17.

[15] Cf. M. Liverani, "Histoire Politique de cette cité," in "Ras Shamra," *DBSup* 9:1295-1348: "Ugarit a toujours fait partie du niveau des 'petits rois' (ou 'vassaux')" (col. 1323).

wielded too limited powers to entertain an absolutely autocratic rule. These rulers might profess divine origin; they were "sons of the god"; they had "sucked the milk of the goddess Anat"[16] and claimed divine authority. Yet concretely the small size of the city-state safeguarded a human face—or at least a commercial face—for Canaanite kingship. "It is characteristic of Phoenician as well as of Philistine organization that the power of the king tended to be kept in check by the 'elders,' who met as a kind of senate in order to consider matters of importance to the state."[17] To a large extent, Canaanite kings were merchant kings. A good part of the government activity consisted in the economic control of the resources of the country and in the organization of trade:[18] the archives of Ugarit and Ebla are particularly rich in account keeping and stock taking.

Paradoxically, it is the Bible that presents one of the most elaborate pictures of this kind of Canaanite rule. This typical image is not found outside Israel in the likes of Hiram of Tyre or of Rezin (Razon) of Damascus, and still less in the pitiful figures of the five "kings" defeated by Joshua and tortured at Makkedah (Josh. 10). The most graphic description of a Canaanite ruler appears in the biblical report of the reign of Solomon, who "has with some justice been called 'the enthroned merchant.'"[19] He even outclassed his models when, taking advantage of a political vacuum in Egypt and Assyria, and following upon the conquests of his father, David, he gave his kingdom the dimensions of a mini-empire extending from Syria to the Red Sea. For the rest, the biblical account of his reign presents a rather mercantile image. If the description of David's reign is largely devoted to campaigns and conquests, that of Solomon, apart from the construction of the temple, consists mostly in a report of his administrative organization (1 Kgs. 4:1-5:32) and of his commercial enterprises (9:26-10:29).[20] The visit of the queen of Sheba must have had purposes other than an academic consultation on "hard questions" (1 Kgs. 10:1-3). The "hundred and twenty talents of gold, very great quantity of spices and precious stones" could not be only a humble token of appreciation for the royal "wisdom" (10:10). Even the building of the temple implied a great deal of transactions and barter with Hiram of Tyre (1 Kgs. 9:10-14). In no way was the image of King Solomon of Jerusalem at odds with the picture presented by the merchant kings of the Phoenician coast.

---

[16] "Krt the son of El, the offspring of the Kindly One and the Holy . . . who sucks the milk of Aterat, who sucks out the breasts of the Virgin Anat" (C. Gordon, *Ugaritic Handbook* [Rome: PBI, 1947], 125, 20-22; 128, II 26-27). Cf. J. Gray, *The Legacy of Canaan: The Ras Shamra Texts and their Relevance to the Old Testament,* VTSup 5 (Leiden: Brill, 1965), 219-223; idem, *The Canaanites* (London: Thames & Hudson, 1964), 106-109.

[17] W. F. Albright, "Syria, the Philistines and Phoenicia," in *The Cambridge Ancient History,* ed. I. E. S. Edwards et al., 3rd ed. II/2 (Cambridge: Cambridge University Press, 1975), 520.

[18] Cf. Gray, *Legacy,* 224f.

[19] O. Eissfeldt, "The Hebrew Kingdom," in *Cambridge Ancient History,* ed. Edwards et al., II/2, 592.

[20] The Jerusalem Bible aptly gives this portion the title of "Solomon the Trader" (p. 447).

At least as regards fertility cults, there is no evidence that Solomon or the other Israelite kings would have practiced those Canaanite rites. In Mesopotamia, during the New Year festival, the king performed the rite of the sacred marriage to stimulate vegetation and promote human fecundity. The Ugaritic poem describing the victory of Baʿal must also have been associated with a New Year ritual enacting the seasonal revival of nature,[21] a ritual in which the king would have taken an active part.[22] The celebration of a similar New Year festival along parallel lines in Israel remains a moot question. Still more problematic is the hypothesis of the royal participation through fecundity rites and the cultic performance of a "sacred marriage."[23] It might be rash therefore to imagine Solomon entering the temple with his wives and concubines to accomplish with them the ritual intercourse. At least the number of those wives and concubines must have been, to the mind of the common folk, a proof of the royal "capacity to guarantee the functioning of nature."[24] The biblical text gives a broad hint that those foreign wives and concubines supplied what was still lacking in the canaanization of the old king (1 Kgs. 11:1-8). It must have gone further than mere "incense burning" at the altars of the local gods (v. 8).

In the global structure of the books of Kings, the conjugal extravagances of Solomon introduce the decadence of his, and of Israelite, kingship. From now on, "the Lord raised up adversaries against him," such as Hadad the Edomite (1 Kgs. 11:14-22) and Rezon of Damascus (11:23-25). Within the country itself, Jeroboam the Ephraimite (11:26-44) rose up and caused the division of the kingdom. Then, but for a few exceptions, the reigns of the successors will be summarized by the sad comment: "He did what was evil in the sight of the Lord." The decadence was to reach its nadir with the fall of Samaria (2 Kgs. 17) and of Jerusalem (2 Kgs. 25).

A MIXED APPRAISAL

Therefore it is clear that the Bible does not idealize kingship unconditionally. A strong current views it as a process of canaanization. As noted by G. von Rad, unlike the Babylonian dynasties, the Davidic kingship does not

---

[21] "We unfortunately do not know the rites associated with this myth, but we may reasonably infer that there was an accompanying ritual" (Gray, *Canaanites,* 128); cf. T. H. Gaster, *Thespis: Ritual, Myth and Drama in the Ancient Near East* (New York: Harper, 1966), 114ff.

[22] "Les modèles royaux, les héros protagonistes des récits de Keret et de Qhat . . . sont des personnages centrés sur le problème de la fertilité et de la reproduction . . . La validité de la royauté, selon les convictions profondes de la population, consiste dans sa capacité . . . à garantir le fonctionnement de la nature" (Liverani, "Histoire politique," col. 1335, who proceeds to submit that this sacred function was performed by the king and the queen in cultic actions).

[23] See a concise statement of the question in A. Cody, "Religious Institutions of Israel," *NJBC*, 1280f.

[24] See n. 22 above.

"come down from heaven at the beginning."[25] It is the outcome of a very human process, of a concession to human necessities.

Does the Bible present this process as a positive development or at least as a necessary one? Commentators interpret the biblical data in different ways. Considering the revolt of the exodus as the paradigm of biblical authenticity, liberationist exegesis tends to see the development of Israelite monarchy as a breach of the genuine biblical spirit. With it, "there was a radical shift in the foundations of Israel's life and faith . . . The entire programme of Solomon now appears to have been a self-serving of king and dynasty . . . a programme of state-sponsored syncretism, which meant of course the abandonment of the radicalness of the Mosaic vision."[26]

On the other hand, and within the methodology of the same liberationist exegesis, N. K. Gottwald tones down his earlier assessment in *The Tribes of Yahweh*[27] and assures that he does not intend to "moralize or absolutize tribal Israel as a 'golden age' and the monarchy as a 'fall from grace.'"[28]

The current scholarly debate echoes the discrepancy of the biblical accounts themselves. The biblical accounts are not of one mind in their estimate of Israelite kingship. According to Wellhausen, the books of Samuel combined an early promonarchical with a later antimonarchical source.[29] Without being so systematic about the use of defined sources, present commentators can still identify a double current, "the first current presenting greater similarity with foreign monarchies in which the king, said to be 'the son of the god,' was his representative on earth, endowed with superhuman

---

[25] "When the monarchy came down from heaven, the monarchy was (first) in Eridu . . ." (*ANET,* 265, quoted by G. von Rad, *Old Testament Theology,* vol. 1, *The Theology of Israel's Historical Traditions* [New York: Harper, 1962], 308).

[26] W. Brueggemann, *The Prophetic Imagination* (London: SCM Press, 1978), 30. The true God of "prophetic imagination" is "a God uncredentialed in the empire, unknown in the courts, unwelcome in the temple. And his history begins in his attentiveness to the cries of the marginal ones" (p. 42).

[27] N. K. Gottwald, *The Tribes of Yahweh: A Sociology of the Religion of Liberated Israel, 1250-1050 B.C.E.* (Maryknoll, N.Y.: Orbis Books, 1979).

[28] N. K. Gottwald, "Introduction," *Semeia 37,* 7. The collaborators of the same issue of *Semeia* chime in, making reference also to the earlier work of Gottwald: "The common view, or rather the domain assumption, that the monarchy is some kind of aberration or 'alien' institution foisted upon true Israel is partly due to the self-limiting perspective of specialization. The views of Bright and Noth (alien institution), Mendenhall (pagan reversion) and Gottwald (dialectically opposed) fail to explain how significant social change takes place" (R. B. Coote and K. W. Whitelam, "The Emergence of Israel: Social Transformation and State Formation following the Decline in Late Bronze Age Trade," *Semeia 37,* 115). See a good summary of the discussion in K. W. Whitelam, "King and Kingship," *ABD* 4: 40-48; and A. R. Ceresko, *The Old Testament: A Liberation Perspective* (Maryknoll, N.Y.: Orbis Books, 1992), 215-217.

[29] Monarchical source: 1 Sam. 9:1-10:16; 11; 13-14; antimonarchical source: 1 Sam. 7-8; 10:17-27; 12;15. The trend now is to trace sources to the various concrete settings determined by form criticism (ark narrative, story of David's rise in the form of an apology, royal chronicles, etc.).

powers, and the other current, that could be called more 'biblical' or prophet-ical, showing great reservations towards this attitude."[30]

In the line of the first current, the king is said to be endowed with divine wisdom (1 Kgs. 3:28); he is the anointed of the Lord (1 Sam. 24:10; 26:9; 2 Sam. 1:14); he performs sacrifices (2 Sam. 6:13; 1 Kgs. 8:62), blesses the people and organizes the cult. Royal messianism will develop along this line (2 Sam. 7:8-16; Isa. 7:13-25; 9:1-6; 11:1-9; Micah 5:1-3). The Davidic dynasty will become the mediator of the covenant and participate with God in the divine function of the Shepherd (1 Sam. 7:8; Ps. 78:70-72; Jer. 3:15; 23:4-7; Ezek. 34:23-30; 37:22-24).

The second trend gives a gloomy picture of the "ways of the king" (1 Sam. 8:11-17). Drawing a calamitous balance sheet of the dynasty, it denounces the failure of the "bad shepherds" (1 Kgs. 22:17; Jer. 23:1f.; Ezek. 34:1-10; Zech. 11:4-11). The book of Deuteronomy tries to strike a balance. It proposes the ideal of a scribal king who will have his own copy of the law of the Lord and "shall read of it every day of his life" (Deut. 17:18-19). Moreover, the restraint provided by God's word will find a concrete shape in the form of a prophetic presence in whose mouth God will put his words (18:15-18). A plural leadership could certainly ward off the danger of despo-tism. Was this idealistic picture realistic? Anyway it was proposed too late to be given the test of time. The Babylonians were already at the gate.

COUNTERACTION: THE PROPHETS

The case of Solomon had revealed the deep tensions which the Israelite culture underwent when it went the way of the other nations. With new tech-niques and new life setting, new needs and challenges, new social and polit-ical organization, new forms of cult and a new world vision, the Israelites underwent a deep cultural crisis that put their very identity in jeopardy. It was the role of the prophets to react against the danger of assimilation. The attitude of Samuel has already been mentioned; other examples are not lack-ing. Yet a more positive stand toward culture can also be found among the prophets themselves.

PROPHETICAL RADICALISM

Elijah

The "historical books" of 1-2 Samuel and 1-2 Kings are rightly classified among the "Former Prophets" in the Hebrew canon. The acts of the prophets

---

[30] E. Jacob and H. Cazelles, "Ras Shamra et l'Ancien Testament," *DBSup* 9 (1979) col. 1432. On the various reconstructions of the sources of the books of Samuel, see N. K. Gottwald, *The Hebrew Bible: A Socio-Literary Introduction* (Philadelphia: Fortress Press, 1985), 312-318; R. W. Klein, *1 Samuel,* WBC 10 (Waco: Word Books, 1983), xxviii-xxxii.

(Samuel, Nathan, Ahijah, Elijah, Elisha) are intertwined with the annals of the kings of Judah and Israel, and the biblical redactors give pride of place to this continuous prophetic challenge. As a kind of extensive caption to the whole work, the story of the prophet Samuel takes the first seven chapters (1 Sam. 1-7). It remains the major factor in the reign of Saul (1 Sam. 8-13; 28) and of the election of David to the royal succession (1 Sam. 15:34-16:13; 19:18-24; 25:1). From Samuel onwards, prophets function like the voice of conscience for the kings, sometimes in cooperation with the royal power, especially in the case of David, more often in opposition to the abuses of authority. Even before the coming of Elijah, the royal history of Judah and Israel is eminently a prophetic history. As against the tendency to allow the Canaanite inculturation to turn into assimilation, the prophetic voice continuously reminded kings and people of their Yahwistic specificity.

In a particularly fierce manner, Elijah embodies the prophetic resistance to the fast-spreading assimilation. He is one of the major figures in the books of Kings and certainly the major one insofar as the northern kingdom is concerned. The opposition of the prophet to the king is merciless. King Ahab and his wife Jezebel stand for total assimilation to the ethos and policies of Phoenician cities. Ahab is married to the Sidonian princess Jezebel, the daughter of Ethbaal, king of Sidon (1 Kgs. 16:31ff.). She seems to have been "a strong willed woman who had a powerful influence on Ahab, himself not a man of weak will."[31] The royal couple intended to "modernize" the northern kingdom and to bring it to the level of the Levantine city-states. The times of Ahab and Jezebel saw the floruit of Phoenician civilization. Freed from Egyptian suzerainty, first Sidon and then Tyre became the leading trade centers of the Mediterranean world. Their role between 1200 and 750 can be compared with that of Spain and Portugal in the beginnings of the modern times. Though their geographical basis was rather narrow, they became the leading powers of the West. They monopolized trade and industry, developed a mercantile navy, sent explorers to the Atlantic, north up to England and south all the way down to South Africa, founded colonies in Malta, Italy, North Africa, Spain, and the Balearic Islands. A famous text of Ezekiel describes this febrile commercial activity (27:1-25). It lists the countries reached by this trade, records their imports and exports, describes the unceasing flow of caravans, relayed by ships, and evokes the flow of foreigners joining the Tyrian navy, its shipyards, and its army.

Such was the economic model that Jezebel brought from Sidon. Such was also the socioreligious pattern that Elijah fiercely opposed. The biblical text influenced by the deuteronomistic redaction has emphasized the religious aspects of the struggle. Ahab propagated the cult of Baal and planted an *asherah* (2 Kgs. 16:31-33). From the run of the narrative, it would even seem that Ahab bears the responsibility for the crime of Abiram, offering his son

---

[31] J. L. McKenzie, *Dictionary of the Bible* (London: Chapman, 1968), 438.

as a human foundation sacrifice (1 Kgs. 16:34). A direct and systematic persecution of Yahwism is conducted under the direction of the pagan wife
Jezebel (18:3f.). The geographical context in which Ahab moves evokes
Canaanite religion. It is Jezreel (18:45f.; 21:1-13; 2 Kgs. 8:29; 9:30f.) the
very name of which (ʾEl will sow) carries overtones of fertility cult. The climax will be reached on Mt. Carmel, a Phoenician holy mountain,[32] where
the priests of Baal found themselves at home (2 Kgs. 18).

The episode of Naboth's vineyard and the murder of its owner shows that
the conflict extends to all the aspects of human existence. Interestingly, Elijah does not address himself to the economic aspects of Ahab's program. He
has other concerns. He does not belong to the economic and financial establishment of the country, the merchant classes, or the political leadership. The
story of Elijah shows him to be at home with the poor. His contact in Sidon
is in the small village of Sarepta, with a starving widow, a victim of the
famine (1 Kgs. 17:8-24). Elisha, his disciple, is a plowman (1 Kgs. 19:19-
21); Naboth's land could make just a "vegetable garden" for the king (1 Kgs.
21:2). Elijah belongs to the poor of the land. The question he raises concerns
the poor. What will be the social cost of the king's policies? The case of
Naboth recalls that the land has more than economic value and that it cannot be reduced to a matter of transaction or to financial considerations (1
Kgs 21:2, 6, 15). The land is the "inheritance of the fathers" (vv. 2, 4), the
sign and guarantee of social belonging and independence. Elijah fights for a
society in which the rights of the poor prevail over the might of the kings,
for a culture that does not consider the laws of economy to be the ultimate
criterion of value. If he combats for Yahweh against the Baalim, it is because
the Baalim are the gods that represent royal absolutism and the Phoenician
mercantile ideology. Elijah's God is the one who cares for the widows
(1 Kgs. 17:17-24), feeds those who starve (1 Kgs. 17:5f., 14-16; 18:41-46),
and protects the rights of the lowly (21:19-24).

The struggle of Elijah is uncompromising. To Carmel, he opposes Horeb
(1 Kgs. 19:9-19); to Jezreel, the desert (19:1-8); to the fertility cult, a
drought (17:1-18:2); to the grabbing for land, the extinction of the offspring
(21:17-24). There is no place for nuance. It is a combat of unsullied Yahwism against the depravity of Baal. The only form of encounter is the fight
to the death. The religious contest is fought on Mt. Carmel and ends with the
slaughter of the priests of Baal. The political battle is waged in Jezreel by
Jehu, the secular arm of the prophetic movement; it will also end in blood-
shed with the death of Jezebel and the royal family (2 Kgs. 9:30-10:11). For

---

[32] "L'occupation antique des Phéniciens se manifeste par le nom de *Rusa qades* (= . . . *ros
qados)* que les listes égyptiennes depuis Thoutmès III (1479 avant J.-C.) appliquent selon toute
vraisemblance au promontoire du Carmel. Ce vocable de "Cap sacré" indique un culte . . . dont
nous retrouvons la survivance dans le périple de Scylax (iv° s. avant J.-C.) qui . . . signale le
Carmel , montagne sacrée de Zeus: *Carmêlos oros hieron Dios"* (F. M. Abel, *Géographie de la
Palestine,* Tome 1, *Géographie Physique et Historique*, EBib [Paris: Gabalda, 1933], 350f.).

good measure, Athaliah, the daughter of Jezebel, married to the king of Judah, will also be done away with in the following chapter (2 Kgs. 11).

For Elijah, there is no middle way. Either Yahweh or Baal is God (1 Kgs. 18:21). Either one goes to Jezreel in search of ʾel and his consorts or one returns to Horeb-Sinai. It is a dilemma between fecundity and all its attendant gods or the desert, where the Lord is to be found. There does not seem to be a way for a fertility that would be guaranteed by Yahweh.

The Rechabites

Equally intransigent will be the stand of the Rechabites, more than two centuries afterwards. We know of the existence of that mysterious group through the witness of Jeremiah, who mentions them as an example to the Jerusalemites (Jer. 35). Jonadab, their founder (Jer. 35:8, 16, 18), had joined Jehu in the fight against Ahab (2 Kgs. 10:15, 23). They were therefore heirs in direct line to the uncompromising "zeal for Yahweh" of the great Israelite prophet. They turned into a social program what had been for Elijah a cry of protest and tried artificially to reconstruct the conditions of the desert, living in tents, refusing to dwell in houses, to sow, to plant and own vineyards, and even to drink wine (Jer. 35:6-10). Theirs was a radical rejection of any form of acculturation, in the style of the Amish of America.

Their archaic way of life was a prophetic protest with which Jeremiah sympathized. Jeremiah himself was not a member of the group. He lived in the village of Anathoth and did not hesitate to buy land (Jer. 32:1-15). Yet the prophet's fascination with the defenders of the old Israelite tradition shows the lasting nostalgia among the spiritual elite of the country for the days of pure Yahwism. Especially in times of crisis, when the process of assimilation to the surrounding cultures revealed its latent menace, the prophetic voice of the Rechabites came to echo the revolt of Elijah.

Amos

Such was also the voice of Amos at the time of Jeroboam II, a century after Elijah. It was a glorious time for Israel. The Assyrian power was at a low ebb and Israel was left at peace. The northern king had a long undisturbed reign of forty years (786-746). He restored Israel "from the entrance of Hamath as far as the sea of Arabah" (2 Kgs. 14:25). Peace favored trade: access to the Red Sea again made possible the old Solomonic trade with the east and the south. Trade brought prosperity and the luxury of big houses and palaces (Amos 3:15; 5:11), of rich carpeting and furniture inlaid with ivory (3:15; 6:4). Banquets were occasions of drinking and carousing (4:1; 6:6). Art and music flourished (6:5). At long last the country experienced a certain measure of comfort, well-being, and artistic culture.

All that took place under a king who, as a worthy successor of Jehu, favored the cult of the true God. Temples to Yahweh multiplied in Bethel

(Amos 3:14; 4:4; 5:5; 7:10), Gilgal (4:4; 5:5), Dan (8:14) and Samaria (8:14). Pilgrimages drew big crowds and rich sacrifices were performed, subsidized by royal endowments and enlivened by professional musicians (5:21-23). Piety and prosperity had embraced. The reformation of Elijah, translated in political moves by Jehu, seemed to have yielded its fruits. The external observer would have said that a successful synthesis had been effected between Yahwism and the royal ideology.

But Amos was not an external observer. He saw through the hypocrisy of the official cult and denounced the betrayal of the true religion. The God of Bethel and of Gilgal might be worshiped under the name of Yahweh; he was not the God of the Sinai, the God of the covenant whose concern was for justice and for the poor. Wealth had destroyed the covenantal egalitarianism, and the sense of justice had given way to the oppression of the poor by the ruling affluent classes.

> They sell the righteous for silver
> and the needy for a pair of shoes
> They trample the head of the poor into the dust of the earth
> and turn aside the way of the afflicted . . .
> They lay themselves down beside every altar
> upon garments taken in pledge;
> and in the house of their God
> they drink the wine of those who have been fined . . . (Amos 2:6-8)

> Woe to those who turn justice to wormwood
> and cast down righteousness to the earth . . .
> Woe to those who are at ease in Zion
> and to those who feel secure on the mountain of Samaria,
> the elite of a prime nation to whom the house of Israel come . . .
> Woe to those who lie upon beds of ivory
> and stretch themselves upon couches . . .
> they bawl idle songs to the sound of the harp
> and like David invent instruments of music.
> They drink wine by the bowlful
> and anoint themselves with choicest oils
> but are not grieved over the ruin of Joseph (Amos 5:7; 6:1, 4-6)

This kind of religion can only be abhorrent to the God of the desert.

> I hate, I despise your feasts
> and I take no delight in your assemblies.
> You may offer me your burnt offerings and cereal offerings
> I will not accept them . . . I will not look at them.
> Take away from me the noise of your songs;
> to the melody of your harps I will not listen . . .

> Did you bring me sacrifices and offerings
> the forty years in the desert, O house of Israel? (Amos 5:21-25)

From where did the prophet draw those impassioned accents? The prophet of Tekoa does not speak much about himself and his human background, and the little he says is unclear. Commentators have often presumed that Amos's sensitiveness to the plight of the poor was due to his own humble origins. One "among the shepherds of Tekoa" (1:1) and "a dresser of sycamore trees" (7:14), he would have belonged to the exploited class of poorly paid manual laborers. Moreover, coming from Tekoa, a village on the edge of the desert, he would have imbibed the spirit of the wilderness where he used to take his flock: "The poor and invigorating life of the desert left a profound mark on the soul of Amos. This background gave him a liking for simple life and a distaste for luxury, a spirit of proud independence. He drew from there a lively and energetic language, rude but frank and fearless."[33] His invectives against the rich would then be an expression of solidarity with the exploited class to which he belonged.

But present-day scholarship tends to view Amos in another light. The "sycamore trees" that he "dressed" might have been his own. The Hebrew word *noqed* in 1:1 (and may be in 7:14), translated as "shepherd" in most translations,[34] is applied to King Mesha of Moab in Transjordan in 2 Kgs. 3:4, where it can only mean "owner of flocks."[35] This would make him "well-to-do, with his own albeit modest, income,"[36] if not an "economically independent landed aristocrat."[37] This would also explain his broad knowledge of the situation and of the events in western Asia (cf. 1:3-2:3).

If such is the case, the prophetic attitude is all the more striking. The members of his guild could have considered him as a turncoat, betraying his peers, shifting his loyalty from the subculture of his caste to that of the opponents. A cultural conversion underlay the prophetic stand of the Judean *noqed*. Before the oppressive prevalent culture could be condemned in the surrounding society, it had first to be uprooted from the prophet's own heart. Deep in himself, in his societal stance and spontaneous reactions, in his thought and in his language, the prophet had to undergo the revolution he was to proclaim. This was the integral "conversion," the *metanoia*, the complete upheaval in one's heart and mind, social approach, and sense of values, that Jesus would proclaim as the key to the "kingdom."

---

[33] E. Osty, *Amos. Osée,* JB (Paris: Cerf, 1952), 10.

[34] See RSV, NRSV, JB, NJB, GNB, NAB, NIB, but "sheep farmer" in the NEB, "éleveur" in the *TOB* and "schafzüchtern" (sheep rearers) in Luther's translation.

[35] See discussion in J. A. Soggin, *The Prophet Amos,* OTL (London: SCM Press, 1987), 9-12; B. E. Willoughby, "Amos," *ABD* 1:203-212.

[36] Soggin, *Prophet Amos,* 10.

[37] Willoughby, "Amos," 205, and even, according to R. R. Wilson "a member of the Judean upper classes, if he was not actually a part of the political or religious establishments in Jerusalem" (*Prophecy and Society in Ancient Israel* [Philadelphia: Fortress Press, 1980], 268).

PROPHETIC DIALOGUE WITH CULTURES

Amos and Hosea

Yet every prophet is not necessarily an Amos. When Amos called for a return to "justice," he viewed it as a torrent gushing forth and rolling unexpectedly in the wilderness:

> Let justice roll down like waters
> and righteousness like an everflowing stream. (Amos 5:24)

The image evoked by the prophet belongs to the symbolic field of the desert. It recalls Moses striking the rock to make "streams come out of the rock and cause waters to flow down like rivers" (Ps. 78:16). Treating the same theme of "justice" and comparing it also with water, Hosea proposes a different image of the rain:

> Sow for yourself righteousness,
> reap the fruit of steadfast love,
> break up your fallow ground,
> for it is the time to seek the Lord,
> that he may come and rain salvation upon you. (Hos. 10:12)

To express a similar idea, Hosea's rhetoric moves in a different symbolic field. The image is no longer that of miraculous divine interventions in the desert. Hosea uses an agricultural simile, evoking the God-given growth of the seed and fecundity of the earth. The tonality is "Canaanite": it recalls a Ugaritic invocation to Baal:

> Unto the earth Baal rains and unto the fields rains ʿAliyy.
> Sweet to the earth is Baal's rain
> and to the field the rain of ʿAliyy.[38]

Hosea and Amos are almost contemporary. They address themselves to the same situation and their message is similar. Yet their cultural approach is quite different.

Canaanite Motifs

Hosea's reaction to the fertility cults was original and creative. Hosea is as vehement as any prophet in his condemnation of idolatry (Hos. 2:7-15;

---

[38] *Legend of King Keret* C, iii:4-8, in *ANET*, p. 148. When Baal dies, "parched is the furrow of the soil . . . Baal neglects the furrow of his tillage" (*Baʿal and Anat* iv:25-27; ibid., p. 141; cf. *The Tale of Aqhat* C, i:30-36, ibid., p.153).

4:16f.; 8:4-7). His teaching is closely connected with that of the prophetic circles of the north.[39] But unlike Elijah or Amos, he does not just hurl massive condemnations at the cult of Baal. He accepts facing the questions raised by life in the land. The faith of Hosea is strong enough and sufficiently perceptive to see how Yahwism can be lived in an agricultural setting and its culture. Hosea is no Rechabite. He does not deem it sinful to leave the desert and come to terms with the realities of the soil. The peasant associates his existence with the rhythms of nature, expects from heaven life-giving rains and asks from the divinity the fecundity of earth, cattle, and a wife. For a farmer, faith in Yahweh has to integrate those realities. While remaining a staunch Yahwist and in total loyalty to the God of the covenant, Hosea faces the life problems to which Baalism attempted to give an answer. His oracles adopt the thought patterns and the literary forms through which Baalism formulated its vision of human existence and of the world.

There follows a process of bold acculturation and demythologizing which is interesting to trace in the texts.

Yahweh has a "spouse": the conjugal imbroglios of the prophet become the symbol of God's tumultuous relationship with Israel. It was risky to speak of God in terms of matrimonial involvement. In Hebrew, one of the most common words for "husband" was precisely *baʿal* (cf. Hos. 2:18). The image and the phraseology would have reminded people of Baal and Anat. But unlike Baal's consort, Yahweh's spouse was not a goddess but poor sinful Israel.

Yahweh is "like the dew," "like a verdant fruit tree" (14:6, 9). The latter phrase would have brought to mind the sacred trees of Canaan. Hosea makes a daring use of imagery taken from the cycle of nature and close to the Canaanite vegetation myth and ritual. It was risky to use such a language in the context of the prevailing syncretism which infiltrated even the Israelite sanctuaries. The prophet goes still further when he announces that Yahweh will "sow Jezreel" (2:25). This was a distinctly Canaanite phrase. "Jezreel" was one of the most fertile parts of the land of Israel, one of the centers of the Baal cult, the winter capital of infamous Ahab and Jezebel. Its very name ("*ʾel* will sow") evoked the fertility cults, myths, and rites of Canaanite religion. In the context of nature worship, through the symbolism of a sexual rite, the god "sowed" the earth and thus procured fecundity to the land. It was bold language to adopt this terminology in a Yahwistic context and to suggest that the "grain, the wine, and the oil" enriching Jezreel (2:24) are the fruits of the divine insemination of the bride Israel. Yet these are not produced by magic rite. The conjugal union is not effected in a mythic theogamy but "in righteousness and justice / in steadfast love and in mercy" (2:21) while Israel responds "in faithfulness and knowledge of the Lord" (2:22).

---

[39] See H. W. Wolff, "Hoseas Geistige Heimat," in *Gesammelte Studien zum Alten Testament* (Munich: Kaiser Verlag, 1973), 233-243.

We can speak legitimately of a Canaanite legacy in the book of Hosea. But what a transposition! It is no longer a hierogamy celebrated by magic rites and inspired by utilitarian considerations. It is a covenant freely consented to, and inspired by love. The conjugal relationship of Yahweh with Israel is no longer meant to renew the fertility of the earth in the New Year celebrations but to actualize salvation history.[40]

Similarly, in the text of Hosea 10:12 quoted above, comparative religion would easily trace sexual connotations in such words as "sow," "reap," "break up the ground." But it is righteousness that is sown and steadfast love that is reaped. The rain sent by God is a rain of justice. A similar cluster of agricultural themes appears in Isaiah 45:8 ("Shower, heavens, from above, and let the skies rain down righteousness; let the earth open . . ."); nevertheless it is Hosea 10:12 that is closer to the Canaanite origins of the vocabulary.[41]

The last stich is particularly significant: "till he comes and rains down justice upon you." The motif of the god raining down upon the earth is common in the history of religions.[42] But the prophet demythologizes the theme by applying it to a rain of justice.

The picture of Yahweh as one who "rains" his salvation is daring for Hosea in the light of the conception of the activities of Canaan's gods. Indeed he probably had a model for such language in the cult of Canaan. Baal once sent a message to Anath: "Banish war from the earth, put love in the land; pour peace into the bowels of the earth, rain down love into the bowels of the field."[43]

The idea of a raining God in Hosea 10:12 appeared so dubious to the ancient translators that they tried to circumvent it. The Greek LXX version has: "till the fruits of righteousness come upon you."[44] The Latin, closer to

---

[40] C. Hauret, *Amos et Osée,* VS 5 (Paris: Beauchesne, 1970), 64.

[41] See T. Worden, "The Literary Influence of the Ugaritic Fertility Myth on the Old Testament," *VT* 3 (1953): 296.

[42] See n.38 above. Concerning the religions of the Mediterranean world and particularly of Ugarit, see Gaster, *Thespis,* 195f., 209-211, 237f. In Vedic literature, there is for instance the hymn to Parjanya: "Send down for us the rain of heaven, ye Maruts, and let the Stallion's flood descend in torrents. Come hither with this thunder while thou pourest the waters down our heavenly Lord and Father. Thunder and roar: the germ of life deposit . . . Saturate both the earth and heaven with fatness . . . Thou hast poured down the rain-flood" (*Rigveda* V, 83, 6-10).

[43] J. L. Mays, *Hosea,* OTL (London: SCM Press, 1969), 146f. The Ugaritic text is quoted according to the translation of M. Dahood, *Psalms 1-50,* AB (New York: Doubleday, 1966), 281; cf. *ANET,* 136 (C,10-14).

[44] A reading taken as genuine by H. W. Wolff, *Hosea,* Hermeneia (Philadelphia: Fortress Press, 1974), 180. See the elaborate discussion of D. Barthélemy, *Critique Textuelle de l'Ancien Testament,* Tome 3, OBO 50/3 (Fribourg: Editions Universitaires; Göttingen: Vandenhoeck & Ruprecht, 1992), 584.

the Hebrew text, prefers: "he will *teach* you righteousness."[45] Fortunately the Hebrew scribal tradition did not shy away from the prophetic boldness of Hosea.

> [Hosea] adapts the motifs and rubrics of the fertility cult to portray the relation of Yahweh and his people, to diagnose Israel's sin, and to describe the future which God will create. With daring skill he appropriates the language and thought of Canaanite religion while rejecting Baalism itself. By this strategy Hosea achieves a fresh modernism that plunges into the contemporaneity of his audience.[46]

Was it really a planned and deliberate "strategy"? It could be simply an impulse of the Spirit. To put it in human terms, Hosea may have felt the sensual appeal of the Canaanite culture too strongly in himself to embrace the Rechabite attitude, or even the viewpoint of Amos. Some of the sap of Canaan flowed in the veins of Gomer's husband.

At any rate, this turned out to be the way of the Spirit. In the process of acculturation, Hosea's faith in Yahweh was enriched. The historical God of the Sinaitic covenant assumed the cosmic dimensions of the Lord of Nature.

It is true that "Hosea's language unequivocally shows that he is unable to speak of a divine being in a general sense; rather, he speaks precisely of Yahweh, who has [been] attested and proved himself in history as the God of Israel."[47] He shows a remarkable awareness of Israel's historical traditions. References to the exodus are many (2:5, 16f.; 9:10; 11:1ff.; 12:14; 13:4ff.) and go still further back to the patriarchal cycle of Jacob (12:4f., 13f.). No one could doubt the vigorous and intransigent faith of the prophet. Hosea did not open the door to syncretism. Rather, by making a bold use of the new language, he integrated the Canaanite sense of nature in his faith vision. The Sinaitic Yahweh was now perceived in his relation with the cosmos and its forces. He appeared now as a God who could answer the questions and meet the needs of a people living in villages who had adopted an agricultural pattern of life and society.

Applying to God the image of the "husband" implied also a new dimension of the experience of God. In the context of Hosea's thought, the "husband God" is the God of the covenant and not a mythical progenitor. But the new phrase carried the inevitable connotations of paternal love that will be made explicit in 11:1 "When Israel was a child, I loved him." The Holy One

---

[45] A shrewd transposition based on the fact that the Hebrew root *yarah* can mean both "to rain" and "to teach" (cf. *torah*, the teaching). E. Jacob suggests that Hosea could have meant it both ways and that he deliberately used a verb that could convey both the ideas of rain (fecundity) and instruction (covenant) ("L'Héritage Cananéen dans le Livre du Prophète Osée," *RHPR* 43 [1963]: 254).

[46] Mays, *Hosea*, 8.

[47] Wolff, *Hosea*, xxv.

could also be a loving God. The "jealous," demanding God could also be the God of forgiveness. The transcendent holiness of God was not toned down but expressed in terms of a surpassing love:

> My heart is overwhelmed, my pity is stirred.
> I will not give vent to my blazing anger,
> I will not destroy Ephraim again;
> for I am God and not man,
> the Holy One present among you. (11:8f.)

A Reversal of Language

In connection with 14:9, Wolff speaks of "polemical theology . . . in contrast to the syncretism of Canaanite religion."[48] The introduction to his commentary presents a better balanced assessment:

> Hosea's theology develops openly in dialogue with the mythology of his day in a remarkable process of adaptation and polemic against the mythology . . . [It] provides us with a fundamental example of faith's dialogue with contemporary ideology.[49]

Wolff's summary is quite appropriate, yet two terms he uses are questionable: "adaptation" and "polemic." To the specialist in missiology the word "adaptation" sounds obsolete. As for "polemic," is it the proper term in the context of the deep empathy shown by the prophet toward the Canaanite mentality? Hosea assumes the language of Canaan, and this has far-reaching implications. But he reverses its meaning. We could speak of a "conversion" of language, of a *meta-glossa* in the sense in which we speak of a *meta-noia*. While assuming the language of Canaan, Hosea transposes it and reverses the mental structures expressed by speech. This prophetic conversion of language is two-pronged. Addressed to Canaan, it proposes a new conception of God and of the world. Addressed to Israel, it invites them to adopt an attitude of cultural dialogue that would enable them to reconcile their attachment to the land with their faith in the God of the covenant.

MESSIANISM

The synthesis proposed by Hosea found a parallel in the area of political culture also. Along with the criticism of the monarchical establishment, another prophetic current came to terms with the ambient royal ideology. Messianism viewed kingship as the carrier of the saving divine purpose.

---

[48] Ibid., 237.
[49] Ibid., xxvi.

MESSIANISM AS POLITICAL ACCULTURATION: ISAIAH

Isaiah is the main representative of this trend. Like the imagery of Hosea, Isaiah's symbolical field borrows largely from the surrounding cultures. The Immanuel oracles particularly brim with motifs derived from the royal protocols of western Asia and Egypt. In Isaiah 7:14, the exact meaning of the word *almah* ("young woman, virgin?") is still discussed. An important element of the debate is the occurrence of the same wording in the texts of Rash Shamra.[50] "The least we can say is that both phrases are very similar in wording," says L. R. Fisher. After reviewing the various explanations proposed to account for the similarity, he concludes with J. Gray that the "phrase may be . . . 'the stock formula of the announcement of pregnancy.'"[51] It is rather a tame conclusion in view of the oracular context. The text does not deal with each and every pregnancy. The conception and the birth are to be a sign, whichever may be the way in which we understand the sign and what it points to. Nowhere else in the Bible is a pregnancy announced in such terms. The biblical parallels of "birth annunciation" (Gen. 16:11; Judg. 13:3) do not use the mysterious word *almah*.

The following context continues to evoke mythical overtones. The "curds and honey" with which the child will be fed are connected with the discernment of good and evil (v. 15).

> Curds and honey are a choice food (offered to the gods in the Babylonian rituals), a symbol of plenty (cf. Dt 32:13, Ugaritic texts and the similar phrase of "the land flowing with milk and honey" in Ex 3:8, etc.) . . . The phrase will recur in 2 Henoch 8:5 in connection with paradise.[52]

Similar mythical overtones will recur in the following Immanuel oracle in 8:23-9:6, especially in the royal protocol assigning the coronation names to the new prince:

> Wonderful Counselor, Mighty God,
> Everlasting Father, Prince of Peace. (Isa. 9:6).

---

[50] *Hl ʾglmt tld bn*: quoted and commented on by L.R. Fisher, *Ras Shamra Parallels: The Texts from Ugarit and the Hebrew Bible* (Rome: Pontifical Biblical Institute, 1972), 46-49.

[51] Ibid., 49.

[52] *TOB* (Paris: Cerf-Société Biblique, 1988), 779, n. *r*. The relevant texts are quoted in H. Wildberger, *Isaiah 1-12* (Minneapolis: Fortress Press, 1991), 314, and discussed by G. Rice, "The Intepretation of Isaiah 7:15-17," *JBL* 96 (1977): 363-369. The idea often expressed in commentaries that milk and honey would be a food of famine, still available when, due to war or drought, the harvests have failed, is an academic construction issued in places where milky products and sweetmeat are taken for granted. In poor countries, even in normal times, the use of fat and sweet food is reserved for festive occasions. In cultures that know of real poverty, a famine characterized by "curds and honey" would sound like making a feast out of penury.

"The names which are given to the child are just like the 'great names' which were given to the Pharaoh in Egypt when he was enthroned."[53] The most surprising of those "throne names of the Messiah" is that of ʾel gibbor, "mighty God," or literally "God-Hero." This apparent deification of the king is so puzzling in a biblical context that the ancient Greek versions have just dropped the objectionable title.[54] Obviously Isaiah cannot be suspected of polytheism, and therefore ʾel is to be taken "in a rather free way, in the sense of divine beings," as in Genesis 32:25ff.; 33:10; 2 Samuel 14:17, 20; Zechariah 12:8.[55] Yet the fact remains that the tone of the passage reflects the royal ideology of the Semitic world. The same terminology and atmosphere appear in Psalm 45:6.

All this does not mean that Israel and its poets and prophets borrowed their views on kingship from the pharaohs. They shared in the culture and the language of their neighbors. Once they had accepted the principle of kingship, the expression of their messianic faith could not but be permeated with the mental schemes of the ambient culture. It is difficult to stop a court poet when he feels inspired!

Still, even in the context of the royalist milieus, court hyperbole was reined in by the prophetic Yahwistic faith. J. D. W. Watts has suggested that the pericope of Isaiah referring to the birth of the "messiah" in 11:1-6 is in fact a dialogue in which defenders of the monarchical tradition (vv. 5-6) exchange views with bystanders holding a more reserved attitude toward the dynasty.[56] Anyway and even if the text is a homogeneous statement, it concludes as a discreet but clear reminder to the prince that his power is to be exercised in "justice and righteousness" (v. 6) and that all the marvels expected from the messianic rule are to be attributed to the "zeal of Yahweh of Hosts." In the oracle of 11:1-10, mythical motifs still recur in the idyllic description of cosmic harmony in vv. 6-8 for which a number of parallels can be found in texts as widely scattered in space and time as the Sumerian poem of Enmerkar, the *Epic of Gilgamesh* and the *Fourth Eclogue* of Virgil.[57] Yet the main stress is on the abiding presence of the Spirit that endows the messianic figure, no longer with names of majesty as in chapter 9 but with the moral equipment of a sage (11:2f.). His role will no longer be that of the warrior, breaking the yoke and the rod of the oppressor to the accompaniment of "the tramping boot in battle tumult" (9:4f.). He will be a prophetic king. Standing for the poor and the meek of the earth in justice and equity, he will wield as his weapons the "rod of his mouth" and "the breath of his lips"(11:4f.). The royal figure bears no longer the features of the ori-

---

[53] Wildberger, *Isaiah 1-12*, 314; he gives parallel texts from Egypt and Canaan on pp. 398 and 402 and discusses whether the text refers to the birth or the enthronement of the royal scion.

[54] Ibid., 387; he notes that Origen marks it with an obelus.

[55] Ibid., 404.

[56] J. D. W. Watts, *Isaiah 1-33*, WBC 24 (Waco: Word Books, 1985), 129f., 134f.

[57] See texts in Wildberger, *Isaiah 1-12*, 479f.

ental monarch but those of the sage and of the prophet. Moreover, as noted by von Rad concerning the Immanuel oracles,

> it is very significant that this coming anointed one is designated as *sar* and his rule as *miserah*. A *sar* is never an independent ruler, but always an official commissioned by a higher authority; even though he is like a king within his sphere of jurisdiction (Is. x.8), and has greater power than many who have no one above them, he nevertheless remains himself a commissioned official; in the language of the east, he is not sultan but vizier, and as such responsible to higher authority. The anointed one is therefore not "king," but is subordinate to a king, namely Yahweh, to whose throne he is summoned as "governor." This deliberate avoidance of the title of king . . . may again involve an attack on the kings in Jerusalem who were now emancipated from Jahweh and behaving as independent rulers.[58]

The clearest messianic oracles intertwine the most enthusiastic expressions of royal ideology with the prophetic caution against monarchical abuse. If not a dialogue between partisans of different views on monarchy, as suggested by Watts,[59] the Isaian messianic texts embody a tension between the thrust of the political culture of the east and the prophetical resistance to the risks of uncontrolled assimilation.

MESSIANISM UNDER SUSPICION: EZEKIEL

More than a hundred years afterwards, Ezekiel was more sober than Isaiah. Chastened by the crisis that had led to the fall of Jerusalem and put an end to the Judean monarchy, he proposed a messianic perspective that infused some of the critical stand of Amos into the Davidic expectations. Ezekiel 34 is particularly interesting in that it expresses the double-edged attitude of the prophet toward the royal dynasty of Judah. It begins with an indictment of the shepherds who have misused their powers to serve their own interests (vv. 1-10). The situation is such that now God himself has to take the situation in hand, resume the function of the shepherd, gather the scattered flock, and lead it to good pastures (v. 11-16). Nevertheless the Davidic covenant is not canceled: David will again be called to be the "one shepherd" (vv. 23-24), the bearer of the new covenant of peace (vv. 25-31). However, this restoration will not be an integral return to the past privileges and functions. The new David will be "shepherd," "servant" (v. 23), and "prince" (*nasi*ʾ) "among them"(v. 24); he will no longer be a "king" (*melek*) "over them." The blueprint for a reconstituted Israel will see to it that this

---

[58] G. von Rad, *Old Testament Theology,* vol. 2, *The Theology of Israel's Prophetic Traditions,* OTL (New York: Harper & Row, 1965), 172.

[59] See n. 56 above.

*nasi*ʾ is kept at arm's length; his estate will be confined to the outskirts of the Holy City, beyond the territory assigned, around the temple, to the priests and Levites and even to the people (Ezek. 45:7f.; 46:21f.; 48:21). The confidence remains in the promises to David, but it is a discriminating and critical confidence. Acceptance and prophetic reproof are woven in a combined perspective.

CONCLUSION

Following an evolutionary model, Western exegesis has often been inclined to postulate a linear development. The starting point is supposed to be the covenantal egalitarianism of the beginnings. With the centralized kingship of Saul the process of decadence has already begun. Things degenerated further when the royal power was appropriated by the dynasty of David. From then on, in both Judah and Israel, history would have only to recall the progressive collapse of a debased system. Prophetism was then construed as a denunciation of this misappropriation of authority and of the royal establishment in general. This construction fitted in with the sociological Weberian model of charism versus institution.

Indeed kingship represented an adaptation to the political culture of the surrounding countries. The Canaanite and Phoenician Baalim and the fecundity cult gave symbolic expression and religious caution to a political economy based on fertility and wealth. Prophetism upheld other values based on covenantal solidarity, concern for justice, and access to that justice for the poor. Transcending forces of nature, Yahweh was free from them and guaranteed freedom from their economic-political and religious tyranny.

Standing for Yahweh against the Baalim, Elijah fought for Naboth and the widows. The wilderness of Mt. Horeb confronted the Phoenician cultural model, the palaces of Samaria, and the luscious prosperity of Jezreel. So did Amos in his protest against an empty cult to a Baalish Yahweh. In this way, the opposition of Elijah to Ahab and that of Amos to Jeroboam II have an emblematic significance. The two prophets project the sharpest image of the tension between assimilation and dissimilation inherent in the Israelite culture.[60]

But facts are often more complex. Every king is not an Ahab. Within the royal institution, the paradigm proposed by Deuteronomy 17-18 kept its value as an ideal. The monarch was exposed to the controlling influence of such prophets as Nathan or Isaiah. The messianism of Isaiah proposed a prophetic ideal of kingship that embraced the perspectives of the covenant.

---

[60] See A. Deissler, "Das Phaenomenon von 'Dissimilation und Assimilation' im biblischen Offenbarungsgang, dargestellt am Verhältnis von Jahwismus and Baalismus bei Hosea," in Pontifical Biblical Commission, *Foi et Culture à la Lumière de la Bible* (Turin: LDC, 1981), 79-92.

Reciprocally, within the prophetic movement, the attitude of Isaiah reveals a stance that is not downright antimonarchical. Similarly, Hosea tried to integrate the language of fertility in his prophetic vision.

Thus was Israelite culture marked by an inherent polar tension between identification with the surrounding world and a sense of specific identity. This tension expressed itself in the uneasy relationship between kingship and prophetism, but it worked also within kingship and prophetism themselves.

There was therefore a continuous tension between culture and counter-culture, assimilation and dissimilation. In "normal" times, the tension remained latent, but it erupted in violent confrontation at times of crisis. Hosea and Isaiah represent a kind of "classicism," in that they succeeded in keeping an even balance between the two opposing forces of acculturation and Yahwist authenticity. The vision of the two great prophets remains as an ideal of a possible reconciliation between the faith in the holy transcendent God and the regard due to the cultures of a humanity created in his image. But the balance was very fragile, and the "golden age" of prophecy was soon to give place to the castigations of Jeremiah and the collapse of 587.

3

Wisdom and Cultures

Wisdom literature is a privileged locus of cultural encounter: "the bibli-cal books which are classified under this title are but a department of a sapi-ential literature which has covered the entire East."[1] All the introductions to the Bible list a number of parallels to Hebrew wisdom found particularly in Egypt and Mesopotamia.[2] The affinity between Israelite and oriental wis-dom has become such a trite commonplace that G. von Rad thought it was time to reverse the perspective and that his work on wisdom should start with "what is specific (to Israel), . . . the reality of life . . . as Israel saw it."[3]

Actually, this general common stock of oriental and biblical wisdom cov-ers a great variety of viewpoints calling for closer examination. So-called "wisdom literature" is so complex that the validity of a common "wisdom" label has been questioned.[4] Similarities themselves can be accounted for in many ways. There can be historical interdependence, cultural interaction, emergence from a common cultural milieu. Affinities can also simply derive from the universal bewilderment of humanity facing the basic enigmas of earthly existence, life and death, sex and love, poverty and richness, evil and sorrow, youth and aging, labor, sickness, frustrations, and so on. Volumes could hardly cover this vast field exhaustively. We may at least attempt a few soundings to trace some of the various forms of cultural interaction at work in the diverse forms of biblical wisdom literature.

---

[1] H. Lusseau, in A. Robert and A. Feuillet (ed.), *Introduction à la Bible,* Tome 1, *Introduc-tion Générale: Ancien Testament* (Tournai: Desclée, 1959), 625.

[2] See the texts in *ANET,* 401-449; see also the elaborate study of the Colloque de Stras-bourg, *Les Sagesses du Proche-Orient Ancien* (Paris: Presses Universitaires de France, 1963); the concise but detailed survey of J. J. M. Roberts, "The Ancient Near Eastern environment," in *The Hebrew Bible and Its Modern Interpreters,* ed. D. A. Knight and G. M. Tucker (Chico, Calif.: Scholars Press, 1985), 94-95; R. E. Murphy, "Wisdom in the Old Testament," *ABD* 6:928-931.

[3] G. Von Rad, *Wisdom in Israel* (London: SCM Press, 1972), 10.

[4] J. L. Crenshaw, "The Wisdom Literature," in *The Hebrew Bible and Its Modern Inter-preters,* ed. Knight and Tucker, 369f.

THE ORIGINS OF WISDOM: THE BOOK OF PROVERBS

A DUAL ORIGIN

"Where then does wisdom come from?" Divided learned opinion seems to justify the puzzled query of Job 28:12. A few scholars see the original setting of sapiential sayings in the clan or the tribe, transmitting folk wisdom and proverbs in the home tradition. Others think of scribal schools attached to the court of the kings.[5]

If we go by the first hypothesis, we have a case of "emergence" of Hebrew wisdom out of a fund of family and clan experience, shared in common with all the surrounding people who lived under the same geographical, climatic and socioeconomic conditions. Problems of conjugal life and children's education, of neighborhood and inheritance, attitude to work, wealth, sickness, and death are the common stock of human existence. Israel could not live in symbiosis with Canaan, Phoenicia, Transjordan, Egypt, and Mesopotamia without drawing from the age-old experience of this vast milieu while contributing to it as well. The cultural roots of Israelite wisdom would be as deep as those of its language.

But the majority of commentators, impressed by a number of verbal similarities with Egyptian wisdom particularly,[6] think that wisdom could have been a trained professional activity, taught to prospective government officials at the court of the kings. Such was the case anyway in Egypt. Biblical tradition also connects the origin and development of wisdom in Israel with King Solomon, who is known to have entertained close conjugal (1 Kgs. 7:8; 9:24) and administrative contacts with Egypt.[7] There is also the possibility that, originated in the clan or the family, Israelite wisdom would have been cultivated, refined, and formalized in the royal schools.[8]

At any rate, it must be noted that wisdom literature has been more widely found in Egypt and in Mesopotamia than in Canaan. In point of fact, the existence of formal sapiential writings in Canaan remains a moot problem. W. F. Albright has pointed to a number of Canaanite words and expressions in Proverbs, and to Phoenician imagery in the book of Job; he submits also that Qoheleth could have been written "by a Jew who lived . . . probably in South Phoenicia."[9] But the fact remains that "we do not possess any didac-

---

[5] See a summary of the discussion in R. E. Murphy, "Introduction to Wisdom Literature," *NJBC*, 448.

[6] See Instructions of Ptahhotep (ca. 2400 B.C.E.), of Merikere and of Amenemhemet (ca. 2000 B.C.E.), and especially of Amenemope (ca. 1200 B.C.E.).

[7] See R. de Vaux, *Ancient Israel* (London: Darton, Longman & Todd, 1961), 1:122f., 129, 132; idem, "Titres et Fonctionnaires Egyptiens à la cour de David et de Salomon;" in *Bible et Orient* (Paris: Cerf, 1967), 189-201 (= *RB* 48 [1939]: 394-405).

[8] See R. E. Murphy, "Introduction to Wisdom Literature," *NJBC*, 448.

[9] W. F. Albright, "Some Canaanite-Phoenician Sources of Hebrew Wisdom," in M. Noth and

tic literature from Ugarit."[10] The parallels to Proverbs from Rash Shamra gathered by J. Khanjian prove that Ugarit had proverbs, phrases, and a sapiential turn of mind—and indeed can there be a country that would not know wisdom? But this background does not amount to systematic collections and to an organized reflection as in the case of Egypt and Mesopotamia.[11] The existence of a Babylonian wisdom text in a Rash Shamra library, quoted by J. Nougayrol, "confirms the Babylonian origin of Ugaritic wisdom."[12] It shows that "wisdom" traveled extensively in western Asia. If it could be imported from Mesopotamia to Ugarit, it could as well make the journey from Egypt to Israel and vice versa. It shows also that, in its ultimate form as recorded, for instance, in the book of Proverbs, sapiential expression reflected more directly the professional intercommunication between the royal chanceries than the spontaneous expressions of a common human experience.

Therefore it would be an oversimplification to see in the book of Proverbs the unsophisticated expression of early Israelite popular wisdom. There must have been an early level of emergence of a wisdom tradition in symbiosis with that of Canaan. But the collection of *meshalim* contained in the Writings is the outcome of a professional process of selection and arrangement of thought following the norms accepted in the official royal establishment.

As regards its relation with surrounding cultures, the book of Proverbs presents a complex picture. It contains a deep layer of popular wisdom which goes down to the solid bedrock of western Asian cultures. In its present form, however, the collection reveals ways of thinking and writing, values and perspectives of a monarchical pattern of society developing in explicit interaction with surrounding countries and especially with Egypt.

A DUAL ATTITUDE

From its very origins, Hebrew wisdom partook of the dual attitude of ancient Israel. Insofar as it emanated from the deep layers of ancient clans and families, it embodied a West Semitic, Canaanite world perception and also reacted against it. Taken over into the monarchical order, it shared in its ambiguity. Its acculturation to the ways of the nations verged precariously on assimilation or was at least tempted by international syncretism. Sure enough, the Yahwistic spirit survived in the recurring reminder that "the fear

---

D. W. Thomas, *Wisdom in Israel and in the Ancient Near East* (Leiden: Brill, 1960), 1-15 (text quoted here from p. 15).

[10] Ibid., 7.

[11] J. Khanjian "Wisdom," in *Ras Shamra Parallels,* vol. 2, ed. L. R. Fischer, AnOr 50 (Rome: Pontifical Biblical Institute, 1975), 373-400.

[12] J. Nougayrol, "Les Sagesses Babyloniennes: Études récentes et textes inédits," in *Les Sagesses du Proche-Orient Ancien,* 50 (the entire text is quoted from pp. 48-50).

of the Lord is the beginning of wisdom." H. Cazelles rightly asserts that "the power of assimilation of biblical thought enabled it to take what was best in the great civilizations that dominated it politically."[13] Yet the same Cazelles notes the ambiguity latent in the ancient texts,

> which is the ambiguity of Israelite monarchy itself. In a sense, Wisdom is as foreign to Israel as monarchy itself. Abraham, Isaac, Jacob are not said to be wise. The term appears with Joseph (Gen 41:33) in the context of the survival in Egypt . . . We can thus perceive the equivocation of Israelite wisdom in its beginnings. It corresponds to the equivocation that will weigh upon Israelite monarchy and explains the conflicts of the prophets against the sages.[14]

Hokmah (wisdom) and *tsedaqah* (justice) are not synonymous. They are rather the two poles of the tension already noticed between Amos and Hosea, Jeremiah and Isaiah, between an acculturation accepting the necessities of human existence and the stern reminder of the holiness of Yahweh.

Paradoxically, during the postexilic period, the old traditional values embodied in the book of Proverbs will be recalled as a protest against the disorder brought about by the foreign rule and the inner corruption of Judean society.[15] In spite of the return from the Babylonian captivity and the rebuilding of the temple, the situation of the Jewish community remained precarious. It was economically impoverished. Politically it was reduced to the position of a backward area on the outskirts of large imperial powers. All too often those powers turned it into their battlefield. The Israelites' religious outlook also had been upset. With the collapse of the monarchy, they had been deprived of the messianic expectations invested in the Davidic dynasty. This situation resulted in a serious identity crisis. Vis-à-vis this deeply seated disorder, the traditional order evoked by the old Proverbs became a rallying point, an indictment of the surrounding injustice. The hoarders (11:26), fast money (13:11), slanted justice (18:5, 16f.), the vicious solidarity of the wealthy against the humble folk (19:4), the iniquitous relations between rich and poor (22:7, 22), the oppression by despotic princes (28:16; 29:12) were stigmatized in the name of ancestral and "proverbial" values.

Interestingly, some of the traditions thus called upon to stem prevailing disorders had been in the past a concession to the ways of the surrounding cultures. For instance, the description of the capable wife that concludes the

---

[13] H. Cazelles, "Les débuts de la Sagesse en Israël," in *Les Sagesses du Proche-Orient Ancien*, 33.

[14] Ibid., 34f.

[15] See A. R. Ceresko, "The Function of 'Order' (*Sedeq*) and 'Creation' in the Book of Proverbs with Some Implications for Today," *Indian Theological Studies* 32 (1995): 208-236.

book of Proverbs (31:10-31) has more in common with a Phoenician land-lady than with spirited Judith or Deborah or with humble Ruth: she is even praised for having trade relations with the "Canaanite" (v. 24).[16] Similarly the portrayal of Lady Wisdom in the first chapters of the book and especially in chapter 8, cannot but evoke, if not the identity, at least the profile of the various Anat, Ashtart, and similar divine queens who also "sat beside (their Lord) . . . and were daily His delight" (cf. Prov. 8:30) in the Semitic and other pantheons.[17] In the postexilic context, however, it could certainly not be understood as a syncretistic surrender to the Mediterranean cults of the goddesses enthroned by the side of their male consorts. The tragic events that led to the collapse of kingship brought a change to the societal and cul-tural significance of woman. Feminine figures came to be proposed as an antithesis to the male-managed failure of yesteryear. In such a setting, the "structural and thematic focus on women in the book of Proverbs" may have been meant to "reflect and support the kingless sociological configuration of the post-exilic era."[18]

Thus was the acculturation of past ages turned into a protest against cul-tural aggression. What had been openness to the world around in the royal period was used at a later stage to counteract unwanted external influences. Past acculturation became the expression of a resistance to new cultural pressures.

CRITICAL WISDOM

The origins of wisdom as reflected in the book of Proverbs reveal a ten-sion between two perceptions of wisdom. A certain type of wisdom is the fruit of experience. Reasonable and sensible, it has come to terms with the surrounding culture and established order. The other sapiential attitude expresses the anxious restlessness of a soul inhabited by a deep sense of the divine holiness. This tension will continue to stir the Israelite sapiential milieus. In quite different forms, the second kind of wisdom finds expres-sion particularly in the books of Job and Qoheleth. But it was already pre-sent in the book of Amos.

---

[16] The "merchant" of the translations is a "Canaanite" *(kanaʿani)* in the original Hebrew text.

[17] "Chapters viii-ix are full of Canaanite words and expressions and may go back to Phoeni-cian sources more directly than any other material in Proverbs. The wisdom cosmogony in viii 22ff. is full of obvious Canaanite reminiscences" (Albright, "Canaanite-Phoenician Sources of Hebrew Wisdom," 9).

[18] C. Camp, *Wisdom and the Feminine in the Book of Proverbs,* Bible and Literature Series (Sheffield: Almond Press, 1985), 289f.

AMOS

There does not seem to be much in common between Amos the prophet and the sages of Israel. Yet several authors have traced the "spiritual home" of Amos to sapiential circles.[19] The broad range of Amos's knowledge of Palestine and of its foreign neighbors, the quality of his style and the use of rhetorical techniques, certain forms of wisdom literature like the pedagogical instruction (3:1; 4:1; 5:1) and didactic questions (5:20; 6:2, 12; 9:7) point to a sapiential background to Amos's outlook.[20] Amos may not have been the uncouth village shepherd he is often supposed to have been. He might rather have been a flock owner, associated with the well-to-do classes.[21] However, his was not the self-complacent language of upper classes satisfied with the existing social situation. We have only to set in contrasting parallel the uproarious image of the society women he presents in 4:1-3 and the decorous portrait of the capable wife in Proverbs 31.

Amos has heard the "roaring" God; the encounter has made him a prophet (1:2). If his cultural background was the sedate setting of the wisdom schools, it has been overturned by the divine violence. His very language is subverted by prophetic inspiration.

> Surely the Lord God does nothing
> without revealing his secret to his servants the prophets.
> The lion has roared; who will not fear?
> The Lord God has spoken; who can but prophesy? (3:7-8)

The context specifies that the Lord God who roars is the one who brought the people out of the land of Egypt (3:1). The image of the lion itself evokes the desert. In Amos, the God and the culture of Sinai swoop down like a bird of prey on the too smooth adoption of the Phoenician ethos represented by the palaces and sanctuaries of Jeroboam's kingdom. Yet to voice the revolt of the poor and denounce the prevailing culture, the prophet uses the language of this same culture, even if he has to strain it to breaking point.

JOB

Like the rest of wisdom literature, the book of Job is well rooted in the Semitic cultural soil and indeed in the haunting universal quandary over the

---

[19] See H. W. Wolff, *Amos' Geistige Heimat,* WMANT 18(Neukirchen: Neukirchener Verlag, 1964); idem, *Amos the Prophet* (Philadelphia: Fortress Press, 1973); S. Terrien, "Amos and Wisdom," in *Israel's Prophetic Heritage,* ed. B. W. Anderson and W. Harrelson (New York: Harper & Row, 1963), 108-115.

[20] See H. W. Wolff, *Joel and Amos,* Hermeneia (Philadelphia: Fortress Press, 1977), 93-100.

[21] See p. 30 above.

enigma of evil. Mesopotamia had its "Babylonian Job,"[22] Egypt, the "Dialogue of the man tired with life" and the "Complaint of the eloquent peasant."[23] Outside the Semitic world, India has a close parallel to the book of Job in the story of Harischandra.[24] S. Terrien, who devotes a page to this Indian parallel concludes rightly: "The book of Job presents a well marked international character."[25]

The book is typically sapiential. It reaches a culminating point in the famous hymn of praise to wisdom (ch. 28): whether attributed to the author himself or to a disciple, it puts the sapiential seal on the whole work. Moreover, the book exhibits the main features of wisdom literature: encyclopedic knowledge *de omni re scibili et quibusdam aliis* ("concerning whatever can be known and few other things as well"), as Mirandola would have said, sense of nature, lengthy debates going through the pros and cons of the theological debate, richness of vocabulary, didactic clarity, and equally didactic prolixity.

But the smooth sapiential flow is broken by the experience of suffering. The book becomes an exercise in cruel irony, turning classical wisdom into derision and presenting it as a cruel joke played on the poor sufferer. Culture is now ridiculed by the representative of the marginalized. The book has the tragi-comic character of a dialogue of the deaf. On the one hand are those who go along blissfully with the religiously correct line of thought, repeating *ad nauseam* the arguments of official wisdom. Facing them, Job represents all those who, at the hard school of grief, have come to face the mystery of another reality. R. Albertz and J. Gammie have suggested that the setting of the book of Job could be the socioeconomic situation prevailing after the exile when people had to borrow and sell their properties to survive famine (see Neh. 5:1-4).[26] Whatever might have been the historical setting, the book reflects the experience of somebody who "in being forced all the way to the bottom, . . . turns and looks up . . . and sees the world through new eyes."[27] As shown in chapters 29-31 particularly, Job's reversal of fortune leads him to a reversal of language and cultural belonging. As a member of the privileged class, he tended to look at the poor as nonentities, "outcast from the land" (30:8). Now that he finds himself in the same humil-

---

[22] *ANET,* 434-437.

[23] Ibid., 405-407, 444-446.

[24] A legendary king of Ayodhya, he was reported to have given all his properties to the sage Vishvamitra. Reduced to the utmost poverty, he invoked god Vishnu and, after various vicissitudes, he reached heaven, where he lives with his family in a heavenly palace. His story is reported in the *Markandeya Purana* and in the *Mahabharata.* See Fr. Madanu, *Job and Harischandra: Biblical and Puranic Expressions* (Hyderabad: St John's Seminary, 1998).

[25] S. Terrien, *Job,* CAT 13 (Neuchâtel: Delachaux & Niestlé, 1963), 9.

[26] Quoted by A. R. Ceresko, "Gustavo Gutiérrez, *On Job,* Some questions of Method," in *Psalmists and Sages: Studies in Old Testament Poetry and Religion,* Indian Theological Studies Supplement 2 (Bangalore: St Peter's Pontifical Institute of Theology, 1994), 200-202.

[27] Ibid., 194.

iated position, he shares their point of view and finds a new way to speak of
God and of his "justice."[28] "He had gained a new perspective on the meaning of that 'justice' he so boastfully talked about upholding in his former
days (e.g., Job 29:11-17)."[29]

By identifying with the poor and the outcasts, making a joke of the official ideology, laying bare the emptiness of correct piety, the language of Job
embodies a cultural revolution. The official culture of an established society
had plunged its nobodies into despair. In their name and in solidarity with
them, Job strikes at the roots of the oppressive culture. He questions the most
fundamental basis of "justice" and uses the language of "wisdom" to expose
its inaccessibility (Job 28). As Terrien says, "the wise man has become a
prophet and, as a prophet facing the transcendent holiness, he is thrown into
the abyss where one loses oneself."[30] In Job the language of wisdom itself
becomes the carrier of the prophetic challenge to wisdom and to its too comfortable cultural expressions.

QOHELETH

"Like a dark riddle is this little book to us."[31] So does R. Gordis begin his
study of Qoheleth. The book indeed bristles with problems, starting with its
enigmatic title disguised in a surprising feminine form and its alleged, obviously improbable, Solomonic authorship. Equally disputed are its style, its
background, and mostly its significance. The book seems to be a web of contradictions. Is it nevertheless to be considered a homogeneous treatment following a dialogical thought process? Or is it made of the broken trends of a
tortuous spiritual itinerary? Or again, is it a pamphlet adopting the shrewd
tactics of a revolutionary thinker hiding his challenge behind the thin veil of
culturally correct language? On the contrary, should we perceive the hand of
a pietistic corrector covering indecent arguments with the ribbons of pious
banalities?[32]

Whichever may be the case, a few points emerge insofar as attitude
towards the ambient culture or cultures is concerned.

---

[28] Ibid., 190-194. "Job turned the whole OT theology on its head. God, he argues, is an anar-
chist who reverses his own order and destroys his creation (chs 4-14) . . . Job's cry and quest is
for a new image of God and a new language of God . . . Job is sensitive to the needs of the suffering masses and theologizes in solidarity with them, and that made his theologizing more real
and authentic" (Jebamalai Susaimanickam, *Commitment to the Oppressed: A Dalit Reading of
the Book of Job* [Rome: Gregorian University, 1996], 43-44).

[29] Ceresko, "Gustavo Gutiérrez," 193.

[30] Terrien, *Job,* 269.

[31] Anonymous quotation in R. Gordis, *Koheleth: The Man and his World. A Study of Ecclesiastes* (New York: Schocken Books, 1968), 3.

[32] Of late, the key to the secret of the book is claimed to have been found in its formal structure: thanks to rhetorical analysis at last an end would have been put to 2000 years of misunderstanding (see A. G. Wright, "Ecclesiastes [Qoheleth]," *NJBC,* 489f.).

1. Qoheleth is *well rooted in the culture of his times.* The book was probably written during the Persian or the Hellenistic period, but before the great crisis that triggered the Maccabean revolt. The author shows himself "undoubtedly trained in the Wisdom academies."[33] He knows their style and phraseology. Even when turning the table on them by putting it in strange contexts, he uses the conventional religious vocabulary of the fear of God and obedience to his commands. His concluding statement need not be an empty boast:

> Not only was Qoheleth a sage himself
> but he taught also the people knowledge,
> weighing, studying and fashioning proverbs with great care.
> He sought to find attractive words
> and honestly set down words of truth. (Qoh. 12:9-10)

2. A further and moot question concerns *the international components* of this wisdom. Wisdom in general deals with the universal issues of happiness, success, failure, death, morality, and so on. But the wise men approached these issues from a certain cultural angle even if this cultural angle was made of intertwining influences. What could be the cross-cultural background of a Jewish sage of the third century B.C.E.? By that time, Israel had entertained close contacts with Mesopotamia and Persia, the Aramaic world, classical and Hellenized Egypt and whichever countries had been affected by the Greek influence that had followed the campaigns of Alexander. In this tangle of possible influences, it is difficult to point to specific currents. There is a "Babylonian Qoheleth,"[34] and an Egyptian debate on the futility of life.[35] Greek influence is disputed: Epicureanism, Stoicism, Heraclitus, Hesiod, and others have been proposed as models that Qoheleth could have followed.[36] We may follow E. Podechard's balanced conclusion:

> The Hebrews did not live in total seclusion and their thinking did not develop in a milieu that would have been immune from any outside influence. The study of wisdom particularly depended on foreign factors, which explain that the sages of Israel took a viewpoint which was

---

[33] Gordis, *Koheleth,* 28.

[34] *ANET,* 438-440; see also the Dialogue between the Master and the Servant in *ANET,* 437f.

[35] Or "Dispute over suicide," *ANET,* 405-407. See further developments in O. Loretz, *Qoheleth und das alte Orient* (Freiburg: Herder, 1964), 57-134 for Egypt, and pp. 135-217 for Mesopotamia.

[36] Loretz, *Qoheleth,* 48-57 is rather negative: "In the book of Qoheleth, we miss not only the influence of Greek language ... but also the impact of Greek and Hellenistic philosophy, literature, mentality" (p. 56). A more positive assessment can be found in M. Hengel, *Judaism and Hellenism* (London: SCM Press, 1974), 1:115: "Influence from the Greek world of ideas is seen in Koheleth more than in any other Old Testament work." The question is extensively covered by E. Podechard, *L'Ecclésiaste,* EBib (Paris: Lecoffre-Gabalda, 1912), 83-109.

not specifically Israelite, nor even religious. By adopting Aramaic language, the Jews ceased being isolated from the outside world if ever they had been. The international character of this language made it a vehicle for all kinds of influence. Through this channel, some Greek ideas could reach the Hebrew mind, even before the campaigns of Alexander. Anyway, when the Greek period began, Hellenism could not but play its educative function in Palestine as well as elsewhere. Did Qoheleth come under this influence? There is ground for thinking so when we consider the general way in which he questions the purpose and the meaning of life, his tendency to think and reason in abstract terms . . . Eccl may not have come into direct contact with the works of Greek philosophers. But he could not escape the diffuse influence of their methods and ideas.[37]

The book of Qoheleth does not illustrate a deliberate effort of "inculturation." Rather it presents an example of the mutual osmosis which impregnated eastern Europe, western Asia and northeast Africa after Alexander. It would be difficult to analyze all the complex elements of this cultural melting pot and to differentiate or oppose Egyptian, Mesopotamian, Greek, or other elements. It may not even be so outlandish to evoke Buddhist elements.[38] The Indian emperor Asoka (273-237 B.C.E.) sent Buddhist missionaries to the west as well as to the east and, if North India knew a Greco-Buddhist school of sculpture and architecture, the west of Asia could as well have felt the pull of Buddhism. This again does not mean that Qoheleth would have practiced yoga under a Buddhist *muni* or *bhikku* or that he would have pondered over the volumes of the *Tripitaka*. But he did belong to a world in which the Yahwistic faith was exposed to new questions, new currents, and new ways of thinking.

3. This exposure to cultural pluralism could not go without an *anthropological crisis*. When this crisis exploded with the persecutions of Antiochus IV and the Maccabean reaction, it had been simmering for quite some time. This sociocultural background would have been sufficient to stir waves of unrest in Hebrew mentality.

Hebrew thinking itself had also its own inborn ferments of dissent. In his own original way, Qoheleth stands in the line of Amos challenging the religiosity of Israelite establishement, of Ezekiel questioning the standard belief in collective retribution, of Job refusing to accept the smooth understanding of divine justice. The elegant skepticism of Qoheleth hides a real prophetic protest.

A book made of questions, [Qoheleth] is mostly a vast questioning not so much of traditional doctrine . . . , as of oneself and of the dominant

[37] Podechard, *L'Ecclésiaste,* 109.
[38] As suggested by Dillon, quoted by Gordis, *Koheleth,* 7.

culture as well . . . This heir to the Old Testament was immersed in the general cultural ambience of the Hellenistic milieus made of all the various cultures of the Near East. Yet, one must go one step further. Qoheleth may have used the language of contemporary culture open as he was to the world. Nevertheless in his own way and from within the same cultural ground, he has also reversed the meaning of the themes he utilized . . . What is new with Qoheleth is that the reversal brought about by his message is exercised from within the very same cultural process he had adopted.[39]

4. The challenge of Qoheleth was two-ended. To Israel he maintained that the very happiness of the just was an illusion; to the nations he declared that ultimately there is no other truth than the fear of the Lord. To both the message was upsetting. Yet his way of overturning the cultural standards of Israel and of the surrounding world can hardly be qualified as a revolt. It is indeed difficult to qualify the skepticism of Qoheleth. E. Renan credits him with a turn of mind similar to his own: Qoheleth would have been a kind of unfrocked rationalistic rabbi, too skeptical even to wish to topple the apple cart; like Renan, he would have just turned the table on pious language. Gordis suggests that Ecclesiastes was too much a man of the establishment to express feelings of revolt: his would have been a bourgeois type of reaction, disinterested in its lucidity. Or was it a metaphysical disinterestedness akin to that of the Buddha? Or again, should we say that the radical criticism of Qoheleth extends to revolt itself, since revolt itself is nothing but vanity and illusion? Unlike Job, Qoheleth does not voice the cry of anguish of those in despair. He prefers to lay bare the hollowness of comfortably settled happiness. His prophetic questioning does not confront head-on the falsehood which it denounces. From inside the establishment, speaking its language and paying it due respect, *he undermines its certitudes by putting the basic questions arising from concrete life experience.* There is no reason to doubt the sincerity of his conclusion: "Fear God and keep his commandments." But his faith in God is qualified by an acid questioning of correct ideology. A faith that has undergone such a treatment can no longer be used as a prop to the pattern of comfortably settled religion, society, and culture.

ACCULTURATION: THE WISDOM OF SOLOMON

"The book of Wisdom is a good example of inculturation."[40] Indeed, of all the books preserved in the Alexandrian Bible canon, it is the one that corresponds best to what present-day theologians call "inculturation." Its

---

[39] D. Lys, *L'Ecclésiaste ou que vaut la Vie?* (Paris: Letouzey, 1977), 77.

[40] M. Gilbert, "Le Livre de la Sagesse et l'Inculturation," in *L'Inculturation et la Sagesse des Nations*, Inculturation Series 4 (Rome: Gregorian University, 1984), 1.

attempt to express his Jewish convictions in the language and thought patterns of Alexandrian Hellenism brings to mind the later efforts of Ricci, De Nobili, or Beschi to translate the gospel message in the classical language and thought patterns of China or India.

ALEXANDRIAN JUDAISM

Alexandrian Judaism produced a rich literature inspired by the Bible. It was the first time that the Jewish faith met a different culture on the latter's own ground and in its own language. In the Babylonian exile, the transplantation had been imposed by a conqueror and had been lived as a temporary experience. Faith in Yahweh had taken the form of a hope in a return to the land and in a restoration. A few centuries later, in Alexandria, the *golah* had become a fact of life. The Jewish community had made its home in Egypt, adopted its language. It had become a political factor in a city where it occupied two out of the five town districts and could number two to four hundred thousand souls, in a country where they constituted a block of one million out of a total population of seven million.[41] This adjustment to the new setting is evidenced by the sizable literature produced by the Egyptian Jewry and stretching over four centuries. To mention a few, almost at random,[42] pride of place must be given to the Septuagint Greek translation of the Bible in the third century B.C.E. Aristobulus, Artapanus, and Aristeas belonged to the second century B.C.E., the Wisdom of Solomon itself probably to the first century along with Alexander Polyhistor. The floruit of Alexandrian Judaism was reached with its most illustrious representative, Philo, at the turn of the Christian era (13 B.C.E.-54 C.E.). He was followed by 3 Maccabees, Pseudo-Philo, and the *Sibylline Oracles*.

It is not clear whether this large body of literature was addressed to the outsiders, as a part of a Jewish missionary drive, or to the insiders to confirm them in their ancestral faith against the too brilliant lure of Egyptian Hellenism.[43] At any rate, it is obvious that this literature is the expression of the

---

[41] According to Philo, *Flacc* 55. See E. Schürer, *The History of the Jewish People in the Age of Jesus Christ (175 B.C.-A.D.135),* rev. and ed. G. Vermes, F. Millar, and M. Goodman (Edinburgh: T & T Clark, 1986), vol. 3/1, 46-50.

[42] See the elaborate survey of Schürer-Vermes, *History,* vol. 3/1, 470-704.

[43] Ibid., 159-176. The case may have to be considered separately for each author. For Philo, a missionary intention is taken for granted by the old edition of Schürer (II/II, pp. 303-315; II/III, pp. 368, 381); G. F. Moore, *Judaism in the First Centuries of the Christian Era* (Cambridge, Mass.: Harvard University Press, 1927), 1:323-328; B. J. Bamberger, *Proselytism: The Talmudic Period* (New York: Hebrew Union College Press, 1939), 18f., 22f. It is denied by E. Will and C. Orrieux, *"Prosélytisme Juif?" Histoire d'une Erreur* (Paris: Les Belles Lettres, 1992), 81-99, 308-316. As for the book of Wisdom, "the author's purpose was to strengthen the faith of his fellow Jews in Alexandria" (A. G. Wright, "Wisdom," *NJBC,* 511); see Gilbert, "Le Livre de la Sagesse," 5; J. M. Reese, *Hellenistic Influence on the Book of Wisdom and Its Consequences,* AnBib 41 (Rome: Biblical Institute, 1970), 146-151, who adds in note: "This opin-

interface between Judaism and Hellenism and that it represents a type of reaction that differed totally from the massive cultural rejection that was taking place at the same time in Palestine under the leadership of the Maccabees. The attitude of the Wisdom of Solomon toward Hellenistic culture must be perceived in this context. Its positive stand appears in both the form and the contents of the book.

THE FORM AND THE LANGUAGE

"'No existing work represents perhaps more completely the style of composition which would be produced by the sophistic school of rhetoric' as it existed under the conditions of Greek life at Alexandria."[44] Avoiding the translational style of the LXX,[45] the author displays a rich, educated vocabulary.[46] J. M. Reese gives a long list of terms reflecting philosophical,[47] ethical,[48] and psychological[49] Hellenistic language.

The list can be extended to religious language.[50] The most significant example is not confined to the Wisdom of Solomon, which has it in common with the entire Alexandrian Judaism. It is the translation of the divine name YHWH as *kyrios,* the Lord. It was a daring step to replace the cryptic and hallowed denomination of the God of Israel by a term that was plain and easily understood but remained somewhat expressionless. The semantic loss was evident. The exotic aura and the arcane remoteness of the Hebrew word disappeared in the linguistic transfer. Lost also was the sense of uniqueness conveyed by the Tetragrammaton: *kyrios* could be commonly applied to the various deities of the Egypto-Hellenistic pantheon. Palestinian Jews must have felt that the new translation made cheap of the divine name. This sense of disappointment was later echoed by an old rabbi who declared that the day when the Greek translation was done "was a hard day for Israel, like the

---

ion is common among commentators" (p. 146 n. 66): the "ungodly" castigated all through the book are not pagan idolaters but lapsed Jews.

[44] H. B. Swete, *An Introduction to the Old Testament in Greek,* 2nd ed. (Cambridge: University Press, 1902), 268-269, quoting B. F. Westcott in *Smith's Dictionary of the Bible,* 3:1780. The style of wisdom is studied in great detail by Reese, *Hellenistic Influence,* 1-31.

[45] Of the 6,952 words used in the book, 335, that is, 20.75 percent of its vocabulary, do not occur in the proto-canonical parts of Wisdom literature.

[46] His range of vocabulary extends to 1,734 different words, of which 1,303 appear only once (Reese, *Hellenistic Influence*).

[47] Especially in the description of the attributes of wisdom in 7:22-24 and also *pneuma zōticon* (life-giving breath), *systasis* (constitution), *physis* (nature), and so on (ibid., 12-17).

[48] *Kakia* (evil), *apistia* (treachery), *aselgeia* (licentiousness), *philotimia* (ambition), and so on (ibid., 17-21).

[49] "In his detailed description of the effects of fear upon the Egyptians (in Wis. 17:3-18), the Sage incorporates 30 words never found elsewhere in the canonical books of the Old Testament" (ibid., 22).

[50] For example, *apaugasma* (radiance), *paredros* (throne partner), *mystis* (initiate), *pronoia* (Providence), *theiotēs* (divinity) (ibid., 6-12).

day on which Israel made the Golden Calf."[51] It is not only in present-day debates that some find the line too fine between "inculturation" and infidelity. Yet the loss of arcane incommunicability was the price necessarily to be paid if, in Alexandria, the Hebrew God was not to be considered one more weird provincial deity of none but folkloric interest.

Readers of Wisdom not only come across a rich Greek vocabulary; they sense also a Hellenistic turn of mind expressing itself in Greek literary forms. But when it comes to giving more precision to this general feeling, scholars seem to enact the fable of the blind men and the elephant and opinions are divided. Looking from the point of view of the second part of the book (chs. 11-19), some would maintain that, under the Greek veneer, the Wisdom of Solomon constitutes "a very useful illustration of what a midrash is."[52] Sectional Hellenistic forms can easily be identified such as *synkrisis* or parallel constructions, aretalogy, allegory, irony, diatribe, sorites, and so on. As regards the book in its entirety, Reese would consider it an example of the *logos protreptikos,* or didactic exhortation.[53] Gilbert opts for the form of *enkōmion,* or eulogy: the book would be a "Praise of Wisdom."[54] The difficulty of classifying the book in neat categories may be compounded by the intellectual formation of the author trained in both the Jewish and the Hellenistic traditions. The literary genre of the book itself can be given as an illustration of intercultural blend.

THE THEMES

The terminology reflects the argument of the book and the way in which its themes are treated. For instance, the word *athanasia* (immortality) is used five times (3:4; 4:1; 8:13, 17; 15:3) in conjunction with *aphtharsia* (incorruptibility). Both terms suggest an approach to the question of afterlife other than the belief in a resurrection. The difference should not be overrated. The author does not indulge in speculations on the immortal and spiritual nature of the soul. Yet words have their own potency. "Resurrection" sees life after death as a gift of God; "immortality" implies an abiding human capacity to overcome death. The one is theological; the other is predominantly anthropological.

The role given to *sophia,* wisdom, is particularly noteworthy. She mediates relationship with God as in Greek philosophy and particularly in Stoicism.[55] This wisdom is inhabited by a *pneuma,* a spirit described in the

---

[51] Quoted by E. Nida, *Towards a Science of Translating* (Leiden: Brill, 1964), 2.

[52] A. G. Wright, *The Literary Genre Midrash* (Staten Island, N.Y.: Alba House, 1967), 109. But, in his commentary in *NJBC* (p. 511), Wright adopts the position of Reese.

[53] Reese, *Hellenistic Influence,* 117-121.

[54] Gilbert, "Le Livre de la Sagesse," 3.

[55] See C. Larcher, *Études sur le Livre de la Sagesse,* EBib (Paris: Gabalda, 1969), 350-355. The Stoic speculation on *sophia* reaches mystical dimensions in the *Hymn to Zeus* of Cleanthes.

lengthy litany of 7:22-8:1. Curiously, Reese sees in this text a transfer of the Egyptian speculations on the goddess Isis. If the "radiance of eternal light" in v. 26 may evoke an inscription praising the Egyptian goddess "who dwells in the rays of the sun,"[56] the overtones of Greek philosophy are much more evident, particularly in vv. 22-24. Actually, "the author seems to have ingenuously borrowed a certain number of themes of the stoic vocabulary."[57]

A little further on, in 7:26, the "reflection of eternal light" and "the image of his goodness" are more Platonic or Neoplatonic than Stoic motifs[58] or belong to "the cosmological speculations of platonico-stoic eclecticism."[59] Rather than identifying the influence of specific philosophical schools, we may rather say in general terms with H. B. Swete that the Pseudo-Solomon "clearly belongs to a period when the Jewish scholars of Alexandria were abreast of the philosophical doctrines and literary standards of the Greek contemporaries."[60]

ACCULTURATION OR ASSIMILATION?

Swete adds that the book of Wisdom "is the solitary survival from the wreck of the earlier works of the philosophical school of Alexandria which culminated in Philo."[61] The remark is quite pertinent and draws our attention to the sizable mass of Judeo-Alexandrian literature of which Wisdom is just an element. How is it that, out of all that huge literary collection, the Pseudo-Solomon was salvaged only in the Alexandrian canon?

It would not do to explain the privileged treatment of the book by its pseudonymous authority. Many other pseudepigrapha were never received into the canon. We should rather reverse the perspective and ask why, in this particular book among so many other productions, the Egyptian Jewry recognized an echo of the great biblical voices of old. When compared with the rest of Judeo-Alexandrian literature, Wisdom strikes a sober, "biblical" note.

---

[56] Cyme inscription v. 43, quoted by Reese, *Hellenistic Influence,* 45.

[57] G. Verbeke, *L'évolution de la doctrine du Pneuma du Stoïcisme à Saint Augustin* (Louvain: Presses Universitaires, 1945), 233. Cf. Larcher, *Études,* 368-375; idem, *Le Livre de la Sagesse ou la Sagesse de Salomon,* EBib (Paris: Gabalda, 1984), 2:479-514. A stoic background may also be traced in 1:7: "The spirit of the Lord has filled the world and that which holds all things together knows what is said." The author has in mind Genesis 1:2, but "[t]here is a highly probable influence of stoic panpneumatism shaping his biblical convictions" (M. A. Chevallier, *Souffle de Dieu: Le Saint-Esprit dans le Nouveau Testament* (Paris: Beauchesne, 1991), 3:161. This Alexandrian understanding of Genesis 1 differs from the Palestinian one in which "the cosmic function of the Spirit does not seem to be mentioned at all in the older Rabbinical literature" and "the *ruah* of Gen 1.2 is commonly translated 'wind'" (though not in the *Neofiti Targum* of Jonathan) (E. Sjöberg, "*pneuma,*" *TDNT* 6:380).

[58] See Larcher, *Études,* 385-388, who quotes *Rep.* 6.509A, where the sun is called "the image of the idea of Good," and *Rep.* 6.510E on the theme of the "mirror."

[59] Larcher, *Études,* 386.

[60] Swete, *Introduction,* 268.

[61] Ibid., 269.

The encounter between Israel and Hellenistic culture was no smooth and homogeneous process. As could be expected, this encounter resulted in an explosion of various attitudes. On the one hand, there was the safe conservative tendency just to wrap the biblical stories in the Greek garb of epics (Philo the Elder), tragedies (Ezekiel the Tragic) or chronology (Demetrius the Chronographer). Others were more adventurous in their hermeneutic or apologetic zeal. The allegorizing method of Philo tended to do away with the historicity of Jewish faith and to reduce it to Platonic symbolism. Apologists pretended to give Israel the credit for all forms of cultural achievement and, in the process, ended up assimilating Israelite religion to that of the environment. According to Eupolemos (second century B.C.E.), Abraham had taught astrology to the priests of Heliopolis; Moses had invented writing and taught it to the Phoenicians, who passed it on to the Greeks.[62] Artapanus went still further: Moses was Mousaios, the master of Orpheus; he had invented sailing, architecture, and irrigation and organized the Egyptian worship according to the various parts of the country; he could be called Hermes on account of his knowledge of letters, arts, and science.[63] Apologetic had run the full cycle. Moses had become the founder of Egyptian zoolatry! In its attempt to assimilate Egypto-Hellenistic culture, Jewish propaganda had lost its bearings. The biblical message had forfeited its identity "losing all sense of the fundamental distinction between Judaism and the Egyptian or Greek religion."[64]

For Aristobulus, all the sages and poets of ancient Greece—Homer and Hesiod as well as Pythagoras and Plato—were mere plagiarists of the law. When quoting Aratos, he substitutes "God" to the invocation to Zeus: "To God our prelude . . . Filled with God are the streets . . . , the seas . . . : we belong to his race."[65] He does the substitution deliberately and explains: "The power of God penetrates everything and so we have rendered the intended meaning by renaming the two mentions of the name of Zeus."[66] In the same way the letter of Aristeas, while condemning the stupidity of idolatry (134-138), has an embassy telling the Egyptian king Ptolemy concerning the Jews that "they worship the same God . . . as we ourselves . . . though we call him by different names, such as Zeus or Dis."[67]

Alexandrian Judaism stands poles apart from the inflexible fidelity to the Lord shown by the Maccabees in Palestine, more or less at the same time. Even in Egypt, it is doubtful that the religious sense of the local Jews would

---

[62] The writings of many Judeo-Hellenistic writers have been partly preserved in the quotations made by Eusebius, *Praeparatio Evangelica;* for Eupolemos, see 9.26-29 (*PG* 21:721-748).

[63] Eusebius, *Praep. Ev.* 13.13 (*PG* 21:1103-1139).

[64] Larcher, *Études,* 135.

[65] Eusebius, *Praep. Ev.* 13.12.6; cf. Acts 17:28.

[66] Eusebius, *Praep. Ev.* 13.12.7.

[67] *Letter of Aristeas* 15; text *APOT* 2:96.

have accepted the assimilation of Yahweh to Zeus or "Dis" and of Moses to the mythological teacher of Orpheus. Neither would they have been happy to fancy Moses as an Egyptian liturgist. In the beginning of its chapter entitled "Jewish Literature composed in Greek," the new Schürer raises the basic question of how deep was the interaction between Judaism and Hellenism. For some, the two cultures "entered into a process of inner fusion with one another." For others, "no such fusion and drastic change within Judaism took place."[68] There can be no single unified answer to the question. Insofar as the Wisdom of Solomon is concerned, the answer lies in between. On the one hand, it did not content itself with a repetition of the old stories in a new style; the Pseudo-Solomon joined in real dialogue with Hellenistic thinking. On the other hand, he did not show any confused amalgamation and did not go into the adventurous speculations of Philo or of the Apologetes.

> Neither does he adopt the Stoic conceptions on God and the soul, on the eternity of matter, nor does he accept the metaphysical dualism of Orphism and of Plato nor again does he assume the old belief (resumed by Plato and the Pythagoreans) in the preexistence of the soul and its successive reincarnations.[69]

Mostly he denounces the materialism of idolatry. In so doing, his emphasis is less on theoretical refutation than on the ethical consequences of "godlessness." His perception of "godlessness" recalls that of the prophets. Accents of Amos seem to resound when he describes the unrighteous wallowing in their "revelry," taking "their fill of costly wines," without regard for the "widow" and "the grey hair of old age," deeming their "might" to be the only "right" (Wis. 2:6-11; cf. Amos 4:13; 6:4-6; Isa. 22:13; Micah 2:1). Equally "prophetic" is the lengthy evocation of the judgment of the wicked (Wis. 3-5). As for the survey of Israel's history and the criticism of idolatry in chapters 10-18, it is "in perfect harmony with the biblical tradition . . . [The author's] project is always expressed in terms of a genuine Yahwism."[70]

In his study of the "levels of assimilation" among Egyptian Jews, J. M. G. Barclay quotes Artapanus, Ezekiel the Tragic, the Letter of Aristeas, Aristobulus, and Philo as examples of "cultural convergence."[71] On the opposite side, the Wisdom of Solomon is listed, along with 3 Maccabees, *Joseph and Aseneth,* and the Egyptian *Sibylline Oracles,* as representing "cultural antagonism." Barclay justifies this classification by the emphasis on judgment

---

[68] Schürer, *History,* 471.

[69] Larcher, *Études,* 232.

[70] M. Gilbert, *La Critique des dieux dans le livre de la Sagesse,* AnBib 53 (Rome: Pontifical Biblical Institute, 1973), 269.

[71] J. M. G. Barclay, *Jews in the Mediterranean Diaspora: From Alexander to Trajan (323 BCE- 117 CE)* (Edinburgh: T & T Clark, 1996), 127-180.

found in the first part of the book (1:1-6:11) and by the aggressive reinterpretation of Exodus given in the latter part (chapters 10-19) with its unmitigated condemnation of Egyptian idolatry.[72] He concludes:

> Since such conflictual and antagonistic passages form the beginning and end of the *Wisdom of Solomon* in its present form, I understand its primary tone as one of cultural antagonism . . . His passionate invective against Gentile religion and his strong affirmation of the Jews' identity as the people of God might have played a significant role in enabling the Jewish community to hold steady in such difficult days.[73]

Indeed the book of Wisdom could hardly be proposed as a model of interreligious dialogue. Yet we should not lose sight of the other side of the picture. This "cultural opposition" is expressed in flowing Greek style and typically Hellenistic thought patterns. The educated Alexandrian reader of the Wisdom of Solomon might have disagreed with the contents of the book. But he would have appreciated its range of expression and would have found himself at home with its way of speaking and thinking. Given the wide variety of philosophies disputing the attention of Alexandrian literati, he might not have been averse to giving a hearing to this Jewish philosophy, which was expressed with such a sophisticated command of language.[74]

Among the various but confused forms of encounter between the Hebrew faith and Hellenism in Alexandria, the canonizing tradition has retained a book which, at the same time, responded to the need of positively entering into dialogue with the predominant culture while preserving the prophetic spirit of fidelity to the covenant. Put in the mouth of a king and addressed to judges, kings, and rulers (1:1; 6:1, 21-24), the challenge of the sage does not shy away from political confrontation. Inherited from the prophets, his stance denounces the imperialism that gloried in ruling over many nations (6:2) but failed to "rule rightly or to keep the law or to walk according to the purpose of God" (6:4).[75] The book of Wisdom has been presented as an example of cultural "synthesis," "fusing wisdom tradition with a number of other elements . . . as well as Hellenistic culture."[76] But the words "synthe-

---

[72] Ibid., 184-188.

[73] Ibid., 190-191.

[74] Language does matter. In this respect, I would hesitate to go by the distinction proposed by Barclay between assimilation and acculturation. Assimilation would be a matter of social integration concerning "social contacts, social interaction and social practices." By contrast, acculturation would be a matter of "linguistic, educational and ideological aspects of a given cultural matrix" (*Jews in the Mediterranean*, 92). The distinction seems to be artificial. Social belonging expresses itself in language and ideology. Reciprocally language and ideology are important elements of the societal tissue.

[75] Even if the address to the kings is an accepted feature of the Hellenistic tracts on kingship, it remains that "the book of Wisdom does not belong to those tracts written to flatter ruling tyrants" (Reese, *Hellenistic Influence*, 149-150).

[76] Wright, "Wisdom," 512.

sis" and "fusing" have connotations that are too systematic and intellectual. They suggest a deliberate attempt to form a coherent system of thought. The Pseudo-Solomon was not a systematic theologian or a philosopher. He was simply a "wisdom writer," a sage. He stood both within and vis-à-vis the surrounding culture. As in the other works of Hebrew wisdom, he kept a double focus on the God who had spoken in the history of Israel and on the world in which he lived. Some refused to look at this world; others yielded to the fascination of this environment. Still others, obsessed by apologetic concerns, reduced the encounter to an exercise in equivalence of concepts. If the Wisdom of Solomon was received by the Alexandrian Jewish tradition, it was not because it presented a totally coherent synthesis but because it echoed the double abiding dimension of the Jewish faith, a faith in a God who is both holy and close to his people, both immanent and transcendent.[77]

CONCLUSIONS

As regards the relationship between the Bible and culture, wisdom literature constitutes a rich and privileged field of exploration—privileged in that it is characterized by a concrete universalism, an anthropological interest, and an openness to the world and to the human being that set it apart from other biblical currents; rich on account of the variety of its chronological, geographical, social, and cultural settings and of the diversity of outlook it manifests. Our few soundings in representative areas may suffice to authorize a few conclusions.

1. The obvious openness of Hebrew wisdom to the surrounding world arises from different attitudes. The latest of its expressions in the Wisdom of Solomon is a fairly typical example of deliberate *acculturation*. But the slightly earlier book of Qoheleth, written in Palestine and in Hebrew does not evidence such deliberate concern. Insofar as it reflects trends of the surrounding Greek culture, its acculturation is more by way of *osmosis* through symbiosis than of intended interaction. In the earlier stages, when wisdom sayings and writings are the expression of popular sagacity or the formulation of scribal training, Hebrew wisdom *emerges* out of an experience shared

---

[77] On the whole, the conclusion of P. Heinisch remains valid: "As against his younger countryman, Philo, who putting his trust in philosophy, tried to wed Jewish faith and Greek thinking and thereby unconsciously jeopardized or watered down several aspects of Old Testament teachings, the hagiographer (of the book of Wisdom) stood solidly on the ground of Judaism . . . No doubt, [he] indulged in the allegorical explanation of Scripture. But while Philo interjected philosophical views into the biblical text, the hagiographer wants only to remind the pious devotee coming to the Temple and seeing the High Priest in all his festive garments (9,8; 18,24) that he should keep in mind the power of God" (P. Heinisch, *Griechische Philosophie und Altes Testament, II, Septuaginta und Buch der Weisheit* (Münster: Aschendorff, 1914), 87-88.

at the two levels of a common Semitic attitude to life and of the international exchange between royal chanceries.

2. The attitude toward surrounding cultures shows *great differences.* When the interaction takes place unconsciously, it may come close to assimilation, as in the case of certain layers of the book of Proverbs. On the opposite side, when acculturation is an intentional process, as in the Pseudo-Solomon, the limits of the sharing are clearly defined and vigorously expressed. Within the same critical attitude toward accepted standards, there is also a great difference of style between the persiflage of Qoheleth and the tragic protest of Job.

3. Underlying the veneer of shared concern, language, and attitude with surrounding cultures, there runs also a current of *critical defiance.* On the one hand, Wisdom has been shown to be the "home" of the most radical prophets, like Amos. On the other hand, prophetic dissent is never totally absent from wisdom reflection. The position of the Israelite sages is always typified by the double influence of insertion into the world and of a call of the Beyond. Like other biblical writings, it is a response to a God perceived as both immanent and transcendent.

4. The criticism of officially accepted wisdom is not the monopoly of Israelite thought. The parallels to Job and Qoheleth found in Egyptian, Mesopotamian, and other literatures show that *human civilizations have always realized their limitations and have continuously entertained a dynamic critical attitude.* In world history, cultures are never a *ktēma eis aei,* "an acquisition forever." Interestingly, in the case of Job and Qoheleth especially, the challenge to traditional Hebrew wisdom finds its arguments and its expression in motifs borrowed from or at least common with currents of thought of other nations. Qoheleth finds himself at one with the questioning of Greek skepticism, if not of the more distant Buddhist invitation to detachment from *sunyata* (universal vacuity). Job, a non-Israelite Edomite from the land of Uz, is at one with the feelings of the Sumerian arguing with his God; he shares in the existential anguish of the Egyptian *Dispute between a Man and his Soul* on whether suicide could not be the only valid issue.[78] The critical attitude toward culture, inherent in Israelite wisdom, belongs itself to the process of "inculturation." Both anthropologically and theologically, "inculturation" is critical. But its criticism is meaningful only if it issues from a shared cultural perception.

---

[78] See *ANET,* 405-407, 589-591.

4

Abraham and Moses
as Paradigmatic Figures

It may seem paradoxical to conclude our survey of the Old Testament with a chapter on Abraham and Moses as "paradigmatic" figures. Yet precisely because they are primordial and foundational, they have a paradigmatic value. The description given them in the Torah is the outcome of a long process of reflection that developed in the various biblical traditions on the significance of the history of Israel. The purport of these stories reaches beyond their historical interest. To the eyes of Israel, the two great leaders are emblematic of the self-awareness of Israel. Abraham is the archetype of the faith response to God's call and promises. Moses embodies the liberation experience.

This paradigmatic value applies also to the question of cultures. The biblical accounts concerning Abraham and Moses illustrate Israel's standpoint in regard to its relation with surrounding peoples. Both heroes are represented as coming from pagan nations, although they sever their links with them to become the starting point of a new history. Their roots belong in a certain civilization. They move away from that world to start a new culture, a new vision of the world.

ABRAHAM

The Lord said to Abraham: "Go forth from the land of your kinsfolk and from your father's house to a land that I will show you." (Gen. 12:1)

ROOTS

The Pentateuch—or, better, the Torah, as it is called in Hebrew[1]— constitutes the core of the Jewish Bible. It is there that the Israelite identity

---

[1] The word "Pentateuch" is purely descriptive: it refers to the first "five scrolls" of the

is defined in terms of covenant and law. Yet, to reach that point in Exodus and the subsequent books, the Torah takes its own slow leisurely way through the fifty chapters of Genesis. In a kind of extended prologue, it goes back to the "fathers," the twelve patriarchs and their common ancestor, Abraham. The story of Abraham itself is prefaced by stories and genealogies embracing the whole of humanity and the entire then-known world, west and north (Japheth), south (Ham) and east (Shem). This is not the place to analyze the sources and their chronological development. As it is, the present redaction makes an important point. It means that the election of Israel took place in a context of solidarity with and dependence on the surrounding world. Through blessings, promise, and covenant, God made Israel "a people holy to the Lord, . . . chosen from all the peoples on earth to be his people, his treasured possession" (Deut. 7:6; cf. Exod. 19:5-6; Deut. 14:2; 26:18; Ps. 135:4; Mal. 3:17). But the first part of Genesis affirms that this identity cannot be abstracted from the common belonging to the surrounding world of the "generations of Shem" (Gen. 10:21-32; 11:11-32), from the wider circle of the "generations of Ham and Japheth" (10:1-20) and ultimately from the "generations of Adam" (Gen. 5:1-32).

This protracted prologue to the Torah extends to the whole people of Israel what Ezekiel said more specifically of Jerusalem:

> Your origin and your birth were in the land of the Canaanites
> Your father was an Amorite and your mother a Hittite.
>
> (Ezek 16:3)

The people of the election are identified by both call and roots. By call this people belongs to God. Its roots are enmeshed with those of "Elam, Ashur, Arpachshad, Lud (Lydia), Aram (Syria)" (Gen. 10:22) and of all the peoples of the earth. From the outset, the Bible presents a wide span of intercultural links as constitutive of the identity of Israel.

Such was the land that brought forth Abraham. The previous chapters imply a long story of interaction between races, countries, and cultures. Abraham was the son of that multicultural background. God did not teach him a new language, new technologies, new artistic expressions. He did not even enjoin new ethics. Abraham remained comfortable with polygamy and slavery. To a large extent, his saga was that of any Amorite clan leader.[2]

A DEPARTURE

But the call of God takes Abraham away from his cradle. The history of the Hebrew ancestor begins abruptly with a departure: Abram leaves his home and his home country for an encounter with God in an undetermined

---

Bible. The Hebrew word *Torah* has more than legal connotations. It evokes the idea of oracular instruction, teaching, guidance.

[2] Or eponymous figure. The question of historicity does not concern us here.

land. The command and the promise of God in Gen. 12:1-8 play an important role in the narrative. The text is prefixed to the history of the covenant as a powerful symbol, "an introit to the story of the patriarchs in such a way as to link the patriarchal with the primeval story . . . and at the same time to point beyond it to the history of the people of Israel."[3] But this "introit" is in fact an "exit": the story begins with a symbol of egression, of "ex-culturation": "Go . . . leave." The cities of Ur and Haran which Abraham is asked to leave represent the south and the north of Mesopotamia, of the land which, along with the valleys of the Nile, the Indus, and the Yangtze Rivers, saw the emergence of human civilization, of technical progress, city building, political organization and administration, science, and literature. This was what Abram left behind to follow God. The story of the great patriarch, of the archetype of God's people, begins with this secession. Why this foundational exodus?

To account for Abram's departure, the Jewish *midrashim* have described a "conversion" of the young hero. The son of an idol maker, he discovers the vanity of idols through various experiences. Taking a public stance against the religion of his father and of his compatriots, he becomes an iconoclast and a preacher of the true faith. Thrown into a furnace, he comes out unscathed while his accusers die in the flames.[4] L. Woolley has given an archaeological veneer to this edifying fiction by describing at length, on the basis of his excavations, the "polytheism of the grossest type" from which Abraham would have escaped.[5] In a similar mood and evoking the royal tomb in which the king's attendants were buried along with their master,[6] liberation hermeneutics could view the departure of Abraham as a revolt against a cruel tyranny. In a more subdued mood, C. Westermann evokes a "crisis situation" from which the nomadic group of Terah had to be rescued.[7] For others, the movements of Abraham across western Asia fit the pattern of normal nomadic transmigrations[8] or correspond to the traffic of caravan traders.[9]

---

[3] C. Westermann, *Genesis 12-36: A Commentary* (Minneapolis: Augsburg, 1985), 146.

[4] See *Genesis Rabbah* 38; L. Ginzberg, *The Legends of the Jews*, vol. 1, *From the Creation to Jacob* (Philadelphia: Jewish Publication Society of America, 1988), 195-203. A similar tradition has continued in Islam: see Y. Moubarac, "Abraham en Islam," in *Abraham Père des Croyants, Cahiers Sioniens* 5 (1951): 108-112.

[5] L. Woolley, *Abraham: Recent Discoveries and Hebrew Origins* (London: Faber & Faber, 1936), 188-258 (text quoted from p. 192).

[6] See L. Woolley, *Ur of the Chaldees* (London: Penguin Books, 1950), 27-67: "when a royal person died, he or she was accompanied to the grave by all the members of the court: the king had at least three people with him in his chamber and sixty-two in the death-pit; the queen was content with some twenty-five in all" (p. 45). Another death-pit contained the bodies of six men-servants and sixty-eight women (ibid.).

[7] Westermann, *Genesis,* 148.

[8] V. Maag, "Malkût Jhwh," *VT* 7 (1959-60): 129-153: "Gen 12:1 . . . reflects an event that occurs not infrequently . . . in the nomadic way of life: the separation of one part of a tribe from the whole . . . and . . . transmigration to new pasturage" (p. 138).

[9] See W. F. Albright, "Abram the Hebrew: A New Archeological Interpretation," *BASOR* 163 (1961): 36-54; C. H. Gordon, "Abraham and the Merchants of Ura," *JNES* 17 (1958): 28-31.

We can go on speculating on the circumstances of Abraham's migration. The whole question hangs on the moot problem of the historicity of the patriarchal saga in Genesis. What is of more direct interest to the reader is the meaning given to the account by the narrator.[10] What did he want to say to his audience and to the successive generations of readers? Inserted as it is as a kind of caption to the whole history of the people, the reference to the departure of Abraham "is to be understood not only as a historical or geographical note, but as a theological programme."[11] The account of Abraham's vocation does not point so much to the past of the patriarch's experience as to the future of the journey on which he will lead his descendants. "In this call and the road which was taken, Israel saw not only an event in her earliest history, but also a basic characteristic of her whole existence before God."[12]

Most of the commentators emphasize the message of faith conveyed by the account. The call of Abraham is "a test of faith,"[13] with an "intentional pathos in the lingering description of the things he is to leave . . . and a corresponding significance in the vagueness with which the goal is indicated . . . Abraham is the hero of faith."[14]

The stress on the faith of the patriarch is certainly an important feature of the narrative. But Westermann rightly remarks that the words of the divine call in 12:1-3 should not be isolated from their context in 11:27-12:9, a context that describes an itinerary.[15] Faith takes the form of starting on a journey. "The text introduces the metaphor of journey as a way of characterizing the life of faith . . . The life of faith is one which keeps Israel in pursuit of the promise of land."[16]

THE LAND AND THE JOURNEY

This itinerant condition is a deeply seated characteristic of God's people. "The patriarch as alien resident is a *tupos* in which the people of Israel sees a reflection of their own nature."[17] The saga of the ancestors of Israel shows them continuously uprooted from their tribal lands (cf. Jacob, Joseph, and ultimately all the children of Jacob). An "exodus" will be the matrix that will mold the people. Except for the short period of David and Solomon, the settling in Canaan will remain insecure and continuously questioned by the prophets. Ezekiel, enacting the exile prophetically, is "a symbol for the

---

[10] Most of Genesis 12:1-9 is attributed to the Yahwist tradition.

[11] W. Brueggemann, *Genesis*, Interpretation 1 (Atlanta: John Knox Press, 1982), 122.

[12] G. von Rad, *Genesis: A Commentary*, OTL (London: SCM Press, 1961), 154.

[13] G. J. Wenham, *Genesis 1-15*, WBC 1 (Waco: Word Books, 1987), 274.

[14] J. Skinner, *Genesis*, ICC (Edinburgh: T & T Clark, 1910), 243.

[15] Westermann, *Genesis 12-36*, 145.

[16] Brueggemann, *Genesis*, 121.

[17] K. L. Schmidt, *"paroikos,"* TWNT 5:846.

house of Israel" (Ezek. 12:6). Then will come the deportation, the precarious return from Babylonia and the Dispersion. Those main stages of the history of Israel illustrate the fundamental itinerancy of a people whose principal celebration was that of a *pesah*, of a passover.[18]

On the other hand, it is a "land" that God promises to Abraham and the whole story of the patriarch is a quest for that land. So will be the story of his descendants. Like any people on earth, the Israelites feel the need of a land in which they will find their roots. The land will polarize the sense of identity. In their relation with God, the land will symbolize all the divine blessings (Exod. 6:4, 8; Deut. 15:4). As regards their cultural self-consciousness, it is the land that will provide a way of life, a world perspective, a system of symbols, a sense of belonging, and a sense of values.

From the very beginning, land and itinerancy form the two poles of Abraham's life and of Israel's identity. The two aspects are well expressed in the opening verse of the patriarchal saga in Genesis 12:1: "Go from your country": it is the call to follow a God who cannot be encompassed by any locality. "To the land I shall show you": God will give the people his blessings and their identity in the earthly world he created. Like their ancestor, the descendants of Abraham will have to carry in their destiny and culture the two opposite aspects of the initial call. Belonging and transcending will characterize their attitude toward surrounding cultures.

The background of this verse in its present form might have been a prophetic protest against too comfortable a settlement in Canaan at the time of Solomon, too successful an acculturation to the ways of the land, resulting in the canaanization of monarchy and the consequent development of royal absolutism.[19] Viewed from that perspective, the call of Abraham is a call to freedom coming from the God of freedom, a reminder to the people and their leaders to press on and keep on walking toward their eschatological goal. God did not take his people to heaven; nor did he propose to them a purely spiritual ideal. He did give them a land "flowing with milk and honey," heavy with earthly goods, "a land of brooks of water, of fountains and hills, a land of wheat and barley, a land of olive trees and honey, . . . a land whose stones are iron, and out of whose hills you can dig copper" (Deut. 8:7-9). But no institution and no human achievement, however noble they may be, can encompass the mind of the Almighty. He will always be beyond and call his people to that Beyond. Promise and blessing have to remain indefinite because God has no limits. He will always "do far more abundantly than all that we ask or think" (Eph. 3:20). God's people are launched into the never-ending journey of God's ways. The children of Abraham will be an "exodus" people, on a continuous search for a city which is to come (Heb. 13:14; cf. 11:10).

---

[18] See L. Legrand, "L'Étranger dans la Bible," *Spiritus* 102 (1986): 57-67.

[19] Brueggemann, *Genesis,* 122.

MOSES

Moses fled from the Pharaoh and settled in the land of Midian. (Exod. 2:15)

BREAKING FREE

From the very outset, the biblical account finds itself in sharp contrast to world history. World history marvels at "the glory that was Egypt." Like Herodotus of old, today's travelers still stand in awe before its huge monuments. Since the days of Champollion, there has been no end of discoveries of ancient temples, tombs, sculptures, and paintings. The scholarly debates have caught popular imagination, relayed by grand exhibitions and less distinguished pulp fiction. But the book of Exodus has another perception of Egypt, that of the migrants reduced to slavery and toiling to build monuments of no concern to them. Viewed from that angle, the "glory of Egypt" was rather the "misery of Egypt" (Exod. 3:17), the "shame of Egypt" (Josh. 5:9), a "plague" (Amos 4:10), an "iron foundry" (Deut. 4:20). In the Bible, Egypt was basically the country *out* of which Israel had to come if they were to live.[20]

The childhood of Moses typifies this attitude of opposition. The story begins like a fairy tale. The baby that should have disappeared in the genocide survives by God's grace. Ironically he is even brought up by Pharaoh's daughter at the royal court. A later tradition, alluded to in the Acts of the Apostles, added that "he was educated in the wisdom of the Egyptians" (Acts 7:22).[21] For the education of the youth, Pharaoh's daughter would have enlisted not only Egyptian but also Chaldean and Greek masters, in other words, the wisdom, art, and technical competence of the entire *oikoumenē*.[22] Judeo-Hellenistic apologetics went still further. Not only was he supposed to have learned from the best of world cultures; he was even claimed to be their founder. Historical novels written by the Jews of Alexandria described him as the inventor of the alphabet, of agricultural and military techniques, of ship building and chariot transport, as the organizer of Egyptian administration. Egypt owed him its philosophy. He was even said to be the teacher of Egyptian religion,[23] which would make Moses the founding father of poly-

---

[20] The phrase "come/come up out of Egypt" recurs 156 times in the Old Testament (43 times in Exodus and 28 times in Deuteronomy).

[21] See Philo, *Vit. Mos.* 1.20-24; 2.1; Josephus, *Ant.* 2.9.7; Pseudo-Philo, *Lib. Ant.* 9.16.

[22] From the Egyptians, he would have learned "arithmetic, geometry, the theories of rhythm, harmony and measure in music, the use of musical instruments . . . the philosophy of symbols and the traditions concerning divine honors given to animals. As for the ordinary educational curriculum, it was the Greeks who taught him whereas scholars from surrounding countries taught him Assyrian language and the Chaldean science of astrology" (Philo, *Vit. Mos.* 23-24).

[23] See the authors and the texts quoted above on pp. 56-58.

theism and zoolatry! At this stage of enthusiastic appropriation of world culture, one is left wondering whether Moses assimilated Egyptian culture or was assimilated by it. The trend of this kind of literature is significant. It betrays the lure of the "wisdom of the Egyptians," of world culture on a people living as a minority in a foreign country and therefore affected with inferiority complex. The only attitude that is imagined is that of uncritical identification with that culture: apologetics end in assimilation.

The biblical text moves exactly in the opposite direction. It does not describe the process of education of young Moses, nor does it explain how the youth preserved, recovered, discovered, or simply never lost his sense of Hebrew identity. After reporting the miracle to which the child owed his survival, the narrative moves abruptly to the act of rebellion against the oppressive culture:

> Moses went out to his people and saw their forced labour. He saw an Egyptian beating a Hebrew, one of his kinsfolk . . . He killed the Egyptian . . . and fled from the Pharaoh. (Exod. 2:11-12, 15)

Moses discovers and asserts his identity in an act of rebellion. There is no facile, romantic assimilation, as in the apologetic Judeo-Hellenistic novels, but the stark rejection of the dominant culture and of its inherent violence. It built beautiful monuments and mighty cities but enslaved its helots and drove them to death.

The place where Moses fled is to be noted: it is Midian, in the Sinai Desert. Egyptian literature had the classical story of Sinuhe, another runaway courtier, who for some unclear reasons, had to take flight from the royal court. But he went to another city, Byblos in Phoenicia, where he could exhibit his talents in another royal court.[24] For Moses, the place of refuge is the desert, which is to function as a powerful symbol through all the pages of the Bible. This symbol of remoteness is to be kept in mind when studying the biblical stance toward culture. According to the Exodus perspective, Israel identifies itself not with cultural accomplishments but with the protest of the oppressed against the ambiguities of human achievements.

INTEGRATION

Yet the desert is not a *nirvana*, a pure vacuity. It is Midian, rather a mysterious land, the geographical location of which is not quite certain.[25] In Bible history, it appears several times in connection with Moab among the

---

[24] *ANET*, 18-22. The story was very popular in Egypt. "Manuscripts are plentiful and run from the late Twelfth Dynasty (about 1800 B.C.) to the Twenty First Dynasty (about 1000 B.C). There are five papyri and at least seventeen ostraca" (ibid., 18).

[25] Scholars situate it either in the Sinai peninsula (F.-M. Abel) or in northeast Arabia, east of Aqabah (J. L. McKenzie, *Dictionary of the Bible* [London: Chapman, 1968], 574).

enemies of Israel (Num. 22:7-14; 31; Judg. 6-8). Yet Moses is represented as entering into the most intimate form of partnership with Midian through marriage—and that with the daughter of a priest. Acculturation turns even into religious fellowship. A strong current of Old Testament scholarship suggests that the designation of ʾel as Yahweh might have had its origin in the family cult of Jethro, the Midianite priest.[26] This view remains hypothetical.[27] Whichever may be the case, the story of Moses' youth and vocation is meant to trace the deep "Sinaitic" roots of Israel's life, culture, and religion. Faith in God cannot be lived in a vacuum. It is to be woven in the warp and woof of political events, social movements, and family situations, in an ongoing interaction of crisscrossing cultural and religious traditions and expressions. Neither is faith in God simply amalgamated with those currents. In the midst of the prophet's total immersion in the life of his people, the Spirit of the prophet denounces the deadly ambiguities of the most brilliant civilizations, and the God of Moses will continue to be attentive and to draw attention to the cry of the oppressed (Exod. 3:7). This intertwining of culture and counterculture, of incarnation and rejection will remain a basic parameter of the relationship between cultures and faith in the God of the Bible.

IN AND BEYOND HISTORY AND CULTURE

This double prelude to Genesis and to the exodus sets the tone of the whole history of Israel. It will be a history deeply rooted in earthly realities. Unlike in the speculations of Philo, Abraham is not sent on a ecstatic journey to the spiritual world of the "sacred Word" of "wisdom"[28] through "contemplative life."[29] He goes to a concrete Canaan of lands and crops, of drought and wells, of friendly and hostile inhabitants, a land defined by geo-

---

[26] This refers to the so-called Qenite hypothesis, according to which Yahweh would have been the god of the Qenites, a clan of Midian. See the elaborate treatment of J. Kinyongo, *Origine et Signification du Nom Divin Yahvé à la Lumière de Récents Travaux et de Traditions Sémitico-Bibliques (Ex 3,13-15 et 6,2-8)*, BBB 35 (Bonn: Peter Hanstein Verlag, 1970), 6-19, 38-41.

[27] See ibid., 39-41. See also the cautious position of H. H. Rowley, "Moses and Monotheism," in *From Moses to Qumran: Studies in the Old Testament* (London: Lutterworth Press, 1963), 48-63: "I do not take the view that the work of Moses is to be resolved into the mere mediation to Israel of the religion of the Kenites. The divine name Yahweh was probably taken over, and the forms of religion; but a new spirit was given to the religion and a new level to its demands. The sense of Yahweh's election of Israel, of His deliverance, of His claims upon her obedience, were all new, and through the truly prophetic personality of Moses it was established on a higher basis than Kenite religion had reached" (p. 59).

[28] Philo, *Migr.* 28.

[29] Ibid. 47.

graphical and historical coordinates. He will build a family of flesh and blood, knowing the joys and the troubles of human families. Similarly Moses, running away to Midian, enters the family of Jethro and finds new roots in the Sinai culture. Having left a civilization, the archetypal figures of Israel adopt another culture. Their "deculturation" results in a new inculturation.

But this move is not just a twist in history, replacing one sociopolitical structure by another one. It is the starting point of an ongoing impetus. The anomalous shift from a rich to a poor civilization implies an invitation to look beyond settled cultural forms and values. It is the beginning of a *history of faith*, of a faith ready to follow God into the cloud of unknowing, into the "mystery of his will," of "his plan for the fullness of time" (Eph. 1:9-10). The Greek myth of the journey was the Odyssey that brought Ulysses back home at the end of all his adventures. The biblical journey does not go back home; it is an ongoing exodus; it looks forward to the "house of God." Abraham and his children will remain *paroikoi,* "people away from home," pilgrims on their way.

By faith Abraham obeyed when he was called, and went forth to the place he was to receive as a heritage, not knowing where he was going . . . For he was looking forward to the city with foundations, whose designer and maker is God. (Heb. 11:8, 10)

By faith Moses . . . refused to be called a son of Pharaoh's daughter, choosing rather to share ill-treatment with the people of God than to enjoy the fleeting pleasures of sin. He considered the reproach borne by God's Anointed greater riches than the treasures of Egypt, for he was looking ahead to the reward. By faith he left Egypt, not because he was afraid of the king's anger; but because he was steadfast as though he saw Him who is invisible. (Heb. 11:24-27)

Thus are posited, from the outset, the two poles of a biblical attitude toward culture. The children of Abraham live in history and are deeply rooted in and committed to the reality of a world that has been blessed in creation and sanctified in incarnation. They share with the rest of humankind in the mission given by the Creator to "fill the earth and control it" (Gen. 1:28), to "till the soil" (Gen. 2:5) and "give names" to all the cosmic environment (Gen. 2:19-20). Culture, like nature, has therefore a consecrated value.

But the people of Abraham and Moses have inherited and continue to heed the call addressed to their ancestor by the God of the beyond. This call and their response in faith make them a prophetic people of "seers": they see "with far seeing eyes, . . . hear what God says, . . . know what the Most High knows, . . . see what the Almighty sees" (Num. 24:3-4). Beyond the realm of created things, they look up at the ultimate. Through cultures but beyond them, they get a glimpse, ever so dim, of the glory of God. Viewed in this perspective, cultures are relative, they are not the supreme reality. They are turned toward God's plan for the fullness of time and their final value depends on their capacity to be the effulgence of the divine beauty. Ultimately, response to culture will mean responding to the prophetic challenge of faith and turning the eyes toward that plenitude that will always exceed whatever we can imagine, will, or think.

Part Two

The Cultural World of Jesus

The New Testament covers a much shorter span of time than the Hebrew Bible. Unlike the Jewish world of the Old Testament, its geographical horizon, restricted to the Mediterranean area, does not extend to Egypt, Mesopotamia, and Persia. Yet this Mediterranean world of the first century C.E., limited as it was, did present a multiform cultural picture.

To begin with, the Judaism of the first century was far from being homogeneous. Its two main Palestinian and Hellenistic branches presented quite different features.

Palestinian Judaism itself was made of widely various currents. Moreover, the writings of the New Testament stand on both sides of the great divide created by the traumatic events of the First Jewish War. The period anterior to this war was marked by turbulent messianic and apocalyptic expectations. The disaster of 70 brought a deep disruption in Jewish soul, thought, and organization. Deprived of the temple and the cult, Judaism underwent a reconstruction around the Book and the Law. The cultural perspectives of the New Testament will reflect the variety of those diverse settings.

As for the Hellenistic world which the gospel soon entered even before the Pauline mission, it was a complex cultural melting pot in which Greek language, thought, and way of life intermingled with local cultures and religions, which in turn were not immune to distant influences arriving from faraway Mesopotamia, Armenia, Persia, Bactria, and even India. Roman legions stationed on the *limes* of the empire, from the Caspian Sea to the *Sinus Arabicus,* saw embassies arriving from the "Bastarnae and the Scythians, the king of the Sarmatians . . . , of the Albani and of Hiberi and of the Medes" and even "from the kings of India."[1] Trade routes were still more extended: silk came from China via Bactria (Afghanistan), Rhagae (Teheran), and Palmyra; Arabia exported frankincense and perfumes; India

---

[1] According to the *Res Gestae Divi Augusti* (*Monumentum Ancyranum*) §31, quoted in A. H. M. Jones, *A History of Rome Through the Fifth Century 2: The Empire* (New York: Harper & Row, 1970), 14-23.

sent paper and precious stones by way of the Persian Gulf, as well as ele-
phants in large numbers, rhinoceroses, and tigers.[2] Ideas also traveled. History reports that Alexander met Gymnosophists from India. Early Christian
writers remembered those radical ascetics and praised them as "pre-Christ-
ian saints."[3] After Alexander, Buddhist missionaries, sent by the Indian
emperor Asoka, went as far as Egypt and Syria. They might have failed to
convert the Hellenistic kings to whom they were sent;[4] but they could not fail
to impress those whom they met. Trade centers such as Alexandria, Antioch,
and Ephesus were also ideological bazaars where all kinds of influences
intersected. Mystery cults were only one of the many forms of these crisscrossing cultural undercurrents that stirred the so-called "Hellenistic world."

It would be impossible to sort out all the elements of this tumultuous intercultural background. Old Testament research has largely integrated the Asian
world of Mesopotamia and Persia in its perspectives. But surprisingly, New
Testament scholarship, except for a few adventurous speculations in the
direction of Iran with R. Reitzenstein[5] and Mandean Mesopotamia with R.
Bultmann,[6] has remained confined within the narrow Mediterranean dilemma
between Judaism and Hellenism. In the absence of monographs studying this
background more elaborately, we shall restrict our inquiry to a few soundings
hopefully selected in significant areas of the New Testament development. A
first sounding will try to identify the culture of Jesus. For the apostolic era we
shall focus on Paul, since he provides us with rich firsthand personal information. For the postapostolic times, leaving aside the Johannine corpus as
fraught with too many problems, we shall consider the "captivity letters," the
setting of which is precisely the zone of cultural fermentation which the Ionian coast constituted from the earliest dawn of history.

---

[2] See A. A. M. Van der Heyden and H. H. Scullard (eds.), *Atlas of the Classical World* (Edinburgh: Nelson, 1963), maps 51 (p. 127) ("Trade in the Empire") and 59 (p. 163) ("Transport of
Animals for the Roman Arenas").

[3] See K. Ziegler and W. Sontheimer, *Der Kleine Pauly, Lexicon der Antike* (Stuttgart:
Drucken-Müller, 1967), 2:892-893. They might have been Jain monks rather than Brahmins, as
usually supposed.

[4] See P. Väth, *Histoire de l'Inde et de sa Culture* (Paris: Payot, 1937), 57-58.

[5] R. Reitzenstein, *Das iranische Erlösungsmysterium* (Bonn, 1921), quoted by E. Cothenet,
Introduction à la Bible. Nouveau Testament (Paris: Desclée, 1977), 3:103.

[6] R. Bultmann, "Die Bedeutung der neuerschlossenen mandäischen und manichäischen
Quelle für das Verständnis des Johannesevangelium," in *Exegetica: Aufsätze zur Erforschung
des Neuen Testaments* (Tübingen: J. C. B. Mohr, 1967), 55-104 (= *ZNW* 24 [1925]: 100-146).
In the heyday of the *Religionsgeschichtliche* school, daring attempts were made to extend the
New Testament horizon up to India. See a survey of those audacious speculations in G. A. van
den Bergh van Eysinga, *Indische Einflüsse auf Evangelische Erzählungen*, FRLANT 4 (Göttingen: Vandenhoeck & Ruprecht, 1909), 7-27. The Indian "influence" was supposed to have
been direct when Jesus was assumed to have become a disciple of a Buddhist *Bhikshu*, in India
between the age of twelve and thirty (Eitel, Jacolliot, Notovitch). In a more sober but as gratuitous a manner, an indirect influence was presumed to have been mediated through the Essenes
(Hilgenfeld, Burnouf).

5

Jesus the Jew

Culture and Subcultures

Studies on "inculturation" often bypass the case of Jesus of Nazareth and proceed at once to Paul's taking the good news to the Gentile world. The implicit point of reference is the "missionary" situation in which a ready-made Christianity encountered a "pagan" world and culture. Paul's statement: "to the Jews as a Jew" and to the Greeks as a Greek (cf. 1 Cor. 9:20f.) has been given as the motto of a genuine missionary attitude at the image of the one who made himself "all things to all people . . . for the sake of the Gospel" (vv. 22f.). Yet it should be obvious enough that, from a Christian point of view, the stand of Jesus Christ deserves prior consideration, to say the least.

CAN ONE SPEAK OF JESUS' CULTURE?

The study of Jesus' culture meets with special difficulties. First, the word "culture" seems hardly to fit Jesus' situation if the word culture is taken in its narrow sense of "refinement by education and training."[1] We know nothing of Jesus' education. The few books that have attempted to break the seal of silence on the thirty formative years of the Nazarean are reduced to conjectures and generalities.[2] Yet culture has a broader meaning. It connotes the entire mental setup acquired through the geographical, ethnic, linguistic, familial, professional, social, and religious environment, covering among other fields food and cuisine, forms of work and recreation, ways of dress-

---

[1] *Oxford Dictionary,* 2:1248; or according to Webster *Dictionary,* "intellectual refinement" resulting from a "training by which man's moral or intellectual nature is developed." See p. xiii above.

2 See the survey of the evidence in J.P. Meier, *A Marginal Jew. Rethinking the Historical Jesus,* ABRL (New York: Doubleday, 1991), 1:252-278.

ing, daily and yearly rhythms of life, type of imagination, symbolic fields, and so on. In this sense Jesus of Nazareth belonged to a specific culture which can be analyzed and which has significant repercussions on his message.

Another difficulty comes from the problem of the "historical Jesus." The task is not easy. When approaching questions touching the "historical Jesus," one feels like being in the proverbial position of rushing in where angels fear to tread, angels in this case being the scholarly academy. It is not so long ago that the Bultmannian school had declared the historical Jesus a restricted zone. Any attempt to reach beyond the "Christ of faith" to recover some of the human cultural components of Jesus' psyche would have come directly under the suspicion of naive psychologizing. Presently, new lines of approach have gone beyond Bultmannian skepticism, and a "third search for the Jew of Nazareth" is being pursued.[3] Indeed, the new quest for the historical Jesus has come back with a vengeance. The fear now is no longer that of entering a forbidden area but of finding one's way in a bewildering variety of opinions. Jesus has been "rejudaized," either as a mainline Israelite or as a "marginal Jew." He has been presented as a revolutionary, either of the Marxist or of the Weberian obedience, as a wandering charismatic, as a Mediterranean Jewish peasant, or, on the contrary, as a middle-class building contractor and even as a disciple of Cynic philosophers. Even the psychologizing reconstitution has received a fresh coating of modern psychoanalysis in the works of F. Dolto and E. Drewermann.

It would be easy to trace the "hidden agenda" underlying these reconstructions. There are the obvious agendas of Judeo-Christian dialogue, of liberation theology, of feminism and of various forms of "inculturation." Those who profess those agendas retort to their critics that the implicit agendas of Western academics, with their male-dominated, spiritualizing, dogmatic, or existentialist orientation, are still more nefarious for being insidious.

As a matter of fact, the various lines of approach make use of solid scientific tools and contribute to sharpen our knowledge of Jesus' background. Particularly insofar as "culture" is concerned, the use of more refined sociological and anthropological tools brings our attention to the complex variety of possible cultural interactions. Main cultures are composite, less homogeneous than they claim to be, exposed as they are to the influence or the resistance of subcultures and countercultures, both enriched and challenged by them.

The outcome is that we can no longer put the historical Jesus between brackets as an unknown inaccessible X, irrelevant to faith in Christ. Jesus the

---

[3] See the survey of B. Witherington, *The Jesus Quest: The Third Search for the Jew of Nazareth* (Downers Grove: InterVarsity Press, 1995); J. M. Borg, *Jesus in Contemporary Scholarship* (Valley Forge, Pa.: Trinity Press International, 1994); S. Freyne, "The Quest for the Historical Jesus: Some Theological Reflections," *Concilium* (1997/1): 37-51; E. Vallauri, "Volti di Gesù negli studi più recenti," *Laurentianum* 39 (1998): 293-337.

Jew can be known through his human Jewishness and this Jewishness is an incontrovertible element of the Christian perception. From the point of view of history, it would be as insensible to sever Jesus from his Jewish milieu as to dissociate Gandhi from the Indian background. From the point of view of Christian faith, belief in Jesus Christ cannot be dissociated from the Palestinian humanity of Jesus. Whatever may be the historical value of the genealogies in Matthew 1 and Luke 3, they intend to assert the full Jewish selfhood of Jesus, "son of David, son of Abraham" (Matt. 1:1). Or, to put it in Johannine terms, "the Word was made flesh," meaning that he was made a *Jewish* flesh. The Word found human expression in a Jewish culture. This Jewish culture of Jesus is both a bridge to his historical identity and a constitutive element of the Christian confession of the incarnated Word. At the same time, this "Jewishness" should not be oversimplified. Jewish identity at the end of the Second Temple period had many facets. Moreover "Jesus the Jew" was also "Jesus the Galilean" and a "rural Galilean" at that, who did not have the same cultural Jewish background as a priest of Jerusalem or an Essene monk of Qumran. Those various aspects will have to be considered. We shall therefore proceed with a study of the Jewishness of Jesus, the better to situate the specificity of the "marginal" Jew he was.

REDISCOVERING THE JEWISHNESS OF JESUS

Rediscovering "Jesus' Jewishness" has been one of the major lines of development of New Testament research after the Second World War.[4] This rediscovery results from the convergence of a variety of factors. The collective remorse consecutive to the Holocaust led to a reconsideration of the deep-seated causes of Christian anti-Semitism. Its roots went deeper than popular prejudices and unenlightened catechesis and homiletics. Christian theology and exegesis themselves carried their share of responsibility insofar as they had dissociated Christianity from its Jewish sources. All too often they had expressed the Christian message in terms of antithesis of or opposition to Judaism. The "old" Testament was supposed to have become obsolete now that it was superseded by the "new" dispensation, and so Judaism could only be a kind of foil to set off the originality and uniqueness of the new religion. These misinterpretations were both the result and the cause of anti-Jewish prejudices. They were also a betrayal of the New Testament data. New Testament scholarship was now to give priority in its agenda to the rediscovery of the fundamental Jewish belonging of Jesus and of early Christianity. At the same time, the spirit of dialogue entered the theological

---

[4] See the survey of D. J. Harrington, "The Jewishness of Jesus: Facing some Problems," *CBQ* 49 (1987): 1-13; and the "Annotated Bibliography" given in J. H. Charlesworth (ed.), *Jesus' Jewishness: Exploring the Place of Jesus in Early Judaism* (New York: Crossroad, 1991), 271-279.

landscape calling for a more honest and positive assessment of the spiritual richness of Jewish tradition. On the part of Jewish scholars like D. Flusser, G. Vermès, Jacob Neusner, S. Safrai, and others, the same spirit of dialogue resulted in original contributions to the research on Jesus and Christian origins.

The reassessment of the Jewish background of the Gospels was stimulated by archaeological discoveries that have shed new light on the history of first-century Judaism. The most spectacular of these finds was that of the Dead Sea Scrolls. The controversies that surround them bear testimony to the ongoing interest they raise even in public opinion. Other finds have remained confined to scholarly circles but are no less important, for example, the discovery of the library of a Gnostic monastery at Nag Hammadi in Egypt. New Targums were found not only in wilderness caves but also . . . on the shelves of the Vatican Library. Excavations of biblical sites in Jerusalem and Galilee contributed also to a better knowledge of the environment in which Jesus lived.[5] Less spectacular finds are no less important. Not only did archaeologists throw a finer mesh on the various tracts of the land of Jesus. They used also a more precise methodology based precisely on a redefinition of "culture." The object of interest extended beyond the realm of "elite or higher culture" as found in monuments and inscriptions. Studies explored "popular or lower culture" as well, as expressed in the daily life of humble folk, their housing and clothing, furniture, food habits, kitchen pots, agricultural implements, cultivation patterns, and so on. Even a first-century fishing boat of the Lake of Galilee has been retrieved and submitted to minute investigation. At Masada and Murabbaᶜat, it is not only the letters and manuscripts that have attracted scholarly interest but also the sandals, mats, clothes, plaits and cosmetic equipment, tools and weapons, plates and jars, olive stones and grains of cereal, and dates and walnuts left by the Zealots and the companions of Bar Kokhba.

Combining those data with more accurate sociological and anthropological models, historians have now returned with renewed attention and confidence to the rich information available in the writings of Josephus and of other Palestinian and Hellenistic Jewish authors as well as in the Gospels. A clearer perspective has now been reached on the situation in Palestine before and after the disaster of 70. There is no going back to a naive reconstruction of the "historical Jesus." But we are now in a better position to situate "Jesus the Jew" in the cultural setting of the eastern Mediterranean world. This better knowledge does not simplify the task, for the Judaism of the end of the Second Temple period appears now as quite a complex reality. The main cultural trends opened on a great variety of subcultural forms. It is not

---

[5] The data have been gathered by J. H. Charlesworth in *Jesus within Judaism: New Light from Exciting Archaeological Discoveries,* ABRL (New York: Doubleday, 1988), and summarized in *Jesus' Jewishness,* ed. Charlesworth, 78-83.

enough to speak of Jesus the Jew. There were many ways of being a Jew in those days.

THE JEWISH CULTURE OF JESUS

LAND

Jesus of Nazareth was born and brought up in a specific culture that was made mostly of land, language, and law. As a son of the *land of Israel*, Jesus was an eastern Mediterranean villager. His food habits were Mediterranean, based on wheat (not on rice or taro), olive oil (not butter or lard), fish (more than meat), figs, dates, and pomegranates (rather than apples or bananas). His symbolic world was shaped by this setting. With his country people he made merry with grape wine, not with beer or *sake*. Fecundity and well-being were symbolized by vineyard and fig trees, not by coconut or mango trees. The works and toil he knew were those of a Mediterranean peasant on hard and rocky soil, in dry climactic conditions. His life followed the rhythms of Mediterranean seasons, marked by the double revival of nature in springtime, during the month of Nisan, and in the autumn month of Tishri, at the fall of the first rains. This rhythm was consecrated by the respective feasts of Passover and Tabernacles. The human distinctiveness of this setting is acutely perceived by the followers of Christ, who, living under other skies, have to struggle with bread and wine in their cult and with a liturgical cycle that runs awry of their true life rhythms.

LANGUAGE

This setting conditioned *Jesus' language*. A child's mother tongue carries centuries of history, lore, homely wisdom, and adaptation to the soil. So did Jesus' language, Palestinian Aramaic.[6]

It was a Semitic language. Speaking it, Jesus assumed the peculiarities of the Semitic way of speaking and thinking. Semitic languages are concrete, favoring verbs rather than adjectives. Sentences are short and follow each other in quick succession, rather than in an orderly architecture of subordinate clauses.[7] Prosody follows the rule of parallelism: the parts of the discourse balance or contrast each other often with the help of assonance. Many

---

[6] See the careful assessment of Meier, *Marginal Jew*, 255-268; J. A. Fitzmyer, "The Study of the Aramaic Background of the New Testament," in *A Wandering Aramean: Collected Aramaic Essays* (Missoula, Mont.: Scholars Press, 1979), 1-20 (= *Jésus aux origines de la Christologie*, ed. J. Dupont, BETL 40 [Gembloux: Duculot, 1975], 73-102); idem, "The Languages of Palestine in the First Century A.D.," in *Wandering Aramean*, 29-56 (= *CBQ* 32 [1970], 501-531).

[7] Grammarians speak of "paratactic" versus "syntactic" grammatical structure.

of these characteristics can easily be traced, for instance, in Jesus' parables or in the rhetoric of the Sermon on the Mount.

This Semitic language had become the dominant vernacular and literary language of western Asia. After the Babylonian exile, Aramaic had progressively superseded Hebrew as the popular Palestinian dialect. Speaking Aramaic, one assumed, even though unconsciously, the postexilic centuries of contact with the nations west of the Indus River. Though with substantial dialectal differences, Jesus shared the language of Persia, Mesopotamia, Armenia, Palmyra, Edessa, and Arabia and partook of their mental horizons. Concretely this meant that Jesus could easily dialogue with the Syro-Phoenician woman (Mark 7:25-29) and that he felt linguistically at home in the foreign Decapolis and in the territory of Caesarea Philippi.

But this Aramaic was Palestinian, which means that it underwent *a strong influence of Hebrew*. On the basis mostly of the Qumran discoveries, attempts have even been made to prove that Hebrew had been revived after the time of the Maccabees and could have been the language of Jesus. Given the distinctive character of the Qumran writings, these attempts fail to convince.[8] Yet the fact remains that Jewish Aramaic could not but bear a definite Hebraic stamp. Its main literary written and oral expression was found in the Targums, translations of the biblical readings at the Sabbath synagogue service. The Aramaic spoken by Jesus not only contained Hebrew loanwords and grammatical constructions; it was also and mostly charged with the ethos and pathos of the Law and the Prophets, with the centuries-old dramatic dialogue between the people and the God of the covenant.

Influences from Greek and Latin on Jesus' Aramaic might have been less consequential. Yet nothing is totally insignificant in the makeup of a human psyche. Martin Hengel has shown how deeply "Judaism" and "Hellenism" interacted in Palestine itself.[9] Jesus' Greek may have been "of a practical, business type, and perhaps rudimentary to boot."[10] He might have needed a translator (Andrew or Philip?) when contacted by "Greeks" (John 12:20-22). He must have been somehow affected by the ubiquitous Greek inscriptions[11] and the kind of Greco-Aramaic jargon that could be heard in the streets of Sepphoris, Tarichae, or Tiberias.[12]

---

[8] See Fitzmyer, "Languages," 44-46.

[9] M. Hengel, *Judaism and Hellenism: Studies in Their Encounter in Palestine during the Early Hellenistic Period* (London: SCM Press, 1974).

[10] Meier, *Marginal Jew,* 268.

[11] "In several cases the Greek inscriptions on these ossuaries have outnumbered those in Aramaic and in Hebrew" (Fitzmyer, "Languages," 35, who, among other evidences, quotes also a Greek inscription of Nazareth showing the penetration of Greek even into obscure corners of rural Galilee). For an assessment of the complex linguistic situation particularly in Galilee, see R. A. Horsley, *Archeology, History and Society in Galilee: The Social Context of Jesus and the Rabbis,* Valley Forge, Pa.: Trinity Press International, 1996), 154-175.

[12] Like the "Hinglish" (mixed Hindi and English) used in the "Bolywoods" ("Bombay

In short, Jesus' language, as Semitic, carried with it the resources of the geographical, historical, and genetic fabric of western Asia. As strongly influenced by Biblical Hebrew, it vibrated with the spiritual intensity of the Law, the Prophets, and the Sages; as Aramaic tinged with some Greek coloring, it evoked a history of half-enforced and half-accepted intermingling with the nations. It was a rich cultural background that Jesus inherited with his mother tongue.

LAW

Paul, who, apart from the crucifixion, has little to say about the humanness of Jesus, nevertheless emphasizes that Jesus was "born under the law" (Gal. 4:4). Indeed, the Torah was a fundamental aspect of Jewish cultural identity. It regulated the cult as well as social relations, extended to hygiene, diet, calendar, trade, financial transactions, agricultural techniques, and so on. The question of Jesus' attitude toward the law is complex and has not been simplified by Paul's polemical statements in Romans and Galatians. There is no doubt that Jesus' attitude toward the law embodied a unique authority and liberty. Yet it is equally certain that Jesus the Jew lived within the framework of the law.

Cult and Piety

Luke specifies that Jesus was circumcised eight days after his birth (2:21), presented to the temple "according to the law of Moses." John describes Jesus' ministry as a continuous roving to and fro between Galilee and Jerusalem, according to the rhythm of the Jewish calendar. Even in the chronology of the Synoptics, Jesus made his final journey to Jerusalem to celebrate the Passover. He is frequently described as attending the synagogal service on the Sabbath day (Mark 1:21; 6:2; Luke 4:16, 31; 6:6; 13:10). His understanding of the Sabbath might have been uncommon; yet he could not be blamed for not being a good practicing Israelite.

Not only was he a practicing Israelite; his was a genuinely Hebrew piety. He used the traditional forms of biblical prayer, the *todah,* or thanksgiving

---

Hollywood") of India! Horsley distinguishes between written and spoken languages in a given area and, within those languages between bi- or multilingualism involving people speaking several languages and *diglossia* when the use of different languages is determined by socioprofessional settings. The present writer has lived for several years on the linguistic border of two Indian states where questions of land ownership and transactions were treated in one language (*Telugu,* language of the caste of the local landowners), questions of labor in another language (*Kannada,* language of the caste of local agricultural workers), while the official state language (*Tamil*) played the role of general *lingua franca.* In addition to that, an important Muslim minority spoke *Urdu* among themselves and with outsiders from the north! And this multilingualism was practiced by people who were often illiterate.

(Matt. 11:25-27), and the cry of lament (Matt. 27:46). Even the Lord's Prayer carries many reminiscences of targumic prayers.[13]

Teaching

In his teachings, Jesus used traditional forms of Hebrew rhetoric such as wisdom sayings (Mark 8:36f.; 9:42; Matt. 5:14f.). The *mashal,* or enigmatic aphorism (Mark 7:14-21; Luke 9:57-60; 14:34f.), could be enlarged into the dimension of a parable. He made frequent use of biblical quotations, applying to them the traditional techniques of interpretation: the *midrash,* or biblical exposition (Matt. 5:21-48; Mark 7:6-13; 10:4-9); the *targum,* or adaptative translation (Mark 4:11f.; Luke 4:18-21); the typically rabbinical form of exegetical riddle presenting an apparent antinomy between two texts (Mark 12:35-37). The very newness of his teachings was expressed through the medium of classical forms. Popular opinion held him to be a rabbi (Mark 9:5; 10:51; 11:21; 14:44f.).

This raises the question of whether Jesus had undergone any formal training in Jewish rhetoric and logic. The question presents many facets. Is there archaeological and historical evidence that literacy was widespread in the first half of the first century C.E. in Palestine? Was there a school, a *beth hassefer,* attached to village synagogues? Were the later prescriptions of the Mishnah on compulsory school attendance from the age of five[14] already valid in Jesus' times? These questions are the subject of scholarly debate.[15] There are only three Gospel texts that report Jesus writing or reading. In Luke 4:16-30, Jesus performs the Sabbath reading at the synagogue of Capernaum; in John 8:6, Jesus writes a mysterious message on the sand; and, in John 7:15, "the Jews marveled at his learning" (*grammata oiden,* literally, "he knew letters"). This is not much, and all the less so since, in each case, there is ground to suspect redactional reconstruction rather than direct witness. But, whether it was due to formal training or not, the fact remains that Jesus was called "Rabbi" and that he taught in synagogues (Mark 1:21, 39; 6:2; 13:10; John 6:59; 18:20) and engaged in learned discussions with "lawyers" and Pharisees (Mark 2:6-10, 18-22, 23-27; 3:1-4; 7:1-23; 10:1-12; 12:35-37). The scribes themselves recognized his authority and consulted him (Mark 12:28-34; Luke 20:39f.).

The natural conclusion from all this is that, sometime during his childhood or early adulthood, Jesus was taught how to read and expound

---

[13] See C. G. Montefiore, *The Synoptic Gospels* (1927; reprint, New York: Ktav, 1968), 100-105; G. Friedlander, *The Jewish Sources of the Sermon on the Mount* (1911; reprint, New York: Ktav, 1969), 152-165; M. Black, *An Aramaic Approach to the Gospels and Acts* (Oxford: Oxford University Press, 1967), 233.

[14] Jehuda ben Tema said: "At five years, the Scriptures (*mikrah,* literally, "reading"); at ten, the Mishnah; at thirteen, the commandments; at fifteen, the Talmud" (*Aboth* 5.21). With its references to Mishnah and Talmud, the text is obviously a later addition.

[15] See the survey of Meier, *Marginal Jew,* 268-278, 300-309.

the Hebrew Scriptures . . . Yet there is no indication of higher studies at some urban center such as Jerusalem . . . One therefore has to allow for a high degree of natural talent—perhaps even genius—that more than compensated for the low level of Jesus' formal education.[16]

This cultural background is to be taken into account for an adequate understanding of the Gospels. In common Christian understanding, scribes and Pharisees were the villains. They were supposed to represent soulless legalism versus Jesus' freedom and rigid casuistry versus human concern and love. The texts appear in another light, however, when set in the context of debates within Judaism.

A typical example can be found in the "woes against the scribes and Pharisees" in Matthew 23. The Matthean text calls for careful assessment. First, it extends to "scribes *and Pharisees*" what Mark 12:38 and Luke 20:46 say of scribes alone. Second, the comparison with Mark and Luke shows that Matthew has synthesized what the other Synoptists report in different contexts. The massive impact of an entire chapter of woes is a Matthean rhetorical construction, achieved, in Matthew's usual way, by making a discourse out of fragmented logia of Jesus. The setting of Matthew's polemic against scribal Judaism has been shown to be the tensions that developed between the rabbinic and the messianic reconstruction of Judaism subsequent to the disaster of 70.

As regards Jesus' logia recorded in the "discourse," they may look biased and smack of anti-Jewish prejudice. They have indeed all too often been interpreted in that spirit as if the Judaism of the early Christian times did not have such impressive figures as Hillel, Gamaliel, Akiba, Johanan ben Zakkai, and many others. But Jesus' words are not to be viewed in isolation. Jeremiah had already used a similar language:

> How can you say: "We are wise and the law of the LORD is with
> us?"
> But behold the false pen of the scribes has made it into a lie
> The wise men shall be put to shame . . . ,
> Lo, they have rejected the word of the LORD
> and what wisdom is in them? (Jer. 8:8f.)

The warning against "those who preach well but do not practice"[17] remained a traditional locus of rabbinic literature, which analyzed seven types of hypocrisy among the Pharisees, particularly among those who "carried their piety on their shoulder" (*y. Berakot* 14b). After quoting a long list of texts, Moshe Weinfeld concludes: "It appears that the critique of Pharisaic

---

[16] Ibid., 278.

[17] Johanan ben Zakkai, quoted by Moshe Weinfeld, "The Charge of Hypocrisy in Matthew 23 and in Jewish Sources," in *The New Testament and Christian-Jewish Dialogue. Studies in Honor of David Flusser,* ed. M. Lowe, *Immanuel* 24-25 (1990): 54.

hypocrisy was a common phenomenon in Judaism of the first centuries of the common era. When the authors of the Synoptic Gospels wrote about Pharisaic hypocrites, they were using material that was widespread in Pharisaic lore itself."[18]

The woes pronounced by Jesus in Matthew 23 are not a condemnation of the scribes and Pharisees *en bloc*. Still less are they a condemnation of Judaism in general. Neither are they to be taken as an expression of fanatic antagonism. They are an echo of the language of the prophets, itself frequently resounding in Judaism. It was the kind of "in-language" which only kindred souls could use toward each other.

Equally misunderstood is the controversy concerning the plucking of grain on the Sabbath (Mark 2:23-28 and par.). It is usually interpreted as a claim of freedom from the law or as an illustration of the superiority of human concern over ritualism. Jesus quotes the example of David breaking the law and eating the Bread of the Presence to justify his disciples. This was a classic topos of debate in the Jewish *halakah*. It was argued that overwhelming hunger (*hulmus*) could be a case of *piqquah nefesh*, of "saving life," which made it permissible to violate a commandment.[19] The same principle of "saving life" was used by Jesus in the case of the man with a withered hand (Mark 3:4 and par.). Rabbis had already formulated the principle that "to you the Sabbath is given and not you to the Sabbath."[20] The point at issue therefore is not freedom versus the law or human concern versus legalism. It is a reminder of the old prophetic principle: "I desire mercy, not sacrifice" (Hos. 6:6; Matt. 9:13; 12:7). Jesus recalls the hierarchy of the commandments of the Torah:

> In God's eye the hunger of the poor is more important than the Sabbath and imposes a more important religious duty than does even the Sabbath . . . The focus of attention is not on criticism of the Sabbath but on the hunger of the poor . . . Mk 2:23-27 is saying precisely what the Beatitude on the poor in Luke 6:20-21 says: that everything that God has promised to Israel by way of salvation belongs to the poor . . . We should not think of the relationship of the earliest Jesus tradition to the Pharisees or comparable Jewish groups as being one of theological confrontation at the level of dogmatic principles.[21]

The interpretation in terms of law versus freedom was in fact culturally conditioned by the Lutheran debate and the advent of modern humanism,

---

[18] Weinfeld, "Charge of Hypocrisy," 58.

[19] See M. Kister, "Plucking on the Sabbath and Christian-Jewish Polemic," in *New Testament and Christian-Jewish Dialogue*, ed. Lowe, 37-38.

[20] *Mekhilta de-Rabbi Ishmael*, quoted by Kister, "Plucking," 40.

[21] L. Schottroff and W. Stegemann, "The Sabbath Was Made for Man," in *God of the Lowly: Socio-Historical Interpretations of the Bible* (Maryknoll, N.Y.: Orbis Books, 1984), 125, 127.

which favored human concern over legalism. It was a typical case of later cultural setting unconsciously affecting the exegesis and hermeneutics of a text. A better knowledge of the cultural context to which Jesus' teachings and deeds belonged has now led to a more accurate comprehension of his message. Interpretation is always enclosed within a cultural horizon. Genuine exegesis must first take the original setting into account. Only then can there be a valid hermeneutic meeting of horizons. Only when the "flesh" is accepted in its Jewish cultural genuineness can the authenticity of the Word reach out to the world.

The long and short of the discussion is that, even when Jesus criticizes the Jewish tradition, he does it from within this tradition itself. Dissent from his native culture stems from his very immersion in this culture. Jesus' prophetic attitude is not that of an outsider. Like Jeremiah and the other prophets of Israel, Jesus belongs to the culture which he transcends. In fact, the divine call to transcendence takes him to more genuine depths of his cultural identity.

SUBCULTURES

Land, language, and law shaped the humanity of Jesus, who, a Jew from first to last, followed a Jewish way of living, of speaking, of teaching, and of praying. But it is not enough to speak of Jesus the Jew. His Jewishness must be specified in terms of the variety of subcultures that constituted the Judaism of the first century, prior to the disaster of 70. We are better aware now of the pluralism that prevailed in Judaism before to the fall of Jerusalem. The destruction of the Holy City and of the temple, the end of the cult and the collapse of the immediate messianic expectations provoked a deep crisis. Johanan ben Zakkai and the Jamnia movement restored Judaism by giving it a new identity, focused on the law and on the rabbinic authority that gave it regulative interpretation. This is the somewhat homogeneous Judaism we know through the Mishnah and the Talmud. No such regulative authority operated before 70, that is, in the days of Jesus and Paul. W. D. Davies can speak of the "hospitable, comprehensive, theological tolerance and fluidity of Judaism before 70 A.D."[22] Any global culture is a mosaic of subcultures conditioned by geographical divisions, professions, social rank, sex, and so on.[23] Small as it was, Palestine was big and varied enough to pre-

---

[22] W. D. Davies, *Jewish and Pauline Studies* (London: SPCK, 1984), 97.

[23] In India, for instance, a preamble to "inculturation" is the question of whether there is such a thing as an Indian culture at all. To which the answer can be both yes and no. Yes, since there is obviously a strongly characterized Indian culture. Whether landing in Bombay, Delhi, or Madras, it is clear that one is not in Hong Kong, New York, or Paris. All over the country, there prevails an impalpable yet powerful common atmosphere. Yet those who come to know India more closely can legitimately wonder whether there is anything in common between

sent a complex picture. The Galilean and professional factors of Jesus' culture are sufficiently important to call for the special chapter that will follow. Presently we shall take a closer look at the social position of Jesus insofar as it was determined by the religious stratification of the people among whom he lived. In the theocratic setup of ancient Palestine, this religious classification was an important social element.

The political-religious map of Palestinian society is drawn by Josephus in several parts of his writings; see *Jewish War* 2.8.14; *Antiquities* 13.5.9; 13.10.5-6; 17.1.2-4; 20.9.1. It consisted of three main groups, the Pharisees, the Sadducees, and the Essenes, to which Josephus reluctantly appends the faction of the freedom fighters going back to Judas the Galilean. In a spirit of adaptation to his Greek readers, Josephus calls those parties *haireseis* (usually translated "sects") or "philosophies." Both designations are inaccurate. They were not "philosophies." Their positions were not based on metaphysical speculations but on religious ground, on their understanding of the Torah. Consequently, they identified themselves more by a praxis than by theories. Neither were they "sects," distinct from the official orthodoxy and rigidly opposed to each other. In Jesus' day, there was no officially defined Jewish "orthodoxy," and the boundaries between the *haireseis* were rather fluid. For instance, the Essenes of Qumran were also Zadokites, which is just another spelling of Sadducee ("sons of Zadok"). "Faction" would suppose a well-structured organization, which was equally lacking. We could speak of "movements" insofar as they expressed a specific vision of society, a collective program of action, and a political influence.[24] Now what was the position of the Jesus movement in that complex socio-politico-religious configuration?

SADDUCEES

The least affinity was with the Sadducees.[25] They formed the priestly group of the "sons of Zadok," who held a monopoly over the high priesthood of the Jerusalem temple. At the time of Solomon's succession, their ancestor, Zadok, priest at the royal court, had made the "correct" option against Abiathar, who had backed the other pretender, Adonijah (1 Kgs. 1:5-26). Zadok's successors, Zadokites or Sadducees, had therefore inherited the

---

Bombay urbanites and villagers of Central India, between Tamilians and Punjabis, between "sanskritized" brahmins and outcaste *dalits*.

[24] The term "current" would be too vague. On the various forms of "association" in Palestine and Greece, see A. J. Saldarini, *Pharisees, Scribes and Sadducees in Palestinian Society: A Sociological Approach* (Wilmington, Del.: Michael Glazier, 1988), 62-75. The *haireseis* mentioned by Josephus represented "political forces," which, for the Pharisees, might have been particularly active in Galilee (pp. 295-297).

[25] On the Sadducees, the basic work is that of J. Le Moyne, *Les Sadducéens,* EBib (Paris: Gabalda, 1972), with a survey of the research on pp. 11-26; see also Saldarini, *Pharisees,* 298 n. 1.

privilege of their ancestor. Jesus, born to a family that claimed Davidic ancestry in the tribe of Judah, did not belong to the priestly tribe of Levi and had no ancestral tie with the Sadducees. Living in Galilee, he had hardly any contact with them. References to the Sadducees are rare in the Synoptic Gospels. The discussion with "Sadducees and Pharisees" on "the signs of the times," followed in the same chapter by the warning against the "leaven of the scribes and Sadducees," is the only passage where the priestly clan is referred to repeatedly (five times in Matt. 16:1-12). The text is likely to be redactional.[26] The controversy with the Sadducees on the resurrection, during the last days of Jesus in Jerusalem, has a better setting (Mark 12:18-27) and may well have been the only actual encounter of Jesus with the priestly clan before his passion. Surprisingly, John, who reports several journeys of Jesus to Jerusalem, makes no mention of the Sadducees.

Like any good Jew, Jesus went to the temple and prayed there with devotion. But his attitude toward the temple was closer to the criticism of Amos (see 4:4-12; 5:21-27) or Jeremiah (see 7:11-15; 19:3-15; 26) than to the enthusiastic prospects of Isaiah and Micah (4:1-8). When Isaiah is quoted in the Gospels, the reference is not to the glowing Zion texts of 2:2-4; 4:2-6; 29:1-8; 37:22-32 but to the Servant songs (Isa. 42:1-4 = Matt. 12:18-21; Isa. 53:4 = Matt. 8:17; Isa. 61:1f.= Luke 4:18f.), the warnings of Isaiah 6:9f. (= Matt. 13:14f.), or the promises made to the "Galilee of the Gentiles" in Isaiah 9:1f. (= Matt. 4:15f.). In fact, Jesus' strategy is based on Galilee, not on Jerusalem, and his "mountain" is not the hill of Zion but the "mountain" of Galilee (Matt. 5:1; 17:1; 28:16). In short, Jesus did not feel comfortable with the Sadducee outlook, and neither would they have felt comfortable with his. It all ended with the tragedy of the trial.

The Essenes

This Zadokite background must be kept in mind when assessing the possible relationship between Jesus and the Essenes. Like any new discovery, the appearances of the Dead Sea Scrolls gave rise to wild speculations. At last the missing link was alleged to have been found between Judaism and Christianity; Jesus would have been a member, if not the leader, of the sect of Qumran, his teachings alleged to be a pale copy of esoteric Essenism. Even his death and resurrection would have been anticipated by the Teacher of Righteousness, the founder of the sect.[27] Since little was known about

---

[26] "As in 3,7 with John the Baptist, Pharisees and Sadducees appear again together. This association in 16,1-12 is stereotyped. One need not ask how the Jerusalem Sadducees find themselves on the shores of the lake of Gennesareth and what they have to do with Jesus. Possibly Matthew wants to . . . recall a parallelism between Jesus and the Baptist: they have the same opponents" (U. Luz, *Das Evangelium nach Matthäus 2 (Mt 8-17)*, EKKNT 1/2 [Zurich: Benziger; Neukirchen: Neukirchener Verlag, 1990], 444).

[27] A survey of those hypotheses can be found in Millar Burrows, *More Light on the Dead*

Essenes, barring a few notes of Josephus (*Jewish War* 2.8-13) and Philo (*Quod omnis probus liber sit* 12-13; *Hypothetica* 11.1-8), the field had long been wide open for free conjectures. In the course of centuries there had been no dearth of daring speculations.[28] The Dead Sea Scrolls revived the old Essene hypothesis. Ultimately, when the dust began to settle on the initial commotion, fanciful hypotheses were put to rest. The texts of Qumran are certainly impressive and revealing. They cast much light on Christian origins and on the New Testament, but "evangelical" they are not.

The Qumranites and the Jesus movement share in a similar radicalism, a vivid eschatological atmosphere and a tense messianism. Having in common the conviction of constituting the community of the "new covenant," they throw an equally forceful challenge to a sinful world. But the world perception in which this message is expressed denotes a totally different turn of mind. The gap can be illustrated by comparing the parables of Jesus and the *Temple Scroll* of Qumran. Both represent the respective favorite medium of expression of what the ideal Rule of God should mean. Yet there can hardly be a greater contrast in cultural sensitivity. Differences in contents are obvious.[29] Formal differences are equally significant. In the priestly perspective of the *Scroll,* God's intervention in the new covenant (col. 2) focuses on the new temple (cols. 3-46). In this context, rules of purity will be still more stringent than the Pharisaic regulations (cols. 47-54), in a context of Holy War (cols. 1; 61.12-63.4) with crucifixion (or impaling?) promised as the punishment for the traitors (cols. 64.6-13). In Jesus' language, God's intervention takes place in the context of rural daily life, of sowing and harvesting, fishing and building, stitching and kneading the dough, feeding and feasting, settling the accounts for daily workers or of debtors. The mental horizon of these two movements is poles apart.

Another significant dissimilarity can be found in the reference to the "poor." Both Jesus and the Qumranites view their movement as in continuity with the "Poor of Yahweh." The Righteous Teacher identifies himself as the "poor One" (1QH 5:13-15), and his successors are also "the poor," the "poor of grace" (1QH 5:22). New Testament scholars were thrilled to find the Matthean phrase "poor in spirit" (*ᶜanewai ruah*) in the *Hymns* of the community (1QH 14:3) and in the *War Scroll* (1QM 14:7).[30] But again these verbal and theological similarities hide a dissimilar outlook on life, society, and the world. For Jesus, the poor are the blind, the lame, the lepers, the all and sundry humble folk found on the Galilean byways (cf. Matt. 11:5; Luke

---

Sea Scrolls (London: Secker & Warburg, 1958), 64-110. Since then, scholarship has given a wide berth to this kind of speculation, but there is no end to the imagination of novelists.

[28] An interesting survey of pre-Qumran evidence and of the speculations anterior to the discovery of the Scrolls can be found as an appendix to J. B. Lightfoot *Epistles to the Colossians and to Philemon,* 3rd ed. (London: Macmillan, 1879), 349-419.

[29] See a summary in Charlesworth, *Jesus within Judaism,* 72-75.

[30] Cf. also the *ruah ᶜanawah,* the "spirit of poverty" in 1QS 4:3.

14:21); at Qumran, the poor are the members of the sect rejected from their rightful place in the temple and persecuted.[31]

These formal differences are quite interesting insofar as they reveal the world vision implied in language. Jesus and the Dead Sea community move within the same religious inheritance and to some extent share in the same religious radicalism. But they represent different subcultures—that of a frustrated Jerusalem clergy, on the one hand, and that of the poor Galilean peasant, on the other.

ZEALOTS

Zealots constitute another group with which Jesus has been identified. We know of the Zealots particularly in the context of the Jewish War, during which they became the soul of the resistance to the Roman legions. Their last stand on the rock of Masada paints a tragic and glorious picture of their fierce commitment to freedom and readiness to die rather than surrender.

From the time of Reimarus onward, the identification of Jesus as a Zealot has been as recurring and popular a topic as the Essene hypothesis.[32] It is equally confusing, if not more so, as the confusion is compounded by intertwining historical, exegetical, and ideological issues.

The *historical problem* is that of the exact chronology of the Zealot movement. Did it exist already some forty years before the Jewish War, at the time of Jesus? Is it not an anachronism to speak of Zealots in the first half of the first century C.E.? Was Judas the Galilean, who launched a revolt in Galilee in 6 C.E., a "Zealot" in the formal sense of the term? Can we identify with the Zealots the *sicarii* against whom young Herod fought? Or were they just highway robbers?

Exegetically, are we entitled to reconstruct the Gospel texts in such a way as to make the Jesus' movement another form of the culture of violence represented by the Zealots and the *sicarii*? Particularly, as regards the passion story, is it legitimate to see in the so-called Jewish trial of Jesus a gratuitous creation of early Christian anti-Judaism and to reduce the case of Jesus to a political matter?

This opinion, frequently held by Jewish scholars and quite a few Christian authors, is not lacking in exegetical arguments, since the Gospel account of Jesus' Jewish trial does present difficulties. But exegesis cannot escape

---

[31] See G. Lohfink, *Lobgesänge der Armen, Studien zum Magnificat, den Hodajot von Qumran und einigen späten Psalmen,* SBS 143 (Stuttgart: Katholisches Bibelwerk, 1990), 23-37.

[32] The classic statement of the case is that of S. G. F. Brandon, *Jesus and the Zealots: A Study of the Political Factor in Primitive Christianity* (Manchester: University Press, 1967). The opposite opinion is defended in the scholarly thesis of M. Hengel, *The Zealots: Investigations into the Jewish Freedom Movement in the Period from Herod I until 70 A.D.* (Edinburgh: T & T Clark, 1989), with an abundant bibliography (updated to 1987) on pp. 410-434 (the original German edition goes back to 1961).

ideological motivations. If the Jewish trial were to be a redactional composition, the Jewish people could be cleared once for all of the guilt of Jesus' rejection. Jesus, a Zealot, would have been condemned by the Roman authorities alone, Israel having no share in the miscarriage of justice. In this century, which has seen the horrifying consequences of anti-Semitism, we can but sympathize with efforts to exonerate the Jewish people from the senseless label of "deicide." A lurking anti-Jewish bias has indeed affected Christian exegesis; it might even have already crept into the composition of the Gospels, particularly of John. But can we set right the record by giving way to another bias?[33]

Another ideological twist comes from the *liberationist perspectives* inclined to emphasize the political dimensions of the good news, of the kingdom, and of Jesus' trial. Here again the accusation of "ideological bias" can be made by classical exegesis, to which the liberationists retort that the "purely religious" or "spiritual" academic interpretation of the Bible is equally biased and constitutes a conservative maneuver to ward off challenge to the status quo.

As regards the historical problem, M. Hengel has studiously reconstituted the history of the freedom movement in Palestine from its inception with Judas the Galilean at the time of the census of 6 C.E. up to its climax with the Jewish War and the fall of Jerusalem in 70. He has particularly demonstrated the affinity of the Zealot movement with the Essenes and its links with the Pharisees, particularly of the Shammaite school.[34] This means that Zealotism was not just an excrescence on the tissue of Palestinian society, the emotional reaction of a few marginal agitators. It gave expression to a deep-seated social malaise, a radical "zeal" for the God of Israel and a faith conviction that God expected human cooperation with the eschatological advent of his kingdom.

Had those feelings crystallized into an organized movement in Jesus' day, some forty years before the crisis of 70? Recent studies tend to doubt it.[35] Yet there is no doubt that "there was a good deal of social unrest, including

---

[33] The case concerning the "Jewish involvement" in Jesus' trial is reviewed in great detail in R. E. Brown's encyclopedic study *The Death of the Messiah: From Gethsemane to the Grave* (New York: Doubleday, 1994), 1:328-397. For the political angle, see pp. 676-722 with bibliography on pp. 665-666.

[34] Hengel, *Zealots,* 70-73, 261f., 280-282, 289f., 333f., 377-379; R. A. Horsley, *Galilee: History, Politics, People* (Valley Forge, Pa.: Trinity Press International, 1995), 256-282.

[35] "Closer analysis of our sources . . . has indicated that, although there was indeed widespread revolt in 4 B.C.E. as well as in 66-70 C.E., there was little violent insurrectionary activity anywhere in Jewish Palestine in the interim . . . The group actually called the Zealots did not emerge until the middle of the Jewish revolt, apparently in Jerusalem during the winter of 67-68" (Horsley, *Galilee: History, Politics, People,* 259; see also by the same author, "Popular Messianic Movements around the time of Jesus," *CBQ* 46 [1984]: 471-495).

periodic protests over particular abuses and some distinctive types of popular movements."[36]

Jesus' movement grew in this atmosphere of social restlessness. Jesus experienced the mounting impatience of the Jewish masses in the face of the Roman colonial system and its socioeconomic consequences. Discharged legionaries and clients of Roman administrators received land as their reward, and the Israelite tribal land system was more and more encroached upon by huge *latifundia* owned by foreign landlords. The parables of the talents (Matt. 25:14-30) and of the shrewd steward (Luke 16:1-9) refer to this situation of absentee landlordism. He sympathized with the restlessness of the peasant class turned into a landless proletariate. This mood could express itself in the form of open rebellion. Jesus echoed this mood in the parable of the rebellious tenants (Mark 12:1-12 and parallels) or in the allusion to the Galilean riot crushed by Pilate (Luke 13:1-5). More commonly the mutinous spirit took the form of popular stories ridiculing and mimicking the *compradors,* who enriched themselves cheating both their masters and their customers. Connivance with this caustic humor can be sensed in the parables of the tricky steward (Luke 16:1-9) or of the merciless debtor (Matt. 18:23-35).

Some of the Gospel logia might also echo Zealot (or pre-Zealot?) slogans, such as the one on being ready to carry the cross (Matt. 10:38; 16:24) or the sword sayings (Luke 12:51-53; 22:35-38). Jesus' suspicions toward the rich were also likely to be part of the Zealot profile.[37] The theme of the kingdom itself was open to many interpretations depending on the kind of apocalypticism one had in mind. Even if it was not Jesus' own understanding, it could certainly be understood in the sense of the Song of Deborah: "Let all thy enemies perish, O Lord" (Judg. 5:31), a feeling frequently echoed in the Psalms (37:20; 68:2f., 22) and, closer to Jesus' times, in the Psalms of Solomon (2:20-31; 17:23-45).[38]

Finally and mostly, Jesus was condemned and executed as a political agitator. This condemnation was a miscarriage of justice. Nevertheless even a misunderstanding supposes some ground for it. In the case of Jesus, the ground was his connivance with the aspirations and the restlessness of the poor and the uneasiness this collusion was bound to cause among the higher classes of society. Without going to the radical excesses of R. Eisler or

---

[36] Horsley, *Galilee,* 259.

[37] Brandon, *Jesus and the Zealots,* 145.

[38] "'King' . . . is a very nervous word in the mouth of any Jewish public figure . . . It is clear that these are edgy times indeed, and that an image fundamental to Jesus' teaching—that of Kingdom—is politically loaded . . . When such a theme is center stage in the teachings of a charismatic figure, the body politic is bound to have a nervous stomach" (B. J. Lee, *The Galilean Jewishness of Jesus: Retrieving the Jewish Origins of Christianity* (New York: Paulist Press, 1988), 75f.).

S. G. F. Brandon, present-day exegesis, especially in the Third World, redis-
covers the political implications of Jesus' stand and death and denounces the
spiritualizing reading of the Gospel as a subtle manipulation to silence the
texts.

Yet, when all has been said, there remains a vast difference between Jesus
and the Zealots. For the Zealots, the sword was the way to the advent of the
kingdom. For Jesus, it was love.[39]

This will sound like a sentimental rendering of the Gospel message only
if we fail to realize that evangelical love is no mere sentimental feeling. Seen
in the context of the risks Jesus took to stand and die for the sake of the good
news to the poor, the love of the Servant appears to be more violent than the
sword and mightier than armies. A reconstruction of Jesus' story that would
eliminate love would empty it of any meaning. It would reduce the saga of
the Galilean to the ridiculous fiasco of a quixotic villager going to the conquest of Rome with the help of a small party of brainless nitwits. There
would then remain the task of finding out who the genius was who invented
the mystery of an *agapē* more potent than any power. Jesus might have been
closer to the Zealots and more distant from them than usually presumed by
both tenants and opponents of the Zealot hypothesis. To a good extent he
shared in their world vision, but, within a common cultural perspective, his
basic option was totally different.

THE PHARISEES

In the collective Christian memory, "scribes and Pharisees" are the "enemies of Jesus." They embody the antithesis of what he stood for. They stand
on the opposite side of the debate in the controversy stories of the Gospels
and are the butt of Jesus' criticism.

For the sake of accuracy, it should first be noted that scribes and Pharisees
are not to be identified, though they were often associated. Scribes were men
of learning; Pharisees were men of praxis. Scribes specialized in explaining
the law, Pharisees in observing it. In the Matthean Sermon on the Mount, the
first part in 5:21-48 concerns the "righteousness of the scribes": it takes a
midrashic form, proposing a radically new *interpretation* of the law. The second part in 6:1-18 is addressed to the Pharisees: it concerns the *deeds* of
righteousness: alms (vv. 1-4), prayer (vv. 5-15) and fasting (vv. 16-18).

The Gospel of Matthew may be responsible for the confusion often prevailing in Christian imagination insofar as it tends to blur the difference

---

[39] "For Jesus, the fundamental principle for interpreting the Law was not 'No Lord but God'
(the Fourth Philosophy) nor the command 'Be holy' (Pharisees, Essenes) nor the concern for
proper Temple worship (Sadducees) but the command to love God and to love one's neighbor,
including one's enemies, as oneself (Mark 12:28-34 and parallels)" (D. Rhoads, "Zealots," *ABD*
6:1052).

between scribes and Pharisees and to lump them together as Jesus' antagonists. Yet even Matthew knows of a scribe ready to follow Jesus (Matt. 8:19).

Mark's Gospel takes better note of the distinction between the two groups and presents a more balanced picture of their attitude toward Jesus. On the one hand, the scribes (2:6; 3:22) and the Pharisees (2:16) question Jesus' ways (2:6, 16; 3:22); Pharisees plot against him (3:6), try to trap him (8:11; 10:2; 12:13), are the leaven one must beware of (8:15) since they are hypocrites (12:15) as well as the scribes (12:38-40), representing nothing but soulless legalism (2:18; 7:1-22). Nevertheless, Mark presents another side of the picture. Some of the scribes and Pharisees are found among those who "followed" Jesus (Mark 2:15).[40] Scribes join with Jesus' disciples in an attempt to perform an exorcism (9:14-18). They approve of Jesus' teaching on the resurrection (12:28) and shortly afterwards (12:28-34), Jesus and a scribe are at one in a happy dialogue on the main commandment of the law. In spite of all his strictures, Jesus could tell a scribe: "You are not far from the kingdom of God" (v. 34). In the controversies reported in Mark 12:18-34, it would seem that in the context of Sadducee Jerusalem, Jesus turns to the scribes as practical allies.

But it is Luke's Gospel that shows the Pharisees in the most favorable light. In the third Gospel Jesus is found repeatedly invited by the Pharisees to sit for meal at their table (7:36; 11:37; 14:1). They warn him also when they come to hear that Herod intends to do away with him (13:31).[41]

To this Lukan positive appraisal must be added in the Fourth Gospel the dignified picture of the Pharisee Nicodemus, the crypto-disciple who comes to consult Jesus at night (John 3:1-21), defends him in the Sanhedrin (7:50-52), and joins with Joseph of Arimathea to give Jesus a decent burial (19:39). John hints that his case might not have been isolated. At the end of Jesus' ministry, just before the passion story, John reports that "many even of the authorities began to believe in him" (12:42).

A statistical detail is significant. The Essenes are never mentioned in the Gospels; the word "Zealot" recurs only once (as a surname of Simon in Luke

---

[40] At least according to the reading of Sinaiticus and of other manuscripts that put the division after v. 16a and read: "there were many who followed him, even the scribes of the Pharisees." This reading is accepted by H. B. Swete, *The Gospel according to St Mark* (London: Macmillan 1898), 41f.; E. P. Gould, *The Gospel according to St. Mark,* ICC (Edinburgh: T & T Clark, 1912), 42; A. Plummer, *The Gospel according to Saint Mark,* CGTC (Cambridge: Cambridge University Press, 1914), 89. Largely rejected by subsequent commentators, this reading has been recently resumed by R. A. Guelich, *Mark 1-88:26,* WBC 34A (Dallas: Word Books, 1989), 97f., 103. It was also accepted in the first edition of the French *TOB.* The second edition has joined the mainstream of translations that keeps the Pharisees in their role of mere opponents.

[41] "On this point, Lk may be closer to historical reality than Mk and especially Mt for whom the Pharisees tend to become systematically Jesus' adversaries, on account of the polemics of the early Church. The finer assessment of Lk may be due also to the influence of Paul, who went on priding himself in his Pharisaic past (Ph 3:5; cf. Ac 23:6; 26:5)" (*TOB* [Paris: Cerf-Les Bergers et les Mages, 1972], 217).

6:15) and "Sadducee" also only once in Mark and Luke (but seven times in Matthew). But the presence of Pharisees is referred to eighty-seven times (respectively for each Gospel: 29 + 12 + 27 + 19).[42] This cannot be entirely due to redactional causes. After 70, it was with the "doctors of the law" that the Christian community had to debate its identity. The Sadducees having disappeared with the temple, the Pharisees "remained practically alone . . . They no longer had any reason . . . to call themselves Pharisees . . . They were quite simply Jews, or rather, they were *the* Jews. Pharisaism and Judaism were now coextensive."[43] Yet Pharisees are frequently mentioned in the Gospels. The reason for this frequency can only be that they were actually quite present in Jesus' ministry. They were a major element in Jesus' intellectual and religious horizon. It was mostly in relation to and in contrast with them that Jesus articulated his views.

Josephus presents them as the representatives of a "philosophy." Writing for Greeks, he had to put the picture in terms adapted to the Greek academic scene. Actually Pharisees were both less and more than a philosophical school.

They were not philosophers skilled in speculative thinking. As J. Jeremias puts it,

the Pharisaic communities were mostly composed of petty common-ers, men of the people with no scribal education, earnest and self-sacrificing; but all too often they were not free from uncharitableness and pride with regard to the masses, the ʿamme ha-ares who did not observe the demands of religious law as they did, and in contrast to whom the Pharisees considered themselves to be the true Israel.[44]

And again,

The Pharisees were the people's party; they represented the common people as opposed to the aristocracy on both religious and social mat-ters. Their much-respected piety and their social leanings towards sup-pressing differences of class, gained them the people's support and assured them, step by step, of the victory.[45]

---

[42] Only the "scribes" (*grammateis*) are mentioned almost as frequently (22 + 21 + 14 + 0 for a total of fifty-seven, to which can be added *nomodidaskalos* and *nomikos*: 1 + 7). In the case of the reference of the scribes, there may be a redactional element. After the disaster of 70; Judaism had to focus on the Book, and the role of the doctors of the law and of the scribes became predominant. It was also the time when the Christian movement had to identify itself in relation to and often in conflict with Judaism. This was a setting that increased the redac-tional interest in Jesus' discussions with the "doctors." This is the reason for which the Gospel of Matthew, the setting of which is more specifically the definition of Christian identity in the post-70 period, amplifies the role of the "scribes" and tends to identify "the scribes and the Pharisees."

[43] M. Simon, *The Jewish Sects at the Time of Jesus* (Philadelphia: Fortress Press, 1967), 29.

[44] J. Jeremias, *Jerusalem in the Time of Jesus* (London: SCM Press, 1969), 259.

[45] Ibid., 266.

A committed laity, the Pharisees did not constitute a philosophical school. But their active commitment to the ways of the Lord was more impressive than mere intellectual dedication to the Torah. Heirs to the Hasideans (Hebrew *hasidim,* the pious) of the Maccabean times (see 1 Macc. 2:42; 7:13), they had the courage to stand against the powers that be in the name of their fidelity to God and to the covenant. They led the resistance to the Hasmonean abuses and paid their opposition with their life when eight hundred of them were crucified by Alexander Janneus. They were again in the forefront of the agitation against the census of 6 c.e., and one of them, Zadok, joined Judas the Galilean as co-leader of the first anti-Roman liberation struggle.[46] During the Jewish War, they first defended a policy of moderation: it belonged to God and not to the sword to bring his rule. But when the situation became desperate, they made common cause with the Zealots and displayed the same heroism. It is impossible to know the proportion of Zealots, of Essenes, and of Pharisees that made the heroic last stand in the Masada fortress. They were all united in death.

This practical devotion to the law explains also their specific doctrines: according to Josephus, they shared the belief in the resurrection, in angels, and in free will (*Ant.* 13.3). Basically these views rested on the conviction that the written Torah had to be completed by the oral law. In other words, unlike the Sadducees, they thought that the tradition of the fathers (*paradosis tōn paterōn* [*Ant.* 13.297; cf. Mark 7:4f.; Gal. 1:14]) had to enliven the letter of the law. Living the law in the context of a lay commitment and in close contact with the realities of life, they felt the need to go beyond a dead letter and to share in the vitality of a living spiritual lineage.

The life of the Pharisees was that of ordinary lay people sharing in the various avocations and concrete problems of the common folk. But it was also a life inspired by a fierce attachment to God and to the demands of the covenant. At different levels they belonged both to the world and to God and they related both belongings by means of a creative tradition that translated their faith in terms of daily chores, of rules on commercial dealings, of what could and could not be done.[47] The ritual of the temple and its laws of purity came down to matters of kitchen pots and clothing; the sanctification of time was effected not only through the yearly cycle of feasts but in the weekly rhythm of the Sabbath celebration.[48]

The culture of the Pharisees was at the same time worldly and godly. It was so deeply rooted that it was the only current that survived the disaster of 70. It became the solid basis on which shattered Judaism could be recon-

---

[46] On the affinities between the Zealot movement and the Pharisees, especially of the Shammai school, see M. Hengel, *The Charismatic Leader and His Followers* (Edinburgh: T & T Clark, 1981), 23f., 55f.

[47] See J. Ernst, *Das Evangelium nach Markus,* RNT (Regensburg: Pustet, 1981), 92.

[48] "We should not underrate the fact that the leading principle of Pharisee piety, the application to daily life of the prescriptions of holiness made only in view of the cult, was a religious achievement of first magnitude" (Ernst, *Markus;* cf. Jeremias, *Jerusalem,* 256-258).

structed after the debacle of the Jewish War. It is no surprise that "they were extremely influential among the townsfolk" (Josephus, *Ant.* 18.15). Had they also a formative influence on Jesus? We know next to nothing about Jesus' education and the influences that played on him. If, during Jesus' youth, there was an impressive anonymous figure in the neighborhood of Nazareth that influenced the mental and spiritual growth of the young carpenter, he is more likely to have been one of the village Pharisees than an Essene from the Dead Sea shores.

At any rate, Jesus' frequent discussions with the Pharisees make it clear that they had a common ground of argument. With the Sadducees, there was little to disagree about since there was little contact. With the Pharisees, on the contrary, recurring dissension was still a form of familiarity. It was a kind of family quarrel.

But dissension there was. On two points mainly, Jesus' basic options ran counter to the Pharisaic spirit. In his dealings with people, his was not the stand of the judge condemning as "accursed this rabble that does not know the law" (John 7:49). His was rather the manner of the Servant, sympathizing with the poor, the sinners, and the marginal populace. In his relation with God, Jesus shunned the legalistic approach that made the Almighty an accountant of good works and merits. The God in whom he put his trust was the God of the good news, his attitude one of filial reliance on the Father of mercies.

In terms of the connection between culture and faith insight, we find that, with the Sadducees and the Essenes, Jesus had little common cultural ground apart from the generally shared Jewish background. The temple and its cult were not the focal point of his world and faith perspective. Along with the Essene Zadokites, and in the prophetic lineage of Amos and Jeremiah, his temple piety was of the critical type. It looked forward to an eschatological cleansing of the temple establishment, even if this cleansing implied its destruction. In that sense, he was at one with the Essenes in their religious radicalism but he lived it in a totally different mental world.

With the Zealots and the Pharisees, it was the opposite. He partook of their popular subculture made of contact with the realities of people's daily life, of sociopolitical restlessness, and of intense apocalyptic expectancy. But his faith orientation ran in the opposite direction.

In short, with respect to the religious, social, and cultural background, Jesus was deeply a man of his times. Yet he was unique. He was at the same time rooted in and a challenge to the culture and the subcultures of Palestine and Galilee.

THE "PEOPLE OF THE LAND"

Like the Pharisees, Jesus lived among the common folk and was one of them. Unlike the Pharisees, he sympathized with their forlorn situation. For him, the "crowd" was an object not of "curse" but of his and God's "compassion . . . because they were like sheep without shepherd" (Mark 6:34). Ultimately, it was with those "accursed" people that he identified best. They were those who did not belong to any of the "sects." They were called the *ʿam ha-ʾarets,* the "people of the land." A mixed lot of simple honest souls and of professed sinners, of poor people struggling to make both ends meet and of corrupt publicans, they had this in common that they were more concerned with the cares of daily life than with theological issues. Identifying with them, Jesus was a "marginal Jew" only insofar as they were rejected to the margin of self asserting Judaism. But this "marginal group" formed the majority of the population and, in this sense, Jesus belonged very much to the mainstream of Jewish society.

The next chapter will study what this identification with the "people of the land" meant concretely for Jesus, the Galilean villager. Let it suffice, at this juncture, to note the relative importance of the sapiential style in the Gospels. Wisdom sayings are typical expressions of folk culture. In the Gospels, it is found particularly in the so-called Q material, the material common to Luke and Matthew, consisting mostly of *logia.* It can be found in various forms:

- *Maxims*: "Whatever you wish others to do to you, so do to them" (6:31 = 7:12); "Let the dead bury their own dead" (9:60 = 8:22).[49]
- *Questions*: "Can a blind man lead a blind man?" (6:39 = 15:14); "Which of you by being anxious can add a cubit to his life span?" (12:25 = 6:27); "If salt loses its saltness, with what can it be salted?" (14:34 = 5:13).
- *Warnings and promises*: "By the measure you use you will be measured" (6:38 = 7:2); "Even the hairs of your head are all numbered" (12:7 = 10:30); "Do not lay up for yourselves treasures on earth where moth and rust consume and thieves break through and steal" (12:33 = 6:19).
- *Generalizations about human conduct*: "A disciple is not above his master nor a slave above his master" (6:40 = 10:24); "No one can serve two masters" (16:13 = 6:24); "The laborer is worth his wages" (10:7 = 10:10).
- *Generalizations from nature*: "The tree is known by its fruit" (6:44 = 12:33); "Consider the lilies, how they grow. They neither labor nor spin; yet, I tell you, even Solomon in all his glory was not attired like one of these" (12:27 = 6:28f).[50]

---

[49] In the following list, the first quotation refers to Luke and the second to the parallel text of Matthew.

[50] This classification and the examples (among many others) are borrowed from C. E. Carlston, "Wisdom and Eschatology in Q," in *Logia: Les Paroles de Jésus. The Sayings of Jesus. Memorial Joseph Coppens,* ed. J. Delobel, BETL 59 (Leuven: Peeters-University Press, 1982), 101-119. Cf. J. S. Kloppenborg, *The Formation of Q: Trajectories in Ancient Wisdom*

The same study can be extended to Mark as well.[51] It is also a matter of common sense that the sick only are in need of physicians (Mark 2:17), that the wedding celebration is no time for fasting (2:13f.). Again, it is a "parable" (3:23) that divided kingdoms and families go to their ruin, that a robber must first neutralize the sturdy owner of the house he came to loot (3:25-28).

It should be noted that these sapiential sayings do not belong to the sophisticated genre of court wisdom as was the case in the Old Testament. They are the expression of rugged rural experience. It may even verge on rustic coarseness when, in Mark 7:18f., it refers to the digestion process ending in the latrine.

The use of this language is significant. It shows Jesus being at one with the experience, culture, and turn of mind of the "people of the land," accepting their common sense as genuine "wisdom" and as an adequate expression of the kingdom.

> Jesus shares in the human condition to such an extent that an important part of his message flows naturally in the stream of human wisdom . . . Is it not . . . an anticipated expression, in a different form, of the prologue of the letter to the Hebrews or of what the fourth gospel will express in a more abstract language: "The *Logos* was made flesh"? In other words, the wisdom language becomes one of the theological *loci* in which the Gospel tradition expresses the mystery of the Incarnation of the Son of God. In Jesus Christ, the divine Wisdom assumes totally and by the same token raises human wisdom to new heights and gives it new value. This has a major importance for the dialogue with non-Christian wisdoms.[52]

To which can be added that, the wisdom of the Gospels being that of the "people of the land," the dialogue it opens with other wisdoms is thereby invited to give privileged value to the wisdom of the "little ones" of the world.

Collections. Studies in Antiquity and Christianity (Philadelphia: Fortress Press, 1987); R. A. Piper, *Wisdom in the Q Tradition: The Aphoristic Sayings of Jesus,* SNTSMS 61 (Cambridge: University Press, 1989).

[51] See J. Schlosser, "Jésus le Sage et ses Vues sur l'Homme d'après l' Évangile de Marc," in *La Sagesse Biblique: De l'Ancien au Nouveau Testament,* ed. J. Trublet, LD 160 (Paris: Cerf, 1995), 321-356.

[52] M. Trimaille, "Jésus et la Sagesse dans la 'Quelle,'" in *La Sagesse Biblique,* ed. Trublet, 318f.

6

The Galilean Villager

Culture and Counterculture

The improved awareness of Jesus' human identity tends often to remain expressed in terms of general Jewishness. But Jesus was a *Galilean* Jew. The Jewish "flesh" taken by the Word was more specifically a "Galilean flesh." To identify the cultural identity of Jesus, the Galilean particularity must also be taken into account. The difference mattered quite a lot, even for Jesus' contemporaries (see Mark 14:70; Matt. 26:69; John 7:41, 52; cf. 1:46). The emphasis on this particularity goes back to the oldest Christian tradition. The titles of "Galilean" and "Nazarean" were given to Jesus and to his followers. They reflect the surprise caused by a messianic claim originating in Galilee. Liberation theologians also have shown a revived interest in the Jesus of flesh and bones and in his historical options in favor of the poor. They may have failed sometimes to devote enough attention to what those *Galilean* poor could have been.[1] Research on Galilee of the first century C.E. has been one of the developing fields of recent New Testament study, combining the resources of history, archaeology, and sociology as well as of literary criticism and Jewish studies.[2]

REDISCOVERING A GALILEAN IDENTITY

This does not mean that all the issues have now been clarified. "The marriage of Galilean studies and historical Jesus research is fraught with its own

---

[1] The remark is made by S. Freyne, *Galilee, Jesus and the Gospels: Literary Approaches and Historical Investigations* (Philadelphia: Fortress Press, 1988), 14-21.

[2] For the growing output of publications, see the bibliography given at the end of Freyne, *Galilee,* 272-291 (up to 1987), which can be complemented up to 1993 by A. Hennessy, *The Galilee of Jesus* (Rome: Gregorian University, 1994), 70-77.

difficulties which have not always been successfully negotiated."[3] The cultural background of Galilee itself remains a moot question. The excavations of Sepphoris, Tiberias, and Beth-shan have seriously altered the image of Galilee as an essentially rural backwater surrounded by the Hellenistic cities of the Decapolis and of the Syro-Phoenician coast. Greek culture had made deep inroads into the "Galilee of the Gentiles." This urban hellenization of Galilee is illustrated, for instance, by the excavations of Sepphoris, a town situated at a short distance of five kilometers to the northwest of Nazareth. Herod Antipas made it his capital, fortified and adorned it in the Greco-Roman style. The theater of the city could accommodate four thousand people, that is, half of the male population. Waterworks, with reservoir and tunnel, brought water to the town. A large villa was unearthed adorned with paintings and refined mosaics depicting a Dionysian procession with its accompaniment of cupids and mythological figures.[4] Sepphoris was not an isolated case. Tiberias was built at the same time and was to replace Sepphoris as the capital of Galilee. During Jesus' lifetime, Herod Antipas followed a steady policy of "modernization" and urbanization of his Galilean tetrarchy. That his policy was somewhat successful is also proved by the prevalence of Greek over Aramaic inscriptions at least in Lower Galilee.[5]

Presuming a continuity between the cities and the surrounding villages, it is easy to imagine the people from the surrounding villages, and particularly from Nazareth, visiting the neighboring city to sell their goods and flocking to the theater of the city.[6] By the same stretch of imagination, we can also envision Yehoshua, the young carpenter of Nazareth, delivering chairs and tables to the Roman garrison of Sepphoris[7] and playing truant to attend the

---

[3] S. Freyne, "Jesus and the Urban Culture of Galilee," in *Texts and Contexts: Biblical Texts in Their Textual and Situational Contexts. Essays in Honor of Lars Hartmann,* ed. Torn Fornberg and David Hellholm (Oslo/Copenhagen/Stockholm: Scandinavian University Press, 1995), 597.

[4] See E. M. Meyers, Ehud Netzer, and C. L. Meyers, "Artistry in Stone: Mosaics of Ancient Sepphoris," *BA* 50 (1987): 223-231.

[5] "One survey of the numerous Aramaic inscriptions from Galilee concluded with the broad generalization that the area along Lake Tiberias and the southern half of Lower Galilee were 'bilingual' . . . while Upper Galilee, which has only a few Greek inscriptions, was dominated by Hebrew-Aramaic" (R. A. Horsley, *Archeology, History and Society in Galilee: The Social Context of Jesus and the Rabbis* [Valley Forge, Pa.: Trinity Press International, 1996], 164). Horsley refers to E. M. Meyers, "Galilean Regionalism as a Factor in Historical Reconstruction," *BASOR* 221 (1986): 97.

[6] E. M. Meyers, "Roman Sepphoris in the Light of New Archaeological Evidence and Research," in *The Galilee in Late Antiquity,* ed. Lee I. Levine (New York: Jewish Theological Seminary of America, 1992), 333.

[7] In this connection, G. Magnani reconstitutes a picture of Jesus the *tektōn* (Mark 6:3) availing himself of the job opportunities offered by the reconstruction of Sepphoris, if not as an engineer at least as a skilled worker and consequently belonging to the "layers of population which, taking into account the lifestyle of those days, could be assimilated to the middle classes of today" (*Vita di Gesù Cristo* [Milan, 1989], 17, quoted by E. Vallauri, "Volti di Gesù negli studi più recenti," *Laurentianum* 39 [1998], 324).

shows at the Roman theater. So was Jesus the Galilean still a true Jew? In this assumed cosmopolitan atmosphere, was not his Jewishness somewhat diluted? Did not the general Mediterranean character of the ambient world obliterate the more specifically Jewish features?[8]

The debate itself testifies to the precision now acquired by our knowledge of first-century Galilee. It shows also that better knowledge brings further problems. To some extent, Mark Twain's witticism holds good for Galilean studies (the word "Galileology" does not seem to have yet obtained recognition!): "The research of many commentators has already cast much obscurity on this subject." The second part of the quip would be too pessimistic: "And it is probable that, if they continue, we shall soon know nothing about it." First, the "darkness" cast by recent study did succeed in doing away with false certitudes like the quasi-pagan climate that would have prevailed in the "Galilee of the Gentiles." Second, out of the scholarly debate and contradictions, outlines of a particular type of Jewishness proper to Galilee come into better focus. Without attempting to cover the entire "Galilean debate" and keeping within the limits of our inquiry into Jesus' cultural background, we may at least explore such cultural components as the religious background, the political climate, the degree of exposure to Hellenism and the social situation. Further precision is still to be brought to the debate. Particularly distinctions must be made between Upper and Lower Galilee, between the subcultures of different classes, and particularly between the "great cultures" of the urban elites and the "small cultures" and even the "countercultures" of village folk.

THE RELIGIOUS BACKGROUND

"Galilee, Galilee, you hate the Torah!" These words of a frustrated rabbi of the third century C.E.[9] are often quoted by the commentators. The qualification of "stupid Galileans" seems also to have been a not uncommon way

---

[8] "Far from being a Judeo-semitic preserve in the midst of ancient Orient, [Galilee] claimed to be a representative part of the Greco-Roman world and more precisely of the *oikoumene,* of the inhabited world or *orbis terrarum* of which August had once for all constituted Rome as the mythical and immortal center . . . Herod established in his kingdom the conditions of an irreversible 'romano-tropism,' for which he set up means of development" (A. Paul, "Nouveau Plaidoyer pour les 'faux jumeaux,'" *NRT* 115 [1993]: 732). Without giving so much importance to the Herodian "romano-tropism," B. J. Malina has also stressed the general features of a "Mediterranean character" ("Dealing with Biblical [Mediterranean] Characters: A Guide for U.S. Consumers," *BTB* 19 [1989]: 127-141; "Is There a Circum-Mediterranean Person? Looking for Stereotypes," *BTB* 22 [1992]: 66-87).

[9] Johanan ben Zakkai, after twenty years in Arav, according to *y. Shabb.* 16.15d. Rabbinic statements need not always be taken literally; they tend to be emotional and humorous. Jerusalem is equally castigated in a similar self-deprecating style: according to a second-century rabbi: "if there are ten portions of hypocrisy in the world, nine of them are in Jerusalem."

of addressing people of the northern province. According to G. Vermès, who quotes such epithets and a few more in the same vein, "they show that the Galileans had the reputation of being unprepared to concern themselves overmuch with Pharisaic scruples."[10] Galileans were considered as typical ⁽am ha-ᵓarets. In plain language, a man from Galilee would have been "a figure of fun, an ignoramus . . . a boor . . . , a religiously uneducated person."[11] Vermès is of the opinion that there could not have been many Galilean Pharisees; the Pharisees mentioned in the Gospels would have been outsiders. If at all they "had acquired some foothold in one or two Galilean cities, . . . their authority was little noticed in rural Galilee, the main field of Jesus' ministry and success."[12]

Further scholarship had a closer look at the matter. The religiosity of Galilee had a rather complicated historical background. Galilee was surrounded by Phoenicians and Syrians. For a long time, it had been cut off from the center of Judaism in Jerusalem. During the Maccabean period, the foreign pressure on the Jews of Galilee had been so strong that Simon Maccabee was sent by Judas to transfer them to Judea "with their wives and children and all they possessed" (1 Macc. 5:14-23).[13] Shortly afterwards, the situation was reversed. Galilee was reunited to a liberated Israel and the Itureans who had settled there had no choice other than expulsion or forcible circumcision (Josephus, *Ant.* 13.318f.). Later on, after the collapse of the Jewish revolts of 70 and 135 C.E., the scribes took refuge in Galilee. Tiberias and Sepphoris became noted centers of rabbinic learning.

But between the reconquest of Galilee in the second century B.C.E. and the rabbinic floruit of the second century C.E., what exactly was the situation in Jesus' day, in the first half of the first century? Scholars, both Christian and Jewish, have tried to piece the evidence.

On the Jewish side, Shmuel Safrai has studied "The Jewish Cultural Nature of Galilee in the First Century."[14] Drawing a long list of "Sages in Galilee" before the destruction of the Second Temple, he shows that Galilee did have its local scribes. "Rabbis visiting from elsewhere would [have found] an audience in public places, as well as being engaged in discussions by the local sages and groups of pupils." He then surveys indications of "Galilean attachment to Judaism," its temple and Torah, to conclude, maybe a little optimistically, that there is "ample evidence both that Galilee had

---

[10] G. Vermès, *Jesus the Jew* (Glasgow: Collins, 1973), 57. The literal interpretation of Ben Zakkai's saying is still followed by M. Hengel, *The Charismatic Leader and His Followers* (Edinburgh: T & T Clark, 1981), 55 (the German original text goes back to 1968).

[11] Vermès, *Jesus the Jew,* 52, 54.

[12] Ibid., 56f.

[13] It might have been only coastal Galilee (see N. J. Mc Eleney, "1-2 Maccabees," *NJBC,* 431).

[14] S. Safrai, "The Jewish Cultural Nature of Galilee in the First Century," in *The New Testament and Christian-Jewish Dialogue. Studies in Honor of David Flusser, Immanuel* 24/25 (1990): 147-186.

close ties with Jerusalem, including the ritual needs of the Temple, and that its religious and social life was rooted in a tradition of the Oral Torah which was indeed superior to the tradition of Judea." Finally, he shows that this evidence tallies with the witness of both the Gospels and Josephus.[15]

On the Christian side, the study of S. Freyne leads to converging results. Studying the Galilean attachment to three main Jewish symbols—the temple, the land, and the Torah—he too questions the validity of the stereotype of a religiously remiss Galilee. But his survey adds nuances to the appraisal of Safrai. As regards the *temple of Jerusalem*, the loyalty of the Galileans was faultless. They did not yield to the lure of the old Israelite sanctuaries and of the new Greek gods; they even took risks when making the traditional pilgrimages to the Holy City, meeting on the way with the hostility of the Samaritans. Yet they were too distant from the concrete realities of the Jerusalem temple to get involved in "an Essene type of protest against the existing priesthood and their conduct." Concerning the *Torah* also, Freyne does not take at its face value the cry of frustration of Johanan ben Zakkai on Galilee "hating the Torah." But, unlike Safrai, he detects little positive evidence of attachment to the scribal and Pharisaic system of devotion to the law. Particularly he finds less heat in the discussion of competing viewpoints: "Because of social as well as economic factors . . . Pharisaism, as an intensification of those basic demands (of the Law), had little attraction for those . . . peasants."

> The priest and his altar were in distant Jerusalem. The freedom fighter with his messianic/apocalyptic hopes and his coins inscribed "for the liberation of Zion" was a product more of Jerusalem and Judean religious, social and political conditions than of those obtaining in Galilee . . . The scribe with his torah-scroll, and his devotees, the Pharisees, were to some extent the indirect result of an alien bureaucracy, now judaised.[16]

Were Galileans "superior to Judeans" in their devotion to the law? Or, while being faithful Jews on the whole, did they react as pragmatic peasants finding the Pharisees' rigid stand "as impractical as it was unattractive"?[17] Will further study and the discovery of new evidence lean on the side of Safrai or of Freyne? What is clear anyway is the basic convergence of both analyses as well as their concurrence with the Gospels' witness. It is not only that Jesus in the Gospels is often presented arguing with "scribes and Pharisees." The discussion itself never bears on the kind of topics that would suggest religious laxity. The contrast between Jesus' polemics and the polemic of the classical prophets is striking. In the Gospels, Jesus does not rebuke

---

[15] Ibid., 170, 180-186.
[16] Freyne, *Galilee*, 180-188, 190, 202, 212-213.
[17] Ibid., 213.

idolatry, apostasy, superstition, sorcery, and witchcraft. What he opposes is a wrong conception of God and of his law. He does not question the religious commitment of his fellow country people. What he challenges is their misguided devotion. Jesus' audience has no problem with the one true God and acceptance of the covenant. In this sense, the Gospels obliquely present a flattering picture of Galilean Judaism. Unlike Elijah in the same area some eight centuries earlier, Jesus did not have to fight for the one Lord and God. He had only to reveal his filial image of God as a Father.

The reservations of Freyne point to a Galilean specificity. Was there a Galilean search for some other forms of Jewish religiosity, a search that could have been the background of the Jesus movement? We have hardly any evidence apart from the Gospels themselves. Elijah is mentioned as often as Moses in the Synoptic Gospels (9 + 9 + 7 for Elijah versus 7 + 8 + 10 for Moses) and more frequently than even Abraham (7 + 1 + 15).[18] At the Transfiguration he appears on a footing of equality with Moses; in Mark he gets even preeminence ("Elijah with Moses," 9:4). Does this indicate a special devotion to the "Galilean" prophet of Jezreel, of Carmel and of Sarepta? In the Galilean messianic perspectives, did he play a greater role than that of precursor?[19] G. Vermès draws our attention to the *hasidim*, literally, the "pious people," charismatic healers and exorcists who displayed another form of Jewish life, more spontaneous and more popular than the rigid attachment to the law of the scribes and Pharisees.[20] Was not this form of Jewish piety given a freer rein in Galilee than in Judea, where the pressure of the official "sects" would have been stronger? Would it not have been at the same time a continuation of the wondrous deeds of Elijah and Elisha[21] and a form of acculturation of Galilean Judaism to the surrounding cults of the Hellenistic healing gods? The existence of such charismatic healers and preachers could constitute the background of Jesus' ministry. Jesus proclaimed his message not only in words but also in deeds. The style of his deeds is closer to the concrete needs of the common folk than the taut attitude of the devotees of the law. This could well point to a Galilean feature of Jesus' cultural background.

---

[18] But less frequently than David (17 + 7 + 13)! It is not only that Elijah is mentioned more often. There is also the fact that Elijah's radicalism and his calling disciples to pursue his work play the role of "prototype" of the charismatic style of Jesus' ministry: see Hengel, *Charismatic Leader*, 5, 15-18.

[19] On the role of Elijah in Judaism, M.J. Stiassny ("Le Prophète Elie dans le Judaisme," in *Élie le Prophète, Études Carmélitaines. Hors Série* 35 [1956]: 199-255), has gathered a rich documentation unfortunately lacking in historical and geographical precision.

[20] Vermès, *Jesus the Jew*, 69-82.

[21] See Barnabas Lindars, "Elijah, Elisha and Gospel Miracles" in *Miracles: Cambridge Studies in Their Philosophy and History*, ed. C. F. D. Moule (London: Mowbray, 1965), 63-79: "The fact that they [Jesus' miracles] are mostly set in Galilee is not without significance," notes Lindars in conclusion (p. 78). He stresses the credulity of the Galileans, people of "mixed stock" and recently converted. This interpretation calls for qualification, but the "significance" remains.

Whichever may be the case with this Galilean specificity, it appears that the Galilee in which Jesus lived was, at least solidly if not deeply, religious. He did not grow up in an atmosphere of indifference. The "Holy Family" did not stand out as an exception in the midst of a godless and lawless society. The Nazarean did not preach in a context of idolatry, superstition, and witch-craft. When his message was not heeded, it was not, as the case had been with Elijah in Jezreel or would be with Paul in Ephesus, because the audience went after other gods. The Galilean culture in which Jesus grew and which he imbibed had a strong religious and Yahwistic component. It had no quarrel with the Jerusalemite brand of Judaic faith. It accepted the distant control of the central cult by the priests and underwent the closer influence of the scribes and Pharisees. Yet, all the while, in a subtle manner, it followed its own Galilean way. This was particularly the case among the ʿam ha-ʾarets, less preoccupied with the finer points of the ritual and of the law, more impressed by the piety of *hasidim* than by the exacting strictness of the lawyers, more concerned also with concrete problems of feeding and healing. Jesus imbibed this Galilean cast of mind. He owed much to the simple folk among whom he lived and in the midst of whom he was brought up before he brought them the good news and called them to conversion.

THE SOCIAL CLIMATE

The socioeconomic situation of Galilee has also been the subject of intensive research,[22] unraveling the many political, economic, and ecological aspects of the question. In the conclusion to the elaborate chapter he devotes to the problem, Freyne speaks of "a dominantly village and peasant ethos which forms a viable subculture in which Jesus lived."[23] This aspect of Jesus' "subculture" deserves closer consideration, as it raises a puzzling problem as well.

GALILEAN URBANIZATION

Actually, Galilee was far from being simply a rural area. It was encircled by a thriving urban civilization. In the west, the prosperous Levantine harbors of Sidon, Tyre, and Akko kept up their historical reputation of commercial centers. A little further south, the harbor of Caesarea had been

---

[22] See E. Meyers, J. Strange, and C Meyers, *Archeology, the Rabbis, and Early Christianity* (Nashville: Abingdon, 1981); R. Horsley and J. S. Hanson, *Bandits, Prophets, and Messiahs: Popular Movements at the Time of Jesus* (New York: Winston Press, 1985); D. W. Bösen, *Galiläa als Lebensraum und Wirkungsfeld Jesu* (Freiburg: Herder, 1985); *The Social World of Formative Judaism: Essays in Tribute of Howard Clark Kee,* ed. J. Neusner, J. Borgen, P. Frerichs and R. Horsley (Philadelphia: Fortress Press, 1988); Freyne, *Galilee,* 135-175.

[23] Freyne, *Galilee,* 175.

recently built by Herod the Great and became the Roman administrative center of Palestine. Damascus in the north, also an old historical city, was the capital of the Decapolis, with Aretas IV as its king. The Decapolis stretched farther southeast. Its very name, the Ten Cities, evoked its basically urban structure. Those trading centers were connected by a tight network of roads, many of which crossed lower Galilee since the plain of Esdrelon and the passes of Yokneam and Megiddo constituted the necessary thoroughfares for west- and southbound traffic. Through this road system and the traffic it carried, the surrounding urban culture could not but infiltrate lower Galilee. The suggestion has even been made that Christian universalism would have been the outcome of the exposure of the Galilean Jesus movement to this cosmopolitan activity. Anyway, the situation of Galilee contrasted with that of Judea. The plains and valleys of Galilee were situated on the highways of western Asia, while hilly Judea looked down at the same highways passing through the lowlands of the Shephelah. The traveler or the merchant passed by the way of Galilee; to Judea he had to go, if at all he had any business there.

Along those roads, Galilee was not deprived of its own cities. If Akko (Ptolemais) and Beth-shan (Scythopolis) were rather peripheral, Sepphoris, Tiberias, Gischala, Jotapata were really Galilean *poleis*. They might not have had the size and the reputation of Tyre, Sidon, and Damascus.[24] Nevertheless they were not insignificant. Herod Antipas, like his father, Herod the Great, though on a lesser scale, wanted to put his country on the map of the Hellenistic world. He conducted an urbanization program, promoting a planned policy of urbanization. He founded Tiberias and decked Sepphoris with new constructions.[25] Just on the other side of the Jordan, his brother Philip upgraded the village of Bethsaida into the *polis* of Julias. Farther north, he made Panias, at the source of the Jordan, his capital, to which he gave the name of Caesarea. More than Judea, Galilee in Jesus' time presented an urban face and leaned to an urban culture.

On this basis, attempts have been made to reconstruct a Hellenistic cultural background to Jesus' message and ministry. Gadara in the Decapolis was just a few miles away from the southeastern shore of the Lake of Galilee, and it seems to have been a breeding ground of philosophers, particularly of the Cynic variety. It was the birthplace of Meleagros, Menippos, Philodemos, and Oinmaos, the first three enjoying a certain notoriety, the

---

[24] See the precisions given by Horsley, *Archeology,* 44f.: the Galilean "cities" cannot compare with the big centers of the Greco-Roman world. For Horsley, the population of Sepphoris and Tiberias must not have exceeded some ten thousand souls. But would such a small population justify an amphitheater that could hold four thousand men? H. W. Hoehner has a much higher estimate of twenty-five thousand (*Herod Antipas* [Grand Rapids: Zondervan, 1972], 52).

[25] His architectural ambitions extended also to Perea, the other part of his tetrarchy, east of the Jordan, where, in the south, he fortified and enlarged Betharamphta to which he gave the name of Livias or Julias in honor of the empress Livia-Julia.

fourth known only through midrashic sources.[26] Could not Jesus' lifestyle be compared with that of the Cynics? Such is the reconstitution proposed by Dominic Crossan and a few others. Jesus' teaching would have been closer to the Cynic kind of countercultural wisdom than to apocalyptic prophetism.[27]

This adventurous reconstruction is largely based on the questionable assumption of a cultural continuum between Galilean cities and villages. The hellenization of a few cities responded to foreign and Herodian influence. Distinctions must be made between the culture of the urban elites and that of the rural peasantry. Relations were rather tense between cities and villages. Economic links were largely one-sided, consisting mostly in heavy taxes to be paid by villagers to subsidize urban development.[28]

The decor on the Herodian royal palace in Tiberias symbolized the alien culture that had suddenly intruded upon the Galilean landscape along with the "in-your-face" city built from revenues regularly taken from the threshing floors and olive presses of Galilean villages by officers who lived lavishly near the palace.[29]

As regards religious attitudes, "are we to suppose that these people abandoned their inherited beliefs and values for those emanating from outside and mediated by centers that were treated with suspicion if not hostility?"[30] Actually, the hostility was such that it escalated into an attack of the surrounding villages on Sepphoris at the death of Herod in 4 B.C.E. and ultimately into the insurrection of 66-67.[31]

---

[26] Philodemos was Epicurean. Menippos (third century B.C.E.) was the author of a *Testament* treated in the comic mood, of *Letters from the Gods,* and of an *Evocation of the Dead*. His influence can be traced in Ovid, Seneca, and Lucian. As for Meleagros, he was the author of satires and epigrammata, often erotic in content. His fame was such that he had imitators down to the sixth century C.E. (See H. Dörrie, "Menippos," and R. Keydell, "Meleagros," in *Der Kleine Pauly, Lexicon der Antike* (Stuttgart: Drucken-Müller,vol. 3 [Stuttgart: Druckenmüller Verlag, 1969], cols. 1171, 1217). Oinmaos is known through *Midrash Rabbah* 65.20.

[27] E. M. Meyers and J. F. Strange, *Archeology, the Rabbis, and Early Christianity* (Nashville: Abingdon, 1981), 57; B. Mack, *A Myth of Innocence: Mark and Christian Origins* (Philadelphia: Fortress Press, 1988), 72-74; J. D. Crossan, *The Historical Jesus: The Life of a Mediterranean Jewish Peasant* (San Francisco: HarperCollins, 1991), 72-88; G. Downing, *Cynics and Christian Origins* (Edinburgh: T & T Clark, 1992).

[28] See Horsley, *Archelogy,* 73-84.

[29] Ibid., 57.

[30] Freyne, "Jesus and the Urban Culture of Galilee," 616.

[31] See Horsley, *Archeology,* 123-130. See the elaborate criticism of the Cynic hypothesis by P. Rhodes Eddy, "Jesus as Diogenes? Reflections on the Cynic Jesus Hypothesis," *JBL* 115 (1996): 449-469. In a rejoinder in the same *Journal* ("Jesus and the Cynics Revisited," *JBL* 116 [1997]: 704-712), D. Seeley proposes a middle way. Though not a Cynic, Jesus could have "combin(ed) parts of Cynic thought with his native Jewish tradition" (p. 711). Against Eddy, he claims that such was the position of Downing, Crossan and Mack whom he quotes: "One might imagine Jesus doing at a popular level what many Jewish intellectuals did at a more sophisti-

A RURAL SUBCULTURE

A rural subculture counteracted this tendency to urban sophistication. Freyne has documented the existence of this tendency.[32] Without resuming his demonstration, let it suffice to show how it applies to Jesus. Several aspects of Jesus' life and ministry reveal his belonging to this solid rural core of Galilean life.

Suspicion toward Herodian "Civilization"

Like John the Baptist, Jesus was suspicious of the type of "civilization" Herod wanted to foster. Without going into the kind of direct confrontation that cost John his life, Jesus calls Herod "a fox" (Luke 13:32) and cautions his disciples "against the leaven of the Pharisees and the leaven of Herod" (Mark 8:15). Amos-like, he shows no sympathy toward those "who are gorgeously appareled and live in luxury in the royal courts" (Luke 7:25; Matt. 11:8). Herodians sensed this antagonism and sought "to destroy him" (Mark 3:6; 12:13).

A Rural Language

Thoroughly rural, the language of Jesus also betrays his social belonging. He spoke of sowing grains and harvesting, of cultivating vineyards and tending orchards; he knew the particularities of the various Galilean types of soil and their flora: wheat, grapes, and figs, thistles, thorns, and other weeds. He admired the beauty of the lilies of the field and the hidden potency of the tiny mustard seed. Equally familiar with the Galilean fauna, he spoke of sparrows and doves, ravens and vultures, hens, chicks, and eagles, snakes, vipers, and scorpions, goats and sheep, foxes and wolves, camels and asses and even of the despised pigs. He knew also about fish, fishing, and fishermen. He quoted the rural proverbs concerning the weather (Matt. 16:2f., 24:27; Luke 10:18; 12:54) and the hazards of farming (Mark 4:1-8 and par.; John 4:35-38).[33]

A noteworthy feature of the parabolic language of Jesus is its "naturalism." Where the Old Testament and the rabbinic writings tend to theologize nature symbolism, Jesus shows a peasant's proximity to the realities of the soil. In Psalm 112:4, "light rises in darkness for the upright." But with good rustic common sense, Jesus knows that God "makes his sun rise on the evil as on the good" (Matt. 5:45). In Isaiah 5:1-2, the choice vineyard is blamed for failing to yield a good vintage. But in Mark 12, the trouble is with the

---

cated level, namely, combining Jewish and Hellenistic traditions of wisdom in order to make critical judgments about the times and propose a religious ethic held to be in keeping with Jewish ideals" (quoted on p. 705 from Mack, *Myth of Innocence*, 74).

[32] Freyne, *Galilee*, 135-175.

[33] See Hennessy, *Galilee*, 24-26.

workers. What goes wrong with the vineyard is not some kind of malefic influence that makes it yield sour grapes. It is the human factor, the socio-political restlessness prevalent in Jesus' day and with which young Herod had already to contend (Josephus, *Ant.* 14.9.2). With Jesus, the symbolic "theme" of the vineyard now vibrates with the pathos of the social unrest affecting Galilean peasantry in Herodian times. A lack of naturalism seems to appear in the parable of the mustard seed in Matt. 13:31f., where the seed becomes a "tree" with branches where the birds of the air make their nest. But these hyperbolic allegorical elements do not figure in Mark 4:30-32, presumably closer to the original wording of Jesus. Mark, and Jesus, knew that the mustard seed does not grow on "trees": it is just a *lachanon,* a vegetable, a shrub where the birds would not find any branches but only a little shade to build their nests. Incorporating the image of the tree in Daniel 4:21, the Matthean text has submitted the original rural metaphor to the midrashic technique. Jesus' language was more genuinely rural. A similar synoptic observation can be made in the parable of the sower. In Luke 8:6, the sower throws part of the seed "on the rock" where "it withers because it had no moisture." One is left wondering why the poor farmer should be so careless as to waste part of the seeds by throwing it on rocks and how, first of all, it could sprout at all if falling on stones. Mark 4:5 has a more professional description: the seed falls not on the "rock" but on "rocky soil" (*petrōdēs*), a ground that has a thin layer of topsoil. A little dew or a slight drizzle would be enough to moisten it, and so "it sprang up quickly because it had no depth of soil." But come the dog days and the young sprouts wither as quickly as they had shot up. We have the story directly from the farmer's mouth.

Peasant or Artisan?

But was Jesus a farmer? Was he not rather a *tektōn,* a carpenter, according to Mark 6:3 (cf. Matt. 13:55)? A surprising element of Jesus' language is that it seems to reveal a type of imagination closer to the farmer's life than to the artisan's. There is no parable dealing with timber, paring and planing, tenon and mortise, hammer, nails, furniture, yokes, and plows. The only two *logia* referring to wood material are the sayings on the "easy yoke" (Matt. 11:30) and the "beam in the eye" (Matt. 7:5), sayings that hardly evoke any high qualification in wood work! A "good tree" giving "good fruits" is the viewpoint of an agriculturist; for a woodworker, the "good tree" would give good timber. The setting of the parables is more the open field than the workshop.[34] In fact the Greek word *tektōn* does not mean exactly "carpenter" but rather "house builder."[35] Actually quite a few words of Jesus refer to build-

---

[34] See L. Legrand, "The Parables of Jesus Viewed from the Dekkan Plateau," *Indian Theological Studies* 23 (1986): 165-166.

[35] See H. Höpfl, "Nonne hic est fabri filius?" *Bib* 4 (1923): 41-55; E. Lombard, "Charpen-

ing techniques: the "house built on the rock" (Matt. 7:24-27), the church
built on Kepha, the Stone (Matt. 16:18f.), the corner stone (Matt. 21:42-44),
the tower in the vineyard (Mark 12:1), the tower of Siloe (Luke 13:4f.) and
the tower builder (Luke 14:28ff.). Jesus' work in his rural setting must have
been rather that of a house builder. The woodwork of those humble mud-
wall huts (see Matt. 6:19) would have been restricted to narrow windows and
a light support of rough rafters with branches laid across for the flat mud
roof. This kind of work did not give the expertise to go to Sepphoris as a cab-
inetmaker for the Roman headquarters and the high officials.[36] More significantly, such an occupation, confined to the limited range of the small village
of Nazareth could hardly have fed a man and his family. We may presume
that a little plot of land would have added its contribution to the maintenance
of the family of Nazareth. Or else a landless Jesus could have lent his services as a casual farmworker at the time of plowing, sowing, or harvesting,
at the time of grape or olive picking, thus adding an occasional shekel or two
to the meager income of his "tectonic" employment.[37]

A Rural Poetry

It is through this language and this culture that Jesus expressed his experience of God. The well-known rehashed distinction between parable and
allegory has a bearing on our inquiry. Allegory belongs to intellectual
learned culture. A story is made to fit with an abstract ideological frame: the
theoretical construction preexists; the story is added to it by way of illustration. Parable is poetry; the further shore is perceived from within the field of
human experience. The parables of Jesus mean that his sense of God issued
from within his human experience of nature, of toil and labor, of the tensions
of human society. He lived the immanent presence of the Father in the most

---

tier ou Maçon?" *RTP* 36 (1948); P. H. Furfey, "Christ as *Tektōn*," *CBQ* 17 (1955): 324-335;
R. A. Batey, "Is Not This the Carpenter?" *NTS* 30 (1984): 249-258.

[36] As suggested by S. J. Case, "Jesus and Sepphoris," *JBL* 45 (1926): 14-26, a suggestion
received with sympathy by Batey, "Is Not This the Carpenter?"; idem, "Sepphoris: An Urban
Portrait of Jesus," *BAR* 18/3 (1992): 50-64.

[37] See Legrand, "Parables." This is still now the pattern of life of the "carpenter" in Indian
villages. The exact social setting of Jesus' life remains a debated question. On Jesus as a small
contractor undertaking work in Sepphoris, see nn. 6-7 above. For Crossan, Jesus, while working among the farms and villages of Lower Galilee, acted as a peasant Jewish Cynic (*Historical Jesus*). S. Freyne suggests that the work of a carpenter implied "a degree of mobility and
status" (*Galilee*, 241). Not finding enough work in his native village, the carpenter had to go
around the farms and villages of Lower Galilee. D. E. Oakman also pictures Jesus as a jour-
neyman but acknowledges additional farmwork for the sake of subsistence (*Jesus and the Economic Questions of His Day* [Lewiston/Queenston: Edwin Mellen Press, 1986], 179-181). M. I.
Finley quotes evidence from Xenophon (*Cyropaedia* 8.2.5) to show that the rural carpenter had
to supplement his income by working as a farmhand (*The Ancient Economy* [London: Chatto &
Windus, 1973], 135; cf. L. Turkowski, "Peasant Agriculture in the Judaean Hills," *PEQ* 100
[1968]: 21-33; 101 [1969]: 101-112).

minute aspects of his daily life and found in them the expression of his insight. His sense of God's transcendence also found its expression not in the allegorical language of royal splendor and astral phenomena but in the unpredictable extravagance of a forgiving Father (Luke 15:11-31), of a host substituting the street beggars for the absentee honorable guests (Luke 14:15-24), of a master forgetting the rules of good accounting to pay undeserving servants (Matt. 20:1-15). There lies a major difference between Jesus' parables and those of the rabbis. Jesus' parables do not illustrate Bible texts. They emerge from the subculture of the common Galilean folk. Apart from their unique message of the Fatherhood of God, they are culturally unique as literary expressions, as theological and mystical language. Martin Dibelius has described the Gospels as *klein Literatur,* a "small literature" which is cast not in the dignified forms of official culture but in such secondary forms as folktales, miracle stories, and cultic legends. In a way his description is accurate. The language of Jesus does not claim to be sized up according to the canons of academic Mediterranean culture, whether Greco-Roman or Judaic. Indeed, it stands away from this kind of civilization. Yet Dibelius was wrong in understanding this classification in a disparaging manner. The language of Jesus in the parables is "great"; it stands out in its poetic vigor. Its greatness is made of authenticity and simplicity. It took a genial creativity to reverse the traditional literary and theological codes and to make folk language the medium of the highest spiritual experiences.

This does not make Jesus a Rousseau or a Tolstoi, idealizing the simple life of the countryside. He knew the farmer's struggle to eke a meager living out of an unfertile soil, the frustration of the jobless anxiously waiting to be hired. Jesus' Galilee is no Arcadia. Its streets were filled with "poor, maimed, lame, and blind" (Luke 14:13, 21). Its villagers would not have been accepted in the bucolic circles of the *Georgics* and of the *Eclogues.* They were rather inclined to oppose the harshness of absentee landowners by hook or by crook (Luke 16:1-8), by laziness (Luke 12:45), or by plain violence (Mark 12:1-9). Jesus' portrait of Galilean rural life echoes the tensions raised by its coexistence with the surrounding urban culture. His "subculture" had elements of a protest against the surrounding exploitative "civilization." His were the language and the culture of the poor of the land.

A RURAL STRATEGY

Of particular significance is the fact that none of the main Galilean centers appears on Jesus' itineraries. A map of the main cities of Galilee, as reconstituted, for instance, on the basis of Josephus's account of the Roman reoccupation of Galilee (Jotapata, Gischala, Sepphoris, Tarichaea, Tiberias), would be exactly the map of the places where Jesus did not go. Tiberias was a new city, recently built on the Lake of Galilee, a beehive of activity with the royal court and its hot-water springs frequented by the aristocracy of the Syrian world. Tarichaea was still closer to the northern shore of the lake, where Jesus exercised his ministry, just a few kilometers south of the traditional site of the multiplication of the loaves and of the mount of the Beatitudes. It was the main fishing center on the shores of the lake. According to Josephus, it had a population of forty thousand souls and counted 230 fishing boats. It was famous for its pickled fish (it is the meaning of *taricheia* in Greek), which were exported far away. Yet it is mentioned only indirectly in the Gospels under its Aramaic name of Magdala. A certain Mary left the town of Magdala to join the group of Jesus' disciples, but there is no report of Jesus having exercised a ministry in this city.

The case of Sepphoris is noteworthy. As we have seen above, Herod Antipas had rebuilt it, made it his capital and turned it into a Hellenistic urban center. It was deeply hellenized, if we assume that the amphitheater held frequent shows and that it was filled to its capacity of four thousand spectators. During his thirty years in Nazareth, Jesus could see the big city a short distance away. We can imagine Yehoshua, the young carpenter from Nazareth, working with his father, Joseph, on some of the construction projects of the budding city. We can as well fancy him, as a teenager, attracted by the lure of the town, attending the shows at the amphitheater. One can always indulge in fantasies, but it is not so easy to give them scholarly credentials. R. A. Batey has tried to make a case for these contacts by tracing logia of Jesus that might refer to theater and to building work.[38] The basis for the case is very slender. Whether the use of the word "hypocrite" supposes a familiarity with Greek theater techniques[39] remains questionable. Finally, there remains the crucial fact that Sepphoris is never mentioned in the Gospels as a setting for the ministry of Jesus. Sustained contacts of Jesus with the neighboring city and a formative influence of its Hellenistic bent on his mind belong to the field of evangelical romancing.

There is nothing in the Gospels' report of Jesus' ministry and in his sayings to suggest that he would have been a patented carpenter to the legions of H. M. Tiberius Caesar garrisoned at Sepphoris. The Gospel data do not tally with an "urban portrait of Jesus." "Jesus maintained his distance from the 'cities' despite his geographic proximity to them."[40] In a Galilee that experienced from outside the influence of surrounding city-states and, from inside, the pull of a growing urbanization, the subculture of Jesus remained attached to his rural roots and to a peasant ethos. One will have to wait for Pauline practical hermeneutics to have "an urban version" of the Christian movement. As for Jesus himself, his world was that of the villages of Galilee, not of its cities.

---

[38] Batey, "Is Not This the Carpenter?" 249-258; idem, "Jesus and the Theater," *NTS* 30 (1984): 563-574; idem, "Sepphoris: An Urban Portrait of Jesus," 52-62.

[39] Batey, "Jesus and the Theater," 563-565.

[40] G. Theissen, *The Gospels in Context: Social and Political History in the Synoptic Tradition* (Minneapolis: Fortress Press, 1992), 14.

CONCLUSIONS

1. *Jesus was a Jew.* His life, action, thought, language, and teachings were totally rooted in Jewish culture. He belonged to it. This fundamental belonging goes far beyond the categories of "inculturation" or "acculturation." "Contextualization" would be equally inadequate insofar as the causative "-ization" would suggest an artificial effort of insertion. In the case of Jesus, there was no effort or insertion. He just belonged to the country in which he was born and to its culture. Speaking from the viewpoint of a "high Christology," John speaks of a "Word made flesh" (1:14), of an incarnation. From the point of view of anthropology, there is just the fact of this native *belonging.*

2. But the "Jewish culture" had *many facets* and there were many ways to relate to it depending on whether one emphasized the law, the land, the temple, or another aspect of Jewish life. In the case of Jesus, we find a tension or a bipolarity between his prophetic stance and his cultural conformity. He is a Jew, a full member of the people of Israel, but he stands often on the fringe of Israelite mainstreams. He is Galilean rather than Judean, a villager rather than a member of the elite of the religious (Jerusalem), administrative (Sepphoris), or economic (Tiberias, Tarichaea) urban centers, an artisan-farmer rather than a priest, a scribe, or a political leader. In this sense, he is a "marginal Jew," who stood outside the pale of well-established interpretations of Judaism. His most authentic Jewishness does not fit any of the set forms of the ancestral faith.

3. If he identifies at all with one of the social groups and its subculture, it is with the "poor of the land," the ʿamei ha-ʾarets. He shares in their life, speaks their language, feels at home with their wisdom, and uses their metaphors. In that sense, he is no "marginal Jew," since the "people of the land" constituted the bulk of the population of Palestine. But here again he escapes neat categorizing. The nonalignment of the common folk with the main currents of Jewish thought was mostly a matter of indifference. In Jesus, there is no indifference. On the contrary, his nonalignment is the expression of a more radical commitment to God and to the coming of his rule. In short, Jesus takes all his interlocutors by surprise.

4. Should we then speak of an "anti-culture" or of a *"counterculture"*? There are certainly aspects of Jesus' approach that show him as a dissenter. Like the Zealots, he shows no sympathy toward the compromising attitude of the Sadducees and of the Herodians. Like the Qumranites, he dreams of a temple that would be a "house of prayer," cleansed from the commercial defilement of Mammon. Yet the word "counterculture" does not seem to do justice to his vision of a new Israel. Counterculture is an antithesis and, as such, continues to give a mirror image of the culture it negates. The Zadokite

opposition to the Sadducee establishment expresses itself in the *Temple Scroll.* In the name of God's rule, the Zealot movement wanted to replace the existing political system with another system, equally based on power and thereby open to corruption. What it would have resulted in, had it been successful, can be gauged by the degradation of the Maccabean struggle into the Hasmonean rule: a magnificent fight for freedom ended ultimately in unrestrained political opportunism. Jesus did not identify with any of the opposition groups. His is an attitude of integral freedom.[41] From within the culture he belongs to and in which he was born, he transcends the cultural as well as the countercultural set patterns. *Even culturally, Jesus stands for a new Israel.*

5. Humanly speaking, Jesus belongs to the race of the creators who open new dimensions of human existence, of the poets who invent new languages, of *the prophets and mystics* who enter the divine sphere and transcend the human perspectives in their commerce with the divine. They are undoubtedly people of their own times and are an expression of the culture of their land. Yet they go beyond it and become, in the midst of their own generations, the explorers of new horizons of being. So was Jesus. He was Jesus the Jew, the Word made a Jewish flesh, but this Word carried along with it all the divine power of creation and the dazzling newness of God's glory (John 1:14).

---

[41] See E. Käsemann, *Jesus Means Freedom: A Polemical Survey of the New Testament* (London: SCM Press, 1969).

Part Three

Paul and Beyond

"Born at Tarsus in Cilicia, but brought up in this city [of Jerusalem] at the feet of Gamaliel" (Acts 22:3), St. Paul represents a typical case of cross-cultural interaction in the New Testament. A "Jew from Tarsus," he was born to a Jewish family but in a Hellenistic city of Asia Minor (Acts 21:39). A Pharisee, son of Pharisees (Acts 23:6), he was also by birth a Roman citizen (Acts 22:25-28). Trained as a Jewish rabbi at the feet of Gamaliel (Acts 22:5), he was an able Greek writer as well. His field of apostolate presents the same bipolarity. It was the Greco-Roman world, but Paul the Jew continued to keep in touch with the important Jewish communities of the Diaspora. He preached and wrote in Greek and used the rhetorical resources of Greek literature, but he handled rabbinic hermeneutic techniques with equal dexterity. After the excesses of the *Religiongeschichtliche Schule* tracing every aspect of Pauline thought to Greek philosophy or mystery cults and a reaction emphasizing the apostle's Jewishness, there is now "a general scholarly consensus that Paul must be thought of as a Jew of the Diaspora."[1] "Hellenistic Judaism" is the phrase commonly used to qualify the kind of hybrid culture that issued from the encounter between Israel and Hellas. But a convenient label is no solution to a problem. The question remains of which term prevailed over the other. Was Saul of Tarsus fundamentally a Jew in Greek garb? Or, on the contrary, was he a renegade Jew who had deserted the ancestral culture and opted for assimilation? Or again, did he try to combine the two elements and how far did he succeed?

No answer can be given a priori. We do not know how much Greek schooling the young Saul had received in his birthplace.[2] Neither are we well informed of the type of Judeo-Hellenistic culture that prevailed in the Cilician Diaspora. If Alexandrian Jewish culture is amply documented, for

---

[1] V. P. Furnish, "Pauline Studies," in *The New Testament and Its Modern Interpreters,* ed. E. J. Epp and G. W. MacRae (Atlanta: Scholars Press, 1989), 332.

[2] The basic study is that of W. C. Van Unnik, *Tarsus or Jerusalem, the City of Paul's Youth* (London: Epworth Press, 1962). The discussion will be resumed in chapter 8 below.

Asian Jewry, scholarship has to acknowledge "the paucity and fragility of our evidence."[3]

As a matter of fact, it is the Pauline letters that constitute the main source of evidence. There has been, in fact, an ongoing debate about whether Paul's work and thought were to be classified as belonging to Hellenism or to Judaism, with the compromise optional variant of Hellenistic Judaism. A surprising feature of present-day Pauline studies is that they seem to develop independently in the two opposite directions, without addressing each other and even attempting to refute each other. A current of Pauline research emphasizes Paul's Jewishness and analyzes its manifestations in his letters, while another line of inquiry shows equal vigor in investigating his dependence on Hellenistic rhetoric and thought patterns. Nowadays, scholars tend to pursue their exploration of both the Jewish and Hellenistic background of the Pauline letters in peaceful mutual ignorance and with equally rewarding results. This apparent cultural ambivalence of the apostle to the nations deserves particular consideration. We shall therefore study the two sides of the diptych separately and then see how they hinge on each other.

---

[3] J. M. G. Ramsay, *Jews in the Mediterranean Diaspora: From Alexander to Trajan (323 BCE- 117 CE)* (Edinburgh: T & T Clark, 1996), 259. Ramsay's study devotes 210 pages to "the Diaspora in Egypt" (pp. 19-228) and only 22 to "the Province of Asia" (pp. 259-281) without a word about Cilicia.

7

Paul the Jew

PAUL'S JEWISH CULTURAL IDENTITY

K. Barth's famed commentary on the Letter to the Romans is almost totally innocent of any reference to the first-century Jewish background of Paul's thought. The purpose of the work being more hermeneutical than strictly exegetical, the great theologian can be excused for evoking Grünewald, Luther, Potemkine and Dostoievsky rather than Hillel, Akiba, or Johanan ben Zakkai. R. Bultmann's scope was more specifically exegetical. Yet, in his *Theology of the New Testament,* his description of flesh,[1] sin,[2] and law[3] dispenses with any consideration of Judaism. The succeeding section on righteousness, apart from the due references to the Old Testament, has only two mentions of the *Psalms of Solomon,* equaled by two quotations taken from Epictetus and the *Corpus Hermeticum.*[4] Insofar as Judaism is concerned, Paul could have been working in a vacuum.

Yet Pauline exegesis had long been aware that it had to take Judaism into account. Without going as far back as St. Jerome, we can at least mention J. Lightfoot, the seventeenth-century predecessor of H. Strack and P. Billerbeck.[5] F. Prat's *Theology of St Paul*, already in 1908, had a few pages on the "traces of rabbinism visible in the Apostle."[6] More elaborate is J. Bonsirven's

---

[1] R. Bultmann, *Theology of the New Testament* (London: SCM Press, 1952), 1:227-238.

[2] Ibid., 238-253. But with a reference to Ovid on p. 248!

[3] Ibid., 257-269. The references are to Goethe (p. 260), Kant (p. 261), and Gnostic myths (p. 269).

[4] Ibid., 270-285. *Psalms of Solomon* are quoted on pp. 273 and 283, Epictetus on p. 277, and *Corpus Hermeticum* on p. 278.

[5] J. Lightfoot, *Hebraicae et Talmudicae Exercitationes on I Cor*, published in 1664 and reprinted in *A Commentary on the New Testament from the Talmud and Hebraica* (Peabody: Hendrickson, 1989), vol. 4.

[6] English translation from the tenth edition by J. L. Stoddard, *The Theology of Saint Paul* (London: Burns & Oates, 1927), 1:36. But Prat goes on immediately to qualify these "traces" as "rare and questionable" on the ground that "the rabbinism of St Paul's time is unknown to

comparative study between rabbinic and Pauline exegesis,[7] which anticipates the structure—including the unbalance—of E. P. Sanders's *magnum
opus* on the same subject.[8]

A shortcoming of Bonsirven's study and of the work anterior to 1950 was
the almost exclusive dependence on "rabbinic literature," an enormous mass
of writings covering many centuries and largely posterior to the crisis of 70
and to the subsequent redefinition of Judaism along Pharisaic lines. The discovery of the Dead Sea Scrolls provided earlier material illustrating nonrab-
binic aspects of Judaism around the turn of the Christian Era. The same
factors that contributed to a rediscovery of the Jewishness of Jesus led also
to a reassessment of the Jewish background of Paul's language, thought, and
mission strategy.

PAUL IN THE CONTEXT OF CONTEMPORARY JUDAISM

The influence of Jewish literary techniques and exegetical methods on
Paul's writings, initiated by Bonsirven, has been further pursued and given
more precision by C. Perrot:

> The Apostle is now better situated in the Judeo-Hellenistic atmosphere
> common to the scribes of his days . . . He actualizes the Scriptures fol-
> lowing the methods of Jewish *midrash* without forgetting the input of
> old Jewish traditions and of the Targums (for instance in 2 Cor 3,7-4,6
> on the veil of Moses). He makes use of the typological interpretation
> widespread in the Dispersion as well as in Palestine (1 Cor 10,1-13;
> Rom 4,18-21; Gal 4,21-31). The Qumran discoveries have confirmed
> those data disclosing surprising affinities between the doctrines of the
> Dead Sea sect and pericopae of the Pauline corpus like 2 Cor 6,14-7,1
> —which is possibly an interpolation—and numerous passages of Col
> and Eph (as in Eph 5,3-17).[9]

---

us." Since the influence of Hellenism is also reduced to "his style of preaching" (p. 39), the conclusion is that "the true origins of Paulinism" are nothing but "the Bible and the teaching of
Jesus" (p. 43).

[7] J. Bonsirven, *Exégèse Rabbinique et Exégèse Paulinienne* (Paris: Beauchesne, 1939).

[8] E. P. Sanders, *Paul and Palestinian Judaism* (London: SCM Press, 1977). In both Bonsirven and Sanders the exposition of Judaism (respectively 254 and 428 pages) is much longer
than its application to Pauline exegesis (respectively 94 and 125 pages).

[9] C. Perrot in A. George and P. Grelot (eds.), *Introduction à la Bible,* Tome III, *Introduction
Historique au Nouveau Testament,* vol. 3, *Les Écrits Apostoliques* (Paris: Desclée, 1977), 20.
See particularly A. T. Hanson, *Studies in Pauline Technique and Theology* (Grand Rapids: Eerd-
mans, 1974), 136-200. A more technical study in terms of rabbinic terminology can be found
in Arne Jarand Hobbel, "Hermeneutics in Talmud, Midrash and the New Testament," in *The
New Testament and Christian-Jewish Dialogue: Studies in Honor of David Flusser,* ed. M.

The affinities between Paul and Jewish writings are not only formal. Referring to the Dead Sea documents, Perrot goes on to say:

The Qumran texts have cast a new light on many important elements of the Pauline writings as in the case, for instance, of the famous antitheses between Spirit and flesh, justice and grace, not to speak of some possible influence of Essene community practices.[10]

It is not just a matter of noting the parallelism of certain themes and concluding to a common general background. It is the entire picture of the Jewish setting of the New Testament which now appears in a new light. The Dead Sea sectarians, the Sadducees, and the Pharisees understood the law in different ways. Pharisees themselves did not form a rigorously homogeneous body: the conflicting views of Hillel and Shammai are only a classic example of the diversities prevailing in the way of understanding and applying the Torah. This pluralism expressed itself in a wide variety of biblical interpretations and in a free exchange of mutual criticism and even of invectives. In this climate of "hospitable, comprehensive, theological tolerance and fluidity of Judaism before 70 A.D.,"[11] Paul's stance does not appear any longer to be that of an outsider, of a convert to another religion burning his former idols:

The discussions of Judaism and Jews in Paul's letters are intramural. They are criticisms of the faith, law, institutions, and worship of Jews not from without but from within . . . In the time of Paul this differentiation did not spell separation . . . His criticisms of the symbols of Judaism no more signify that he had forsaken Judaism than did the bitter attacks of the sectarians at Qumran against the authorities in Jerusalem signify that they had forsaken it.[12]

Paul's criticism of the law particularly could be viewed at that time—and was certainly viewed by him—as part of the multiform Jewish self-searching for identity. To many currents of thought, Paul added his own interpretation in the light of his faith in Jesus as Messiah. This was not necessarily "heretical," all the less so since there was no defined orthodoxy.

Lowe, *Immanuel* 24/25 (1990): 132-146; P. J. Thomson, *Paul and the Jewish Law: Halakah in the Letters of the Apostles to the Gentiles,* CRINT 3/1 (Maastricht: Van Gorcum, 1990).

[10] Perrot, *Introduction,* ed. George and Grelot, III/3: 20. For further developments, see *Paul and Qumran: Studies in New Testament Exegesis,* ed. J. Murphy-O'Connor (London: Chapman, 1969).

[11] W. D. Davies, *Jewish and Pauline Studies* (London: SPCK, 1984), 97.

[12] Ibid., 97. On Paul's sense of identity, see J. D. G. Dunn, "Who Did Paul Think He Was? A Study of Jewish-Christian Identity," *NTS* 45 (1999): 174-193.

LAW AND CULTURE

The knowledge of this Jewish background leads to a better assessment of the Pauline stand on two important points: his attitude toward the law and his mission strategy.

As regards the law, W. D. Davies denounces the too-common identification of the Torah with the commandments. This alleged antinomy between precepts and liberty serves as a basis for the doctrinal antitheses between grace and law, faith and works, which are supposed to form the core of the Pauline gospel. Actually, for Judaism and for Paul, the law, the Torah, did not consist only in commandments:

> At least four aspects of it have to be borne in mind. First, it includes commandments which are to be obeyed . . . Secondly, it encompasses much that is not legal in the sense of commandment: in particular . . . It includes the history of the people of Israel as variously interpreted at different stages . . . Third, . . . the Torah had come to be interpreted as the wisdom after the pattern of which and by means of which God created the world (Proverbs 8) . . . Fourth . . . , the term Torah . . . connoted for Paul as a Jew the whole of the revealed will of God in the universe, in nature, and in human society.[13]

In this sense, the Torah

> could be taken to indicate a whole cultural tradition . . . To submit to or reject the law was to accept or reject a particular culture or way of life in all its intricate ramifications . . . The question of Paul's relation to the law, then is the question of his relation to the whole tradition, indeed, the very culture of the Jewish people among whom he had been born.[14]

From the anthropological point of view, the Torah was culture; from the theological point of view, it was also grace.[15] It was the entire story of God's election of Israel through promises and covenants. On both accounts, it cast deep roots in the heart of the Jewish people and so it did in the heart of Paul the Jew. Paul does not propose to do away with the law but to subordinate it to the love of Christ.[16] Paul acknowledges the privileges granted to Israel, to whom "belong the sonship, the glory, the covenants, the giving of the law, the worship, and the promises. To them belong the patriarchs and of their

---

[13] Davies, *Jewish and Pauline Studies,* 92f.
[14] Ibid., 93.
[15] Ibid., 118.
[16] Ibid., 121.

race according to the flesh is the Christ" (Rom. 9:4). Paul remains convinced that "the gifts and the call of God are irreversible" (Rom. 11:29).

He was proud of Abraham, at home with the Scriptures, grateful for the promises and the covenant. He defends the law that he criticizes. After having explained that it has been an occasion of sin, he specifies that this is not due to the law itself but to sin lurking behind in hiding and looking for its opportunity (Rom. 7:11). The law has been given through the ministry of angels (Gal. 3:19). It is "good" (Rom. 7:13): it is "spiritual" (7:14).[17] It has played a "pedagogical" role (Gal. 3:24). Well understood, it anticipates the revelation of the great command of love (Rom. 13:8-10; Gal. 5:14).

For all the attachment Paul had toward his law and his culture, he submitted it to a scathing criticism, and we shall come to it presently. But it is important to take note that this criticism stems from a true devotion and a sense of belonging. What came first was not the criticism of the law, a subjective experience of failure or an objective analysis of inadequacy. It all started with the experience of meeting and recognizing the Risen Christ, which Paul described as the "revelation" of Jesus as the Son of God (Gal. 1:12), the "illumination" of the glory of God shining in the face of Christ" (2 Cor. 4:6). Viewed in that light, the gift of the law on Mt. Sinai, a "glorious" blessing as it was, lost its absolute character: "What once was splendor has come to have no splendor at all because of the splendor that surpasses it" (2 Cor. 3:10). "Whatever gain I had, I counted as loss for the sake of Christ. Indeed I count everything as loss because of the surpassing worth of knowing Jesus Christ my Lord" (Phil. 3:7-8).

The law was "splendor"; it was "gain." But compared with the revelation of the light of glory and of the infinite richness manifested in Christ, the "splendor" paled and the "gain" was loss.

E. P. Sanders rightly expresses disagreement with a fairly common understanding of Paul's theology:

> For Paul, the conviction of a universal solution preceded the conviction of a universal plight . . . Bultmann wrote that "the view that all men are sinners, which he develops at length in Rom 1.18-3.20, is a basic one for his doctrine of salvation." I should have said that his doctrine of salvation led to a necessary conclusion that all men required salvation.[18]

Paul's "conversion" does not mean that he rejected the law in an act of apostasy. From within the law, he perceived its risks and limitations in the

---

[17] "The passage (Rom 7:7-25) therefore is rightly to be reckoned as an apology for the law" (J. D. G. Dunn, *Romans 1-8*, WBC [Dallas: Word Books, 1988], 377); cf. J. A. Fitzmyer, *Romans*, AB 33 (New York: Doubleday, 1993): "an apology for the law itself" (p. 473).

[18] Sanders, *Paul and Palestinian Judaism*, 474. Bultmann's quotation is from his *Theology of the New Testament*, 227.

light of the Risen One. Ultimately, bringing Pauline thought on the law
within the context of Judaism gives it added significance. The focus of
Paul's message appears in a better light. It consists not in the indictment of
human failure but in the revelation of God's glory manifested in the Risen
Lord. "The Gospel within the Gospel" is really "gospel," a message of good
news.

A REVISED FOCUS ON PAUL'S MISSION STRATEGY

There follows a new understanding of Paul's missionary outlook. The
apostle did not set about to spread a new religion that would replace
Judaism. The Tübingen school of the last century posited a Hegelian dialec-
tical antithesis between the Pauline Gentile church and Petrine Jewish Christianity. Paul was supposed to stand for freedom from the law and Peter for
Judaic legalism. The formation of the canon in the second century would
have effected the synthesis by putting the two apostles on an equal footing.
According to this view, Paul would have reneged Judaism by rejecting the
Mosaic law and would have proposed an acceptance of Jesus Christ free
from any dependence on Israel. This thesis underlies the attempts of the
Religionsgeschichtliche Schule to trace the origins of Paul's theology in Hel-
lenism, mystery cults, Gnosticism, and so on. Names are legion from
Usener, Bousset, Cumont, and Reitzenstein to Loisy, Bultmann, and others.

J. Munck turned the tables on the Tübingen system by showing that, basically, Paul's mission strategy followed the outlook of Jesus, which was that
of the Old Testament and of Judaism.[19] Salvation comes from the Jews, but
the election of Israel is not exclusive. Munck quotes an important article of
Sundkler on Jesus' attitude to the pagans, which concludes that "the opposition between particularism and universalism is the product of a modern cosmopolitan outlook and has nothing to do with the biblical conception of
mission."[20]

On the whole, Israel envisaged an eschatological universalism. At the end
of times, the nations were to rally to Israel and share in its messianic blessings (Isa. 2:2-4; 60:1-16; Ps. 87).[21] It was therefore a shattering blow for
Paul, "great sorrow and unceasing anguish of heart" (Rom. 9:2) to see Israel
rejecting the good news. Indeed it was a "mystery" that the nations should
precede the chosen people in accepting the grace of God. On the other hand,
like Jesus "marveling" at the faith of the centurion (Matt. 8:10) and of the

---

[19] J. Munck, *Paul and the Salvation of Mankind* (London: SPCK, 1959).

[20] B. Sundkler, "Jésus et les Païens," *RHPR* 16 (1936): 499, quoted by Munck, *Paul,* 71.
Sundkler's views have been resumed by J. Jeremias in *Jesus' Promise to the Nations,* SBT 24
(London: SCM Press, 1958), 57-62.

[21] See L. Legrand, *Unity and Plurality: Mission in the Bible* (Maryknoll, N.Y.: Orbis Books,
1990), 15-27.

Canaanite woman (Matt. 15:28), Paul was filled with awe and jubilation to see the unexpected wonder of the response of the nations to the messianic proclamation. Even if the letter to the Ephesians does not come directly from the hand of Paul, it does reflect the thrill of the early Christians, to whom was disclosed "the mystery of Christ, unknown in former generations to the human race and now revealed by the Spirit to his holy apostles and prophets, that through the Gospel, the Gentiles are joint heirs with the Jews, part of the same body, sharers together in the promise made in Christ Jesus" (Eph. 3:4-6; cf. Col. 1:26f.; Rom. 16:25f.).

Admiring the faith of the centurion, Jesus had seen the dawn of the day when the nations would gather from east and west to sit at the banquet of Abraham (Matt. 8:11). Such was also, in the Fourth Gospel, the meaning of the conversion of the Samaritan woman and of the coming of the enigmatic "Greeks" during the last days before the Passover. The time of the eschatological harvest had come (John 4:35; 12:20-24). What had been rather exceptional and in the nature of proleptic signs during the ministry of Jesus became for Paul the basis of his strategy. It was not as though Paul had embarked on his journeys with this clear policy in mind from the outset. He would have rather followed the "normal" course of going first to the Jews. But it did happen that the positive response to his message came from the non-Jews rather than from his own people. What should have been the time of the plenitude of Israel turned out to be the time of the "plenitude of the nations" (Rom. 11:25). The "time of Israel" would come only at the end and would replace the time of the nations as the eschatological time (Rom. 11:11f., 15f., 25f.). It was no longer the nations but Israel that would be expected to respond to God's call "in the latter days."

This change of perspective amounted to a momentous reversal of the biblical conception of time. Yet, in this turnabout, Israel remained central. It was as guests to the "banquet of Abraham," in the company of "Isaac and Jacob" that "the crowds from east and west" were to "sit in the kingdom of heaven" (Matt. 8:11). Similarly, in Paul's outlook, Israel remained the "olive tree," the "root." The nations were only "branches," "grafted" to the original stem (Rom. 11:17-24). In Paul's strategy, the final objective remained Israel. The conversion of the Gentiles was only God's love stratagem: "Salvation has come to the Gentiles, so as to make Israel jealous . . . Inasmuch then as I am an apostle to the Gentiles, I value my ministry with the hope of stirring my fellow Jews to jealousy and so of saving some of them" (Rom. 11:11, 13f.).

The heart of Paul remained totally Israelite and so were his outlook, his understanding of the divine economy, and his mission strategy. Going to the nations, Paul did not turn away from Israel and forswear his Jewish identity. He continued to carry the views and hopes of his people in his mind and in his heart. It was for the love of Israel and for their salvation that he went to the nations.

A CRITICAL STANCE

Nevertheless, for all his attachment to his kinsmen, Paul engaged in a scorching criticism of their—and his—patrimony.

"Gain" and "Loss"

It is true that this criticism was not the primary element of his new vision. The starting point was the Damascus encounter with the Risen Lord that gave Paul the "knowledge of him and of the power of his resurrection" (Phil. 3:10). But this new "knowledge" overturned all his mental world. What he thought to be "gain" now appeared to be "loss" (3:8). Having discovered the "righteousness that comes from God through faith in Jesus Christ" (3:9), he saw the emptiness of a "righteousness of his own," however blameless it might have been (3:5, 9). Seeing in the mystery of the Lord's death and resurrection the full meaning of "life," he understood that what he called life was death (3:11-21). The pride he took in belonging to the chosen people was only reliance in the "flesh" (3:3-5). The first chapters of the letter to the Romans are a kind of elaborate commentary on this initiatory experience more concretely described in Philippians 3. In 2 Corinthians, he reports the experience in terms of "glory." Once he has been given to behold the glory of the Lord (2 Cor. 3:18), once "the light of the knowledge of the glory of God in the face of Christ has shone in (his) heart" (4:6), the blazing Sinai theophany, with all its lightning and thunder, fades into a dim, veiled image, a shadow having "no splendor at all" (3:7-10).

A Cultural Revolution

As regards culture, Paul's criticism of the law is especially meaningful. The law seems to be the focus of what Paul discarded on discovering God's "righteousness" and the free gift of his grace. For all the attachment he had toward the law, Paul could not but find it wanting when compared with his experience of the Risen Lord. Again and again, especially in Romans and Galatians, he belittles the law. "Now God's righteousness has been manifested apart from the law" (Rom. 3:21); "you are no longer under the law but under grace" (6:14); "you have died to the law" (7:4); "the law of the Spirit of life in Christ Jesus has set me free from the law of sin and death" (8:2): quotations could be multiplied endlessly. The *nomos* is referred to seventy-two times in Romans and thirty-two times in Galatians, mostly in disparaging terms: "the law produces nothing but God's retribution" (Rom. 4:15 *JB*); "the law came in to increase the trespass" (5:20; cf. Gal. 3:19). There seems to be a radical antinomy between the "works of the law" and "justification by grace through faith" (Rom. 3:28; Gal. 2:16; 3:2, 5, 12). Paul's language reaches a pitch of violence when he proclaims that "those who depend on the Law are under a curse" (Gal. 3:10). To realize how radical was Paul's rhetoric, we have just to substitute the Hebrew equivalent *torah* for the Greek *nomos* or the English "law" and to keep in mind that, for Israel, the *torah* was the very core of their life and culture.

The unforeseen success of his mission to the *go'im* led Paul to extend the privileges of Israel to them. Having accepted the messianic proclamation without passing through the circumcision, "apart from the law," they were "justified and sanctified" (1 Cor. 6:11; cf. 1:30); they became God's temple (1 Cor. 3:16), formed the *ekklēsia,* the true people of God (Rom. 9:24-26). It was a daring theological and cultural venture to do away with circumcision as a sign of belonging to the covenant and to extend to the "uncircumcised" the promises of the election (1 Thess. 1:4). It upset the whole traditional perspective to transfer the title of *ekklēsia* to a few scattered houses in a small town of northern Greece. *Ekklēsia* was the Greek rendering of the *qᵉhal YHWH*, the gathering of the covenanted people at the foot of Mt. Sinai. Could this small group of *go'im* in a distant country be considered the genuine representative of the true Israel (1 Thess. 1:1; 2:14)? Could "pagans" be "called holy" (1 Thess. 4:3-7), a title reserved to Israel, the "holy nation, set apart to the service of God" (Exod. 19:6; Lev. 19:2). What Paul proposed was a radical revision of Israelite identity. The true circumcision was that of the heart in the Spirit (Rom. 2:23-29; cf. Jer. 4:4; 9:25; Deut. 10:16; 30:6). The promises made to Abraham before the Sinai covenant took priority over the covenant and its law. The descent from Abraham itself was no longer a matter of "flesh," of physical lineage, nor was the physical belonging to the tribes of Israel sufficient and necessary to be the true Israel (Rom. 9:6-7). Faith was all that mattered (Gal. 3:7; Rom. 4; 9:6-9). Finally the law itself was redefined in terms of "walking in the Spirit" (Rom. 8:4-11), so broad a definition that it could equally be spelled out as elimination (Rom. 3:21, 28; 6:14; 1 Cor. 9:20; Gal. 2:16; 3:10-12; 5:18) or fulfillment (Rom. 3:31; 13:8-10; Gal. 6:2) of the law.

Once more it must be stressed that, for Paul, all this did not amount to a rejection of his Israelite faith. He was, on the contrary, convinced that he had at last identified the genuine "Israel of God" (Gal. 6:16), the true "people" of God (Rom. 9:25f.; 15:10; 2 Cor. 6:16). For him, this did not amount to the foundation of another "church" or of a new "religion" outside Israel. It was the disclosure of Israel's true inheritance. But, if for Paul this was a dazzling illumination, for others it was a shocking betrayal. Can a people be identified only by a spiritual belonging? Do not rites, customs, a common way of life—in short, a culture—go to the heart of a people's very being? It was not just a theological revision but the awesome challenge of a cultural revolution that Paul proposed to Israel. We can only sympathize with Peter, wavering between two positions and even with James and the Judaizers, who thought they had to rush to the rescue of the hallowed traditions. The case is closed and the matter simple only for those who have excluded Israel from their Christian perception, which Paul never did.[22] Yet, while assessing the biblical evidence, it must be kept in mind that the radical stand of Paul is not the sole response of the New Testament. The compromising attitude of James has been duly recorded in Acts 15:13-29; neither text nor context suggests that Luke disowns it. Matthew and the letter of James also represent different positions. If we go by the witness of Acts, Paul himself had to concede a middle course in certain concrete situations (Acts 16:3). "Jew with the Jews and Greek among the Greeks" (cf. 1 Cor. 9:20f.) is a generous program but not so obvious a line of conduct in the prevailing situation where Jews and Greeks lived in close coexistence.

IMPLICATIONS

Situating Paul's criticism of the law within the context of Judaism helps also better to perceive its implications. If this criticism had come from outside, from a man alienated from his people, it would express his personal disappointment with his religion and culture. It would have a mere biographical interest. At most it would be a criticism of the Jewish law as such. This is the interpretation usually presumed by those who view Rom. 7:7-25 as an autobiographical description. The passage would echo a juvenile crisis undergone by young Saul struggling desperately with "covetousness," "sin," and "flesh" without finding any support in the law but taboos and prohibitions.[23] Following this interpretation, the Christian reader would have only to sit back comfortably as a spectator and thank the Lord for belonging to a religion supposed to be free from this bondage to the law. In the same line,

---

[22] "The primitive Church and Paul were universalistic as Jesus was, because they knew that the Gospel was for Gentiles as well as for Jews, whereas the later Catholic Church lost that universalism. It no longer divided the human race into Israel and the Gentiles but turned with its message to the Gentiles" (Munck, *Paul,* 71). In fact, the problem of the relationship between religion, culture, national identity, law and land continues to baffle the world of today, its politicians, sociologists, and anthropologists, wherever cultures meet and confront each other, which is almost everywhere on earth. What is to be the fate of "Christian civilization" in the multiracial and plurireligious Western world? What is to be the relationship between Islam and the *shariah* in the "secular" yet predominantly Muslim countries of southern Asia? Between Buddhism and national identity in Sri Lanka and Thailand? Between "Indian-ness" and *Hindutva* in India? The world of today still needs a Paul to expose all these questions to "the power of his resurrection" (Phil 3:10).

[23] This was a fairly common opinion until the study of W. G. Kümmel, *Römer 7 und die Bekehrung des Paulus* (Leipzig: J. G. Hinrichs, 1929; reprinted in *Römer 7 und das Bild des Menschen im Neuen Testament,* TBü 53 [Munich: Kaiser, 1974]). "Most interpreters now agree that it would be a mistake to take the passage autobiographically . . . The thought is rather of childhood of man, the mythical period of the human race's beginning" (J. D. G. Dunn, *Romans 1-8,* 382). For a detailed survey of the various interpretations of Rom. 7:7-25, see C. E. B. Cranfield, *A Critical and Exegetical Commentary on the Epistle to the Romans* (Edinburgh: T & T Clark, 1975), 342-347.

the preacher illustrates this enslavement to the Jewish law with examples concerning Sabbath observances and dietary regulations and the matter ends with reinforced—and sterile—good conscience and superiority complex.

Reducing Paul's criticism of the law to the external aspects of the Jewish law would "trivialize Paul's insight"[24] and miss its full significance. Coming from inside Judaism, Paul's criticism throbbed with a deep attachment to the tradition of the fathers. It is in comparison with the greater "splendor" manifested in Christ that the "splendor" of Sinai betrays its meanness. Yet, while losing in comparison, "splendid" it remains: five times in as many verses (2 Cor. 3:7-11) Paul will apply the word *doxa,* glory, splendor, to the Sinaitic dispensation.

Paul does not envisage another "law," another culture that would be superior to that of his people. Unlike the Jewish apologists of Hellenistic Judaism,[25] he may not speak of a superiority of the Jewish way of life over that of the nations; he does not compare his *Ioudaïsmos* (Gal. 1:13f.) with other socioreligious systems. But nothing in his language would suggest an inferiority complex.

In other words, it is the "law" at its best, as a culture that Paul loved, in which he took pride and to which he was attached by all the fibers of his Hebrew soul, that Paul found wanting because it falls short of the glory of God. It is not only the Jewish law as such, the Hebrew way of life, but any culture that stands exposed. The implication of Paul's stance is that, no less than the Jewish "law," that is, than the Jewish socioreligious system and way of life, the glory of any human culture appears as transitory, pale, unsubstantial, has a "splendor that has no splendor at all by contrast with the glory that transcends it" (2 Cor. 3:10). Paul does not exempt other cultures from the radical assessment he made of the God-given law of Sinai. The diatribe against the Greco-Roman world in Romans 1 must be taken with a pinch of rhetorical salt and may not correspond exactly to the ideal of a sober analysis of Mediterranean society. It is at least a forceful theological statement of the universal human impotence in the face of the grace of God. Whatever will be said of the inadequacy of the law at a later stage applies to all the cultures of the world.

It is true that such an appraisal reflects Paul's rhetorical dramatization and antithetical turn of mind. Could we also reverse the picture, bringing to bear on the indictment of the Greco-Roman world in Romans 1 the same qualification that Paul applied to the Torah and extending to world cultures what Paul says of his Judaism? Would it be undue inference to assert that any culture has glory, that it is "good," "holy"? Would Paul's views authorize the nations of the world to take pride in their "laws" as Paul did in the Torah? Insofar as the texts of Paul are concerned, we would go beyond exegesis to

---

[24] Fitzmyer, *Romans,* 465.

[25] For the rich apologetic literature of Alexandrian Judaism, see pp. 55f. above.

theological conclusions. It is only the Lukan Paul who draws that kind of conclusion. The Athenian speech in Acts 17 attributes to the Greek poets a pedagogical role parallel to that of the law (vv. 27f.).[26] With its emphasis on continuity and his perception of the history of salvation, the Lukan work presents a more optimistic approach, closer to the spirit of *Gaudium et Spes,* the Pastoral Constitution on the Church in the Modern World from the Second Vatican Council. The next chapter will show that Paul himself, when not extolling the utmost transcendence of the divine "glory," has a more positive estimate of human values. Here, as with other aspects of the biblical message, there is place for pluralism.

Yet Paul's radical standpoint is not to be dismissed as mere rhetorical emphasis. The splendor of human cultures, like that of the Sinaitic law, is of a "fading" nature. Archaeology has amply illustrated the mortality of human civilizations. Paul's assessment of the law is the expression of an intense discovery of the divine loving power. In the same way the Hindu mystics speak of everything as *maya,* emptiness, illusion, unreality, in the face of the only final plenitude of the One who is *Saccinanda,* authentic Being, pure Freedom and eternal Bliss. As Paul himself says, until "we see face to face," whatever present splendor we see now is only "the puzzling reflection of a mirror" (1 Cor. 13:12).

---

[26] See pp. 159ff. below.

8

Paul the Greek

However conservative his family might have been, a Jewish boy of Tarsus in Cilicia was not born to the same brand of Judaism as his co-religionist born in Jerusalem. It was a Judaism that had experienced a long exposure to the ambient Greek way of life. Even if we go by W. C. Van Unnik's interpretation of Acts 22:3 and accept that the entire process of Paul's education from his early childhood onwards took place in Jerusalem,[1] the fact remains that the apostle wrote his letters in quite a becoming type of Greek. His grammar is adequate. He displays an apt choice of words. His style, if not always elegant, is forceful and convincing. If "his knowledge of Hellenism was gathered after his conversion,"[2] in the course of his ministry to the Gentiles, after he became an adult, it must be acknowledged that he did a remarkable job of it.[3] It follows that along with the rediscovery of Paul's Jewish roots, there is scope also for another current of research exploring the Hellenistic background of the Apostle to the Gentiles. In the last decades, this line of investigation has attracted a great deal of scholarly attention. Its results are equally convincing and enlightening.

---

[1] W. C. Van Unnik, *Tarsus or Jerusalem, the City of Paul's Youth* (London: Epworth Press, 1962). We quote the study in the reprint given in *Sparsa Collecta: The Collected Essays of W.C. Van Unnik*, part 1, *Evangelia. Paulina. Acta*, NovTSup 29 (Leiden: Brill, 1973), 259-320. See pp. 138-140 below.

[2] Ibid., 306.

[3] Examples of successful adult enculturation are not rare. The American J. Green has made it to the *Académie Française*, where he has Russian-born Henri Troyat as a colleague. A number of Indian-born authors are distinguished English writers. In India, there is the case of the Jesuit Costantino Beschi 1680-1747), who came to India in 1710, worked as a *sanyasi* among the higher castes of the Madurai Mission, took the Tamil name of Veeramamunivar ("the great and courageous monk"), and wrote a number of books in Tamil and particularly the *Tembavani* (1724), acknowledged as a classic of Tamil literature. Before him, De Nobili (1577-1656) had written abundantly in Tamil, Telugu, and Sanskrit and the English Jesuit Thomas Stevens had composed the *Krista Purana* in Marathi, toward the end of the sixteenth century.

"LIGHT FROM THE EAST"

This approach has the support of an old tradition. It goes as far back as
the spontaneous interpretation of the Pauline letters by the Greek fathers.
The Latin exegetical tradition was particularly impressed by the affinities
between Paul and the Latin philosopher Seneca. A third-century anonymous
author composed an apocryphal correspondence between Paul and the Stoic
philosopher.[4] Jerome, who accepted the authenticity of those letters and
quoted them, called the Latin Stoic "our own Seneca."[5]

Characterized as it was by a return to the literary techniques and human-
istic ethics of Greco-Roman classicism, the Renaissance could have given a
new thrust to the study of the Hellenistic setting of the New Testament. In
fact, the sixteenth century did witness a revived interest in the Greek text of
the New Testament, its manuscripts, grammar, and vocabulary. This interest
could have been extended to a rhetorical approach, which, in the case of the
Pauline letters, would have been particularly fruitful. But the dogmatic pre-
occupations of the Reformation and Counter-Reformation turned Pauline
exegesis away from disinterested literary pursuits. They would have sounded
trivial in the polemical context of those days. Later on, the argument shifted,
according to the mood of the times, to the opposition between rationalism
and supernaturalism, between Hegelianism and Thomism, existentialism
and eschatologism. This latent dogmatic concern continued to turn exegesis
away from literary methods.

In the Pauline field, as in several other areas of biblical research, it was
archaeology that drew scholarly attention to the literary background of the
apostolic writings. Asia Minor was the heartland of Paul's ministry. It was
also one of the most active centers of early modern archaeology. W. M. Ramsay was one of the first to explore this setting of Paul's work, writing, and
thought. He popularized the fruit of his investigations in *St Paul the Traveller and the Roman Citizen* (1895) and *The Cities of Paul* (1907). Those
important books helped to conjure a picture of Paul not only as a theologian
but as the representative of a lively and complex world, as a denizen of the
Mediterranean world, interacting with the culture of his times.

Equally relevant, though a little more distant from Paul's apostolic field,
were the archaeological discoveries of Egypt. Now, unlike Old Testament
scholarship, Pauline studies were not concerned with the mighty pyramids,
majestic temples, and their hieroglyphic inscriptions. Their interest was
rather drawn toward the more humble contents of domestic garbage cast off

---

[4] Published by Alcuin in the eighth century, this correspondence had a great influence in the
Middle Ages; it is quoted by Peter of Cluny, Abelard, and even Petrarch. The first printed edition was made by Erasmus in Basel, 1515. See W. Schneemelcher (ed.), *New Testament Apoc-
rypha*, vol. 2, *Writings Relating to the Apostles, Apocalypses and Related Subjects* (London:
Lutterworth, 1965), 133-141.

[5] *Adv. Jov.* 1.49; the apocryphal correspondence is quoted in *De Vir. Ill.* 12.

some two thousand years ago in the village compost pits. An interesting component of this litter was the discarded pieces of papyrus left over from the artless correspondence of rural folk. Better than the artificial "epistles" of professional writers like Cicero, who wrote self-consciously for posterity, these naive missives revealed what it meant to exchange news and notes in antiquity. A full science was born out of those discoveries. Papyrology studied the texture of the writing material, the graphic *ductus* of the letters, the speed of writing and the use of secretaries, the postal system and the conventional epistolary forms of the Greco-Roman world. It gave also an idea of the kind of Greek non-literati provincials could write in the Roman empire.

The insight gathered from this epigraphic and epistolary material was first systematically gathered by A. Deissmann. As indicated in the subtitle, his *Bible Studies*, which appeared in German in 1895, proposed *Contributions Chiefly from Papyri and Inscriptions to the History of the Language, the Literature, and the Religion of Hellenistic Judaism and Primitive Christianity*. This was followed and further developed in another book: *Light from the Ancient East: The New Testament Illustrated by Recently Discovered Texts of the Graeco-Roman World* (1st German ed., 1908; Eng. trans. 1927). The title is curious: whatever was "east" of Marburg was *the* "East." This perspective reflects the narrow mental geographical horizon of those days: material culled from Turkey and Egypt was considered to be coming from the "East." Old Testament scholarship knew that the "Orient" extended much farther east, to Mesopotamia and Iran, if not beyond. At least a window had been opened out of the Hegelian landscape of nineteenth-century New Testament scholarship.

Through this window, new lights began to gleam but also new problems to arise. In view of the similarities found between New Testament Greek and the lowly papyri and ostraca of Egypt, Deissmann concluded that Christianity must have developed in the lower strata of Greco-Roman society. More recent research has questioned this conclusion. Anyway, now at least one had raised the question of the social setting of the New Testament. The Pauline letters were not born out of a human vacuum, suddenly filled with abstract theological controversies. They were not just to be a matter of debate between the tenants and the opponents of the Augsburg Confession and the Council of Trent. They were cultural products, following set literary conventional forms, depending on and reacting to a socioeconomic and political environment.

LINGUISTIC AND RHETORICAL
CULTURAL BACKGROUND

The Language of Paul's Times

The very fact that Egyptian villagers wrote their letters in Greek was striking evidence of the spread of Hellenism even in rural areas and in countries that could boast of so prestigious a culture as that of ancient Egypt. It showed also that there was no such a thing as "biblical Greek" and that the New Testament authors used the *Koine,* the common Greek language of the Hellenistic times.[6] As Deissmann puts it in his autobiography, this amounted to a "secularization of sacred philology."[7]

PAULINE RHETORICS

As regards the rhetorical pattern of the Pauline letters, Deissmann could easily identify the basic structure of the Introduction made of *superscriptio* (sender), *adscriptio* (addressee), and *salutatio* (greeting): X to Y *chaire!* The rest of this modest correspondence was too sketchy to identify a specific structure. The study of Greek rhetoric relayed the data of popular correspondence. Applying the analysis of Quintilian, H. D. Betz traced the standard division of *exordium, narratio, propositio, probatio, exhortatio,* and *peroratio* in the letter to the Galatians.[8] This method was extended to the letter to the Romans[9] and to other Pauline letters.[10]

Another line of study investigated the various literary forms used by the apostle. Paul the Jewish rabbi was influenced by such Jewish forms as the *midrash,* the *pesher,* prayers, targumic ways of quoting the Scriptures. Paul the Greek follows also Greek literary patterns. One of the first publications of R. Bultmann had been a comparison entitled "The Style of the Pauline Rhetoric and the Stoico-Cynic Diatribe."[11] Subsequent scholarship questioned the existence of a genre of "diatribe."[12] But "this does not lead to the conclusion that Bultmann's work is irrelevant . . . Rather what he has shown is not that Paul has been influenced by the diatribe, but that he was influ-

---

[6] "The New Testament authors did not write in a Semitic biblical Greek hardly comprehensible to the Greek speaking pagan contemporaries. They did not use the kind of language that could be considered as inspired in the 19th century" (E. Plümacher, "Deissmann, Adolf," *TRE* 8:406).

[7] Quoted by Plümacher, "Deissmann," 8:406.

[8] H. D. Betz, "The Literary Composition and Function of Paul's Letter to the Galatians," *NTS* 21 (1975): 353-379; idem, *Galatians: A Commentary on Paul's Letter to the Churches in Galatia,* Hermeneia (Philadelphia: Fortress Press, 1979).

[9] See J. N. Aletti, "La *dispositio* rhétorique dans les épîtres pauliniennes," *NTS* 38 (1992): 385-401; and various papers in *The Romans Debate,* ed. K. P. Donfried (Edinburgh: T & T Clark, 1991).

[10] J. L. White, *The Form and Function of the Body of the Greek Letter: A Study of the Letter-Body in the Non-Literary Papyri and in Paul the Apostle,* SBLDS 2 (Missoula, Mont.: Scholars Press, 1972); M. L. Stirewalt, "The Form and Function of the Greek Letter Essay," in *Romans Debate,* ed. Donfried, 147-171.

[11] R. Bultmann, *Der Stil der paulinischen Predigt und die kynisch-stoische Diatribe,* FRLANT 13 (Göttingen: Vandenhoeck & Ruprecht, 1910).

[12] See K. P. Donfried, "False Presuppositions in the Study of Romans" in *Romans Debate,* ed. Donfried, 117-119.

enced by rhetorical usages which were common in the Greco-Roman world."[13]

Further analysis could easily identify other forms such as recommendation, petition, letter-essay, autobiography, *parenesis,* or exhortation, and various forms of ethical material. Paul made also a deft use of Hellenistic figures of speech such as personification, or *prosopopeia,* antithesis, chiasmus, metonymy, anacoluthon, climax, ellipse, hyperbole, and oxymoron.[14]

A study of Hellenistic literature could very well borrow its paradigms of literary forms and figures of speech from the Pauline letters. This does not make Paul a professional rhetorician. His rhetorical exuberance was not the painfully pedantic application of school techniques. It sprang spontaneously from the fervor of his convictions. But it could not have sprung so spontaneously if Paul had not imbibed the rhetorical resources of Hellenistic culture. While taking note of Paul's literary skill, a historian of Greek Christian literature adds: "His genius made up for his lack of culture."[15] The statement is questionable: genius does not function in a vacuum. The eloquence of Paul is not that of an Amos or of a Jeremiah. Paul's genius would have found other forms of expression if it had developed in Persia, India, or China.

A New Symbolic Field

This study of the Hellenistic background of the Pauline letters could be extended to other aspects of his literary technique. But there is more at stake than stylistic forms. A more significant aspect of Paul's penmanship is the symbolic field in which it moves. The symbolic field goes deeply into the cultural psyche of a people. Its implied cultural substratum conditions a whole way of thinking, reasoning, arguing, exhorting. It opens the channels of communication and conviction. Now, when compared with Jesus' symbolic world and with that of the Old Testament, Paul's metaphorical system shows great originality.

It was not only that Greek replaced Aramaic as the medium of communication of the good news. Paul had to supply his urban communities with a new world of images to express their faith. He had to provide them with new parables, new semantic horizons. To the villagers of Galilee Jesus had spoken of fields and vineyards, sowing and harvesting, mustard seed, fig trees, and lilies of the field. Addressing the citizens of the Hellenistic cities, Paul referred to athletic competitions (1 Cor. 9:24-26; Gal. 2:2; 5:7; Phil. 3:12-

---

[13] Ibid., 118f.

[14] See A. Brunot, *Le Génie Littéraire de Saint Paul,* LD 15 (Paris: Cerf, 1955); B. Rigaux, *Saint Paul et ses Lettres,* pp 176-180; Furnish, "Pauline Studies," 322-325; D. E. Aune, *Greco-Roman Literature and the New Testament: Selected Forms and Genres,* SBLSBS 21 (Atlanta: Scholars Press, 1988); A. J. Malherbe, *Ancient Epistolary Theorists,* SBLSBS 19 (Atlanta: Scholars Press, 1988).

[15] M. Puech, *Histoire de la Littérature grecque chrétienne,* I, Paris, 1928, p. 317, quoted by A. Brunot, *op. cit.,* p. 225.

14),[16] rules of elocution (1 Cor. 14:10-11), music instruments (1 Cor. 14:7f.), spectacles in the arena (1 Cor. 4:9), business partners (Phlm. 17), slave market (1 Cor. 6:20; Gal. 4:5). The world he evokes has such urban professions as architects (1 Cor. 3:10-13), judges (1 Cor. 6:4), tutors (Gal. 3:24) and peddlers (2 Cor. 2:17), not to speak of prostitutes (1 Cor. 6:15-16). It has recourse to letters of recommendation (2 Cor. 3:1-3), makes use of mirrors (1 Cor. 13:12; 2 Cor. 3:18) and perfumes (2 Cor. 2:14). It was made of cities and was concerned with citizenship (Phil. 3:20). Even the image of the "body" was not without political overtones: before it had been applied by Paul to the body of Christ (1 Cor. 12:12-17), it was a classical metaphor to express the diversity and unity of the city or of the state.

If Jesus' parables give us a lively image of rural Galilee, Paul's language evokes the altogether different culture of the Hellenistic cities engaged in politics, art, techniques, sports, and learning. When we realize the importance of symbols in language in general, in religions particularly and specifically in biblical rite and epos, this mutation of symbolic register cannot be taken as a trifling stylistic matter. Paul provided the nascent church with a new equipment to come forth from its Palestinian cradle and embark on the wider Mediterranean environment. The change of semantic field might even have induced theological consequences. For instance, commentators have noted that Paul's references to sacraments are rather rare.[17] A reason could be precisely that the predominantly rural sacramental symbolism of water, oil, bread, and wine would not have suited the more sophisticated mental horizon of the urban Hellenistic environment. Paul might have already experienced the difficulties met by linguistic and liturgical acculturation in non-Palestinian cultures, in Asia and elsewhere.

HELLENISTIC WORLD VISION

From the schools or milieus that gave him a knowledge of Greek rhetoric, Paul could not but undergo a still deeper influence from a certain world vision, a certain way of relating to humanity and to the universe. Sharing the language of the nations meant also communing in their *Weltanschauung*, their questions and aspirations. A new flow of studies has now begun investigating the patent or latent connections between Pauline thought and con-

---

[16] See V. C. Pfitzner, *Paul and the Agon Motif: Traditional Athletic Imagery in the Pauline Literature,* NovTSup 16 (Leiden: Brill, 1967).

[17] For instance, in J. A. Fitzmyer's valuable survey of "Pauline Theology" in the *NJBC*, baptism takes only four short paragraphs and the Eucharist five out of a total of 152 sections (or approximately three columns out of a total of seventy). In the much shorter summary of Johannine theology by F. J. Maloney in the same *NJBC* the sacraments are given two full columns out of twenty.

temporary philosophical movements.[18] Connections with Stoicism have already been noted above.[19] Attention has been drawn particularly to the Cynic forms of the Stoic movement.[20] Others think rather of the abiding influence of the older Platonic current,[21] which was soon to revive in the Neoplatonism of Plotinus and Porphyry. It would be wrong to trace rigid lines of dependence. Paul was not a schoolman abiding strictly by the teachings of one master. He imbibed the cultural atmosphere of his times and it was a complex atmosphere indeed amidst the multiple crisscrossing factors of the old, rich, and vast Mediterranean world.

We cannot attempt to cover all the aspects of this conscious or unconscious dialogue of Pauline thought with the Hellenistic world. It will suffice to select two aspects of particular significance: the field of ethics and the Greek quest for knowledge and wisdom.

WISDOM AND KNOWLEDGE

Greek civilization was characterized by a quest for wisdom and knowledge. Paul's diagnosis is accurate: "Greeks seek wisdom" (1 Cor. 1:22) and Greek wisdom consisted in "knowledge." "Wisdom is the knowledge of the things concerning God and man and their respective causes" said a Jewish student of Greek philosophy (4 Macc. 1:16) echoing a similar definition of the Pseudo-Plutarch (*Plac. Phil.* 1.1). Socrates had already set the tone by quoting as his motto the inscription of the sanctuary of Delphi: "Know thyself" (*Charm.* 164de; *Laws* 11.923z; *Phaedr.* 230a; *Phil.* 48c; *Protag.* 343b).

Paul knew that he had struck a chord in the heart of the Corinthians when he thanked God—and praised them—for being "enriched with all speech and knowledge" (1 Cor. 1:5). It might have been a "tongue-in-cheek" statement. The rest of the letter will express serious reservations about this "knowledge" of theirs. The apostle recalls Isaiah's condemnation of the "wisdom of the wise" (1 Cor. 1:19 = Isa. 29:14) and reminds the Corinthians that he proclaimed "the testimony of God without lofty words of wisdom" (2:2), he who announced the folly of a crucified Messiah and the

---

[18] See A. J. Malherbe, *Paul and the Popular Philosophers* (Minneapolis: Fortress Press, 1989).

[19] See the paper of A. J. Malherbe, "Determinism and Free Will in Paul: The Argument of 1 Corinthians 8 and 9," and that of Troels Engberg-Pedersen, "Stoicism in Philippians," in *Paul in His Hellenistic Context,* ed. Troels Engberg-Pedersen (Edinburgh: T & T Clark, 1994), 231-290.

[20] Especially by A. J. Malherbe, *The Cynic Epistles,* SBLBS 12 (Missoula, Mont.: Scholars Press, 1977); idem, *Paul and the Thessalonians: The Philosophic Tradition of Pastoral Care* (Philadelphia: Fortress Press, 1987); idem, *Paul and Popular Philosophers.*

[21] See D. E. Aune, "Human Nature and Ethics in Hellenistic Philosophical Traditions and Paul: Some Issues and Problems," in *Paul in His Hellenistic Context,* ed. Engberg-Pedersen, 291-312.

foolishness of God, wiser than men (1:22-25). Yet, to denounce the alluring words of wisdom (2:4), he crafted a skillful triple chiasmus (1:22-25) in the best tradition of Greek oratory. Mostly, he accepted the dialogue with wisdom and explained how the "folly of the cross" was wisdom indeed, the "secret and hidden wisdom of God" deeper than human thought, revealed in the Spirit (2:6-10). If human wisdom has to face a shattering exposure to the folly of Calvary, the message of the cross can reciprocally be interpreted in terms of wisdom. "Knowing nothing but Jesus Christ and him crucified" may be a paradoxical form of *gnosis*. Yet knowledge it is, since it is a participation in the knowledge of the Spirit, who "searches everything, even the depths of God" and "comprehends the thoughts of God" (2:10f.).

At this point Paul's thought reaches mystical depths. There has been a debate among exegetes on Pauline "mysticism." The solution depends to a good extent on how we define "mysticism." For Deissmann, Pauline "mysticism" was due to an infiltration of Greek pantheism. The Risen Christ was viewed as a sort of ethereal spiritual atmosphere, and the phrase "in Christ" had to be taken in a "local sense" as if the Christian was called to merge into a divine All. The mind of the apostle would have been infiltrated by dangerous pagan elements of Greek culture. This pantheistic interpretation of Pauline thought is now commonly rejected.[22] Paul was no pantheist. The Risen Christ did not turn into a disincarnated gaseous envelope. He remained the crucified Messiah. But through faith, sacraments, dynamic transformation of life and ethic attitudes, the believer is deeply united with him, becomes one "body" (Rom. 12:4f.; 1 Cor. 6:15; 10:16f.; 12:12-14, 27; 2 Cor. 4:10; cf. Col. 3:15; Eph. 4:4), one "spirit" (Rom. 8:9-11; 1 Cor. 12:13; cf. Eph. 4:4) with him, and it is not a misnomer to qualify this identification as mysticism.[23]

These developments in the thought of the apostle need not be attributed to the external influence of Hellenistic factors as if these had been imported from outside. The relationship is deeper and more subtle, seated at the level of shared culture and concerns. It was the interchange with this milieu that changed Paul's outlook. In the letters to the Thessalonians, Christ was viewed as the One whom we would accompany at his return so as to live "*with* him" (1 Thess. 4:14, 17; 5:10). In the letters to the Corinthians, Galatians, and Romans, the standard phrase is now "*in* Christ." The viewpoint is that of the present relationship between him and the believer. The eschatological expectation to be with the Messiah on the last days reflected a Judaic perception. The reflection on what it means presently to live "in Christ" and to share in his Spirit of sonship represents an attempt to express

---

[22] See discussion in A. Schweitzer, *The Mysticism of Paul the Apostle* (London: A. & C. Black, 1931); A. Wikenhauser, *Pauline Mysticism: Christ in the Mystical Teaching of St Paul* (Edinburgh: Nelson, 1960); J. A. T. Robinson, *The Body*, SBT 5 (London: SCM Press, 1952).

[23] See the careful assessment of L. Cerfaux, *The Christian in the Theology of St Paul* (New York: Herder & Herder, 1967), 351-372.

the Christian experience in terms of the Greek introspective mind. It reveals an interiorization of the Christ-event which was hardly perceptible in the early days of the church and which is a dialogic response to the Greek quest for knowledge and truth.

This dialogic attitude is also apparent in Paul's discussion of the resurrection with the Corinthian community. Once the fact of Jesus' resurrection has been clearly restated (1 Cor. 15:1-11) and its importance emphasized (vv. 12-34), the debate begins on what a risen body could be, a notion that the Greeks found unintelligible. The encyclopedic arguments listed on the variety of bodies in nature (vv. 37-41), on the transformation of the seed within the continuity of the species and the interaction of spirit and body (vv. 42-44) evoke more the debates in the Corinthian lecture hall of Tyrannus than the rabbinic arguments at the neighboring synagogue (Acts 19:9).[24]

ETHICS

Taking the world seriously implied also adopting a stand as regards personal conduct, family life, social and political issues, and proposing appropriate ethics. The Gospel proclaimed by Jesus did not provide precise guidelines applicable to life in the Greco-Roman cities. It was basically good news, rather than a set program of life.[25] Moreover, its cultural background was Palestinian. So was also the cultural horizon of the ethics of the Torah. Its framework was still largely valid for the New Israel. Yet it covered too much and too little, being at the same time too minute and not precise enough. It was too minute in that it was a "law of commandments and ordinances" (Eph. 2:15) to be replaced by the "law of the Spirit of life in Christ Jesus" (Rom. 8:2). At the same time, it was too imprecise in that it could not answer the problems of the new situation. Sexual ethics had to be redefined in terms of the new freedom in the Spirit and of enhanced eschatological expectations (1 Cor. 7). As regards society, authorities were no longer Israelite kings and priests but pagan rulers (1 Cor. 6:1-7; Rom. 13:1-7). The social setting was no longer the covenanted people but the *domus* and the socially stratified Hellenistic and Roman cities. The Torah that regulated the life of Israel was, at least theoretically, based on covenantal egalitarianism, extended in a certain measure to the *ger*, the resident alien. But the Christian *domus* in the midst of the Roman empire knew the complex hierarchy of patricians, clients, plebeians, and slaves, of citizens and foreigners. When Paul declared, in Galatians 3:28, that, in Christ Jesus, there was no longer "Jew or Greek, slave or free, male or female," to which Colossians 3:11

---

[24] Without excluding the fact that this kind of reinterpretation of the old Jewish themes had already influenced the Jewish sapiential and apocalyptic thinking (see M. Hengel, *Judaism and Hellenism* [London: SCM Press, 1974], 1:199f.).

[25] See J. Jeremias, *The Sermon on the Mount,* Facet Books 2 (Philadelphia: Fortress Press, 1963).

added "barbarian or Scythian," he did not address an Israelite but a western Mediterranean situation. The Old Testament was too narrowly focused on Israel to give a clear answer to the communities scattered all over the west.

Paul and the early churches among the Gentiles had to work out a Christian line of conduct as the problems arose in the communities. 1 Corinthians reveals the process of ad hoc responses to concrete challenges. The contemplation of the mystery of Christ was certainly the basic motive of Pauline parenesis.[26] But more concrete factors had also to intervene. To start with, common sense had its role to play. Moreover, the influence of Stoicism continued to exercise itself, consciously or not, on Paul's mind. When Paul advocates a life "free from care" in 1 Corinthians 7:32ff. or when he describes the attitude of a slave, obedient yet free (Col. 3:22-25), he has much in common with the ideal proposed by Epictetus, the Stoic philosopher who was himself a slave.[27]

Hellenistic Judaism had prepared catalogues of virtues and vices and lists of domestic duties. The "household codes," which describe the respective duties of the various members of the *domus*, husband and wife, parents and children, masters and slaves, have been the subject of detailed research. These catalogues of duties appear frequently in the epistles (Col. 3:18-4:1; Eph. 5:22-6:9; 1 Pet. 2:13-3:7; Titus 2:1-10) and in the early Christian literature (*Did.* 4.9-11; *Barn.* 19.5-7). Scholars discuss whether these lists derive from Hellenism (Stoicism? Platonism? Aristotle?) or from Hellenistic Judaism.[28] The problem is compounded by the fact that, by definition as it were, Hellenistic Judaism itself was the outcome of a dialogue with Greek thought and particularly with Stoicism. It is impossible to imagine that the early Christian tradition could have insulated itself totally from its Hellenistic environment. Even if the New Testament writers had wished to do so, their readers could not but recognize the familiar ring of popular Greek philosophical *parenesis*. As Malherbe puts it:

---

[26] See H. Cruz, *Christological Motives and Motivated Actions in Pauline Paraenesis,* European University Studies Theology 23 (Frankfurt: Peter Lang, 1990); W. Popkes rightly points out to the "Jesus tradition" in the process of formation of New Testament Ethic (*Paränese und Neues Testament,* SBS 168 [Stuttgart: Katholisches Bibelwerk, 1996], 127-129).

[27] See Epictetus, *Diss.* 3.22.69; 4.7.5; *Manual* 13; 29. See L. Legrand, "Saint Paul et le Célibat," in *Sacerdoce et Célibat: Etudes Historiques et Théologiques,* ed. J. Coppens, BETL 28 (Gembloux: Duculot; Louvain: Peeters, 1971), 322. A concise and balanced exposition of the process of development of Christian parenesis is given by Popkes, *Paränese,* 123-137. After having stated that "early Christian Parenesis took place in the framework of a complex field and duration of time that concerned individuals, groups, languages, cultures and generations" (p.123), he goes on to analyze the main factors that shaped early Christian ethics: the Jesus tradition, the Jewish antecedents, and the Hellenistic conception of world and life.

[28] See a survey of the debate in D. L. Balch, "Household Codes," in *Greco-Roman Literature and the New Testament: Selected Forms and Genres,* ed. D. E. Aune (Atlanta: Scholars Press, 1988), 25-50, with "Annotated Bibliography," pp. 47-50; Popkes, *Paränese,* 33 n. 87, 159-163.

Paul's followers and interpreters took his familiarity with moral philosophy for granted and therefore did not think it incongruous to represent him as *Paulus hellenisticus*. Paul himself used the philosophical traditions with at least as much originality as his contemporaries did . . . Yet for all this he remains *Paulus christianus,* but without that making any the less *Paulus hellenisticus.* After all, like Tennyson's Ulysses, . . . we are part of all we have met. So was Paul.[29]

A one-sided emphasis on Paul's Hellenism would cut him away from the deep Jewish roots from which until the end he drew his identity and the identity of his faith in Jesus Christ. On the other hand, overlooking Paul's Hellenism would miss the far-reaching implications of his going over to the nations. Entrusted with the gospel to the nations (Gal. 2:7-9), the apostle took the gospel to uncharted seas. With Paul, the gospel entered the urban culture of the Greco-Roman world.

This called for a thorough reversal of Jesus' evangelizing praxis. Jesus' mission strategy had been essentially rural, mostly restricted to the confines of interior Galilee. Paul targeted the cities of the west, not only Syrian Antioch and the minor cities of the Anatolian plateau, but the big commercial and intellectual centers of Ephesus, Thessalonica, Athens, Corinth, Rome. Proclaiming the good news to rural Galilee could be done in the style of "itinerant charismatics," moving from village to village, without resources and equipment, relying on local hospitality (see Mark 6:8-11). Launching into the wide world of the nations called for a planned strategy, recourse to financial means, and support of co-workers and local communities. It called also for a new thinking, a new cultural outfit to meet the Greco-Roman environment. Paul supplied this hermeneutic of language, thought, life, and action. There was more than geographical expansion in the move of the apostle to the nations of the west. By reaching new territories and meeting their cultures, the apostle to the nations opened also new vistas and gave Christian faith a new breadth and a new depth.

---

[29] Malherbe, *Paul and the Popular Philosophers,* 8f.

9

Interface

Cross-Cultural Interaction

"Jew to the Jews and Greek to the Greeks" says Paul of his apostolic stance of total availability to all (1 Cor. 9:20). Paul was well aware of his bicultural ambiguity, but this did not mean that he could dissociate the two aspects of his personality and play Jekyll and Hyde alternatively with one or the other role. The reality was that, whether to the Jews or to the Greeks, he was at the same time and completely both Jew and Greek. How were the two related? How did Judaism and Hellenism coexist and interact in Saul of Tarsus? Was the Hellenistic culture grafted on to a Judaic background or vice versa? Did the blend result in confused syncretism or did one of the two constitutive elements prevail over the other?

PAUL'S UPBRINGING

An element of solution would be forthcoming if we knew the kind of education the young Saul underwent. The only text referring to Paul's upbringing is the short autobiographical indication with which the apostle prefaces his "apology to the Jews" in Acts 22:3:

> Born at Tarsus in Cilicia, but brought up in this city [of Jerusalem], instructed at the feet of Gamaliel in the minute knowledge of the ancestral law.

W. C. Van Unnik has submitted this text to minute analysis.[1] He shows convincingly that birth, nurture at home ("brought up"), and formal instruc-

---

[1] W. C. Van Unnik, "Tarsus or Jerusalem, the City of Paul's Youth," in *Sparsa Collecta: The Collected Essays of W.C. Van Unnik,* Part 1: *Evangelia. Paulina. Acta,* NovTSup 29 (Leiden: Brill, 1973), 259-320 (originally published by Epworth Press, London, 1962).

tion ("instructed") form "a fixed literary unit" describing the stages of a child's education.[2] Therefore the text does not oppose a basic Greek education in the Hellenistic setting of Tarsus to a later Jewish rabbinic initiation in Jerusalem. The opposition is between the birth at Tarsus and the whole formative process in totally Jewish surroundings.

> In opposition to the prevailing opinion about this, it must be concluded that although Paul was born in Tarsus, it was in Jerusalem that he received his upbringing in the parental home just as it was in Jerusalem that he received his later schooling for the rabbinate. When and why his parents removed to Jerusalem remains concealed from us because of lack of data. But . . . his removal took place quite early in Paul's life, apparently before he could peep round the corner of the door and certainly before he went roaming on the street.[3]

This would imply "that the tongue in which Paul learned to express himself in the days of his youth was not Greek but Aramaic"[4] His knowledge of Greek and the consequent use of the LXX as his basic Bible would go back to the mysterious years following his conversion.[5] If we were to go by Van Unnik's conclusions, we would have a case of a born and bred Jew passing over to the Greek world and trying to fit in there. It would be an example of "enculturation," of successful adaptation to the new cultural setting. Paul would have been a predecessor of Beschi,[6] a paragon of the ideal missionary who, sent to an alien world, decides to adopt its culture so as to win it over and achieves his purpose.

But Paul's immersion in both the Jewish and Hellenistic culture is too deep to be accounted for in terms of external adjustment. His is not a case of a generous Jewish missionary training himself laboriously in the ways of thinking and speaking of the Greeks. Nor is Paul a Greek applying a thin cover of Scripture quotations and rabbinic tropes to disguise a fundamentally Gentile language. The apostle is comfortably and innocently both Jew and Greek, a perfect example of the crossbreeding that has always been the ferment of cultural development. His bicultural background was the providential equipment that enabled him to be the bridge between the Jewish matrix of the Christian faith and its universal reach.

Actually the philological demonstration of Van Unnik is quite convincing, but his exegetical conclusions are less so. His exegesis of the Lukan text is accurate, but is Luke's version of Paul's speech to the Jews of Jerusalem

---

[2] Ibid., 274.
[3] Ibid., 301.
[4] Ibid., 304.
[5] Ibid., 305f.
[6] See p. 127 above.

to be taken at face value? In fact, the evidence provided by Luke's report of Paul's apology calls for a double level of qualification:

1. It belongs to the form of apology. In Acts 22, Paul addresses the Jews to convince them that he is himself a good son of Israel. His "infancy narrative" will therefore tend to overemphasize the elements of identification with the audience.

2. Luke's own theological perspective stresses the priority of Israel.[7] This leads the author of Acts to emphasize the Judaic features of Paul's identity and ministry. The Lukan Paul is more closely associated with Israel than the historical one. For instance, according to Luke in Acts, the apostle makes it a point to go systematically first to the Jews and then only to the Gentiles. But in Galatians 2:9, the historical Paul recalls the Jerusalem agreement that he should go to the Gentiles, leaving the Judaic constituency to Peter.[8]

The long and short of this inquiry is that we know no more of the formative period of Paul's life than of the early years of Jesus. In a way, the upbringing of young Saul is shrouded in still greater mystery than the childhood of Jesus of Nazareth. Jesus belonged to a fairly homogeneous rural Aramaic environment. Paul's cultural background is far more complex.

THE MILIEU OF HELLENISTIC JUDAISM

If we know too little of Paul's early years to explain his bicultural belonging, we are better informed about the world in which this dual culture developed. At the time of the Babylonian exile, Judaism had spread eastward toward Babylonia and Persia. Then, with the hellenization of the Mediterranean world subsequent to the campaigns of Alexander, Jewish communities, for various political, economic, and ecological reasons, spread southward to Egypt and Libya, northward to Syria and Asia Minor, and westward to Europe. When Saul of Tarsus was born in Cilicia, this encounter of Israel with Hellas had already a long story.

This encounter resulted in different types of reactions. In the context of the Maccabean revolt, unqualified rejection and open warfare (1 Macc. 2:15-28) seemed to be the only alternative to total assimilation (1 Macc. 1:11-15). Such extremist attitudes were exceptional and restricted to the Palestinian homeland. Elsewhere the daily contact with the Hellenistic environment

---

[7] See J. Jervell, *Luke and the People of God: A New Look at Luke-Acts* (Minneapolis: Augsburg, 1972).

[8] R. J. Dillon concludes that Luke's report "is not very plausible" ("Acts," *NJBC,* 760). J. A. Fitzmyer is equally skeptical: "Paul himself never utters a word about this feature of his youth . . . In the long run the only evidence that Paul was trained as a rabbinical figure such as Gamaliel is the statement of Acts" ("Paul," *NJBC,* 1333).

showed that the Greek way of life was not rank devilry. A *modus vivendi* and even a *modus cogitandi* could be found.

As seen above,[9] it was a common notion among Alexandrian Jews that "the philosophers and poets of ancient Greece had undergone the influence of the laws of Moses and witnessed, in some passages of their writings, to the excellence of his teachings."[10] Identified with Mousaios, the father of Orpheus, god of arts and knowledge, Moses was claimed to be "the teaching master of all humanity."[11] This kind of monopolizing apologetics ended finally in syncretism, since, in his wisdom, Moses was supposed to have invented the Egyptian religion.[12]

Occasionally, Philo echoed this Alexandrian apologetics.[13] Elsewhere he proposed a more sophisticated explanation of the harmonies between Judaism and Hellenism. Philosophical knowledge and oracular vision issued ultimately from the transcendent and universal *nous:* "It is heaven which has showered philosophy on us," he said.[14] Commenting on this text, H. A. Wolfson says:

> Philosophy was thus in a sense revealed to the Greeks as the Law was to the Jews . . . Philosophy is just as much a gift of God to the non-Jews as revelation is to the Jews. This is in accordance with his general view, based upon Scripture, that all knowledge comes from God.[15]

In the same vein, in the Wisdom of Solomon, the gift of wisdom, identified with the all-pervasive *pneuma,* is "a breath of the power of God, . . . a reflection of eternal light" (7:22-26). Prophetic revelation and human science are viewed in ultimate dependence on the divine *nous* or *pneuma* and this explains their convergence.[16]

PAUL IN HIS MILIEU

The letters of Paul do not entertain any such speculations. On the contrary, when he evokes Greek culture, the mood is of confrontation rather than of dialogue: "The Greeks look for wisdom but we proclaim a crucified Christ . . . , foolishness to the Nations . . . When I came to you, . . . I did not

---

[9] See pp. 55ff. above.

[10] C. Larcher, *Études sur le Livre de la Sagesse,* EBib (Paris: Gabalda, 1969), 136; cf. M. Hengel, *Judaism and Hellenism: Studies in Their Encounter in Palestine during the Early Hellenistic Period* (London: SCM Press, 1974), 1:165.

[11] J. Jeremias, "*Mōusēs, TWNT* 4:854.

[12] Artapanus quoted by Eusebius, *Praep. Ev.* 9.29.4.

[13] Adding Heraclitus and Zeno to the list of Moses' plagiarists (*Leg. All.* 1.10.8; *Quod omnis probus liber sit* 57).

[14] *De Spec. Leg.* 3.34.185; cf. *De Op. Mund.* 8; *Quis rerum divinarum heres sit* 214.

[15] H. A.Wolfson, *Philo: The Foundations of Religious Philosophy in Judaism, Christianity and Islam* (Cambridge, Mass.: Harvard University Press, 1968), 1:142-143.

[16] Larcher examines the possible biblical, Platonic, or Stoic antecedents of these speculations (*Études,* 367-369). See pp. 52f. above.

come proclaiming the mystery of God in lofty words of wisdom. For I decided to know nothing among you except Christ and him crucified" (1 Cor. 1:22-23; 2:1-2). As for the Greco-Roman world in general, the apostle declares it to be as a flagrant manifestation of "the wrath of God revealed from heaven against all ungodliness and wickedness" (Rom. 1:18). He develops the point in a fierce picture of a society given over to all kinds of degrading passions (Rom. 1:26-32).

THEORY AND PRAXIS

Are we back to the fierce Maccabean rejection of the Greek culture? This passionate rhetoric corresponds to Paul's theological systematization. His was a world vision in black and white, issued from his perception of the absolute newness brought about by Jesus Christ. Paul's theological outlook is commanded by an apocalyptic contrast between good and evil. We are now in the last days, engaged in the eschatological struggle between God and Evil, Sin and Grace, the Wrath and God's saving justice. The world is a prey to sin in its totality (Rom. 3:23). The only reprieve is found in faith, in the reliance on grace which abounded all the more in proportion as sin increased (Rom. 5:20). This fiery apocalyptic condemnation of the old world stands in sharp contrast to the later Lukan perception of a continuous flow of divine grace in an ongoing history of salvation. But did Paul's apocalyptic outlook make him a radical recusant, fanatically averse to the Greco-Roman world in its totality? Two remarks are presently called for to put the matter in a proper perspective.

1. The previous chapter should be kept in mind. Paul did belong to the Hellenistic world. He shared in its language, modes of thinking, ethical values to a good extent, symbolic field, and cosmic sense. His condemnation stems from within a shared culture, as had been the case also with the prophets of Israel and Jesus himself in their attitude toward the Jewish world.

2. A distinction should be made between theory and praxis, and this distinction applies to Paul's attitude toward both Israel and the nations. The apostle's apocalyptic world vision in black and white should leave no room for a balanced estimate of the values of individuals and civilizations. Yet, when it comes to the praxis, Paul is not swept away by his apocalyptic views to the extent of losing sight of actual realities. His may be an apocalyptic turn of mind, but his writings are in no way made of the fantastic visions of the apocalyptists. They constitute an exchange of letters addressed to concrete people in specific circumstances. A personal streak of realism and pastoral contact with living communities saved Paul from the excess of fanatical apocalypticism.

As regards Israel, the time before Christ might have been characterized by the "law of sin and death," from which one had to be set free by the "law of the Spirit life in Christ Jesus" (Rom. 8:2). But in fact, Israel was also represented by the prophets, quoted repeatedly, and mostly by Abraham, taken as a paradigm of the primacy of faith (Rom. 4; Gal. 3:6-14). It is from within the tradition of Israel that Paul repudiates the old law.

Similarly, as regards the nations, if Paul condemns the perversion of idolatry, it is in the name of the knowledge of God "they certainly had" (Rom. 1:21 *NAB*). The world did not come to know God through wisdom (1 Cor. 1:21), but therein precisely lies their guilt. The implication is that wisdom should have led them to God: "whatever can be known about God was clear to them" (Rom. 1:20). They had access to the "truth of God" (Rom. 1:25). In the same way, when enumerating the vices of the nations, Paul uses lists that owe as much to Stoic diatribe as to rabbinic or apocryphal literature and to the rhetoric of Hellenistic Judaism.[17] In the same way that he stood within the prophetic tradition of Israel when criticizing the law, Paul made his own the best of Greek ethics when judging the pagan world. He did not condemn it from outside, from the point of view of some otherworldly celestial sphere. Neither did he stand from within a Judaism that would have been totally separated from the surrounding world. It was Saul of Tarsus, possibly trained at the feet of Gamaliel, but immersed in the Mediterranean culture, who faced the Hellenistic world.

Paul engaged in more "dialogue" with the "pagan" world than he would have probably cared to admit. Like any human being, he could not stand outside the world he belonged to. It was only from within the cultural complex in which he lived that he could respond to the transforming power of the resurrection and witness to it.

CULTURAL INTERPLAY

How did the various elements of Paul's intercultural background interact together? There were various possibilities.

In the simplest case, *one of the cultural components would predominate over the other*. Thus, the *midrashim* on Abraham in Galatians 3:6-9 and 4:22-30 (cf. Rom. 4) evoke the hum of Gamaliel's *yeshiva*. But, in the same letter to the Galatians, the paean to freedom of 5:13 echoes rather the clarion call of Marathon and of the Thermopylae.[18]

---

[17] See the texts quoted by O. Michel, *Der Brief an die Römer,* KEK (Göttingen: Vandenhoeck & Ruprecht, 1963), 68 n. 5; U. Wilckens, *Der Brief an die Römer (Röm 1-5),* EKK 6/1 (Zurich: Benziger; Neukirchen: Neukirchener Verlag, 1978), 109 n. 201. Philo has the longest list with 147 forms of crime!

[18] The theme of "freedom" recurs seven times in Romans and eleven times in Galatians in the following way:

	eleutheria (freedom)	*eleutheros* (free)	*eleutheroun* (set free)
Rom	1	2	4
Gal	4	6	1
LXX	3	19	1	*(cont.)*

In other cases, *the two components complemented or corrected each other*. For instance, when speaking to the Corinthians, he made his own their typically Greek quest for "wisdom." But his Jewish background, allied with the experience of the cross, gave the "wisdom" he proposed a prophetic and apocalyptic tension evidently absent from the Hellenistic experience (1 Cor. 1:18-30; 2:6-16). Reciprocally, this Hellenistic background helped him to transcend narrow Israelite perspectives and perceive the universalistic dimensions of God's plan and the human depth of the mysteries of sin and salvation.

In another form of interaction, *the cultural components worked together in synergy* to corroborate each other. Thus, when Paul proclaims that, in Christ Jesus, there is no Jew or Greek, slave or free (Gal. 3:28; cf. 1 Cor. 12:13; Col. 3:11), the formulation might have been equally indebted to Hebrew covenantal egalitarianism and to Stoic or Cynic disregard of social and ethnic discriminations. Parallels on both sides are equally convincing and not mutually exclusive. Moses and Epictetus were at one in the mind of Saul of Tarsus.

In still other cases, Paul's thinking and language *drift from one cultural field to the other*. Thus it has been noted[19] that the argument in favor of the "unmarried" state in 1 Corinthians 7 begins with apocalyptic considerations referring to the *anagkê* and *thlipsis,* the eschatological "distress" and "ordeal" that mark the end of times, for "the time is running short" (vv. 26-29). Then the argument veers to Stoic ascetic phraseology: "having wives as though they had none . . . , weeping as though not weeping . . . , making use of the world as though not using it," to conclude with a perfect expression of Stoic *ataraxia:* "I should like you to be free of all worries" (vv. 29-32). These verses could almost come from the stylus of Epictetus or Seneca:

The figures given for the LXX leave out the Deuterocanonical books, largely influenced by Hellenistic Judaism. It will be noted that the vocabulary of "freedom" is proportionally rare in the Old Testament: Romans–Galatians alone have almost as great a total frequency of the theme (eighteen times) as the entire Old Testament (twenty-three times). Adding the other Pauline letters, we have a total of twenty-eight uses of the root *eleuther/-os, -ia, -oun.* Even the LXX has hellenized the original Hebrew text by using the stem *eleuther-* to render various Hebrew words. The corresponding Hebrew is still less frequent: the abstract *huf^esha* occurs only once (Lev 19:20), the adjective *hof^eshi* fourteen times in the context of slaves set free and once in connection with "free" animals (two instances give the adjective a different meaning: 1 Sam. 17:25 and Ps. 88:6). In the Hebrew Bible, the root never applies to political or spiritual freedom. It is not that the idea does not exist, but it is expressed by other terms, mostly "redemption" (*ge'ullah*) and "salvation" (*yesha^c, padah*). Significantly, the substantial article on *eleutheria, -os, -oun* by H. Schlier (*TWNT* 2:484-500) has no section on the Old Testament. N. Lohfink notes that the Hebrew sociological terminology of the *huf^eshah* was not used to develop the basic theological idea of exodus as liberation from Egypt. In connection with Deut. 6:20-25 and Lev. 25:42, he observes that the exodus theology developed not on the basis of a concept of "freedom" but on a sense of dependence on God ("*hof^eshi,*" *TWAT* 3:127).

[19] J. G. Gager, "Functional Diversity in Paul's Use of End-time Language," *JBL* 89 (1970): 330-333; L. Legrand, "Saint Paul et le Célibat," in *Sacerdoce et Célibat: Etudes Historiques et Théologiques,* ed. J. Coppens, BETL 28 (Gembloux: Duculot, 1971), 321-330.

"This appears at first sight to be the passage most strongly subject to Stoic influence in all the Pauline epistles, and to commend the ideal of that ataraxy which is secured by dissociating oneself inwardly from one's outward fate."[20] But Paul is not a systematic philosopher: in the same breath he borrows the platonic antithesis between timeless "ideas" and transient appearances: "the frame (*schēma*) of this world is passing away" (v. 31).[21] Finally Paul has to return to the plain language of Christian experience to set things right: the freedom of the unmarried is not a question of indifference but of greater commitment to the Lord (vv. 32-35). This apology for the "unmarried condition" is of particular interest. In a few verses, Paul refers to four cultural fields, that of Jewish apocalyptic, of Greek Stoicism and Platonism, and of plain Christian experience. Did he feel any uneasiness in so groping for a clear formulation? It is not sure at all: each of those fields was for him home ground on which he felt quite comfortable.

Thus did various cultural currents interact in Paul's mind. It may not always be possible to disentangle the threads of his psyche and thought. Cultures are not simple. They are the meeting point of complex synergies and tensions. Even speaking of "Hellenistic Judaism" is an oversimplification. Each of the terms is complex. The Hebrew culture that Paul inherited was made, in equal proportions, of apocalyptic expectations, of attention to the law, and of sapiential insights. If apocalyptic perspectives resulted in a radical condemnation of the present age, the study of the Torah implied a more worldly approach to the details of present life, while wisdom combined the "fear of the Lord" with mundane observations. As for the culture of the Mediterranean world, the classical appellation "Greco-Roman world" suggests an inherent duality further compounded with Syrian, Egyptian, Anatolian, and other influences.

How is this complex cultural interplay to be characterized? The terms "inculturation," "acculturation," and "enculturation" are not suitable. They all refer to an approach from outside. In the case of Paul, he was born and he lived and worked in the midst of the crisscrossing cultural forces that made Hellenistic Judaism. His theological turn of mind might have been inclined to an attitude of confrontation: in the light of the glory of God shining on the face of Christ, all the rest was darkness. Yet the world in which he lived and toiled was a solid reality that could not be bypassed. His origin and his mission belonged to both Jerusalem and Athens (or maybe rather Ephesus). When compared with Jesus, Paul manifests a great originality. Living in the limited confines of Palestine and even of Galilee, Jesus knew a fairly limited cultural horizon. Paul met with a more formidable cultural task. He

---

[20] H. Conzelmann, *I Corinthians: A Commentary on the First Epistle to the Corinthians*, Hermeneia (Philadelphia: Fortress Press, 1975), 133.

[21] "Here we perceive an echo of the great Platonic antithesis between the eternal and absolute ideas and the world of sensory impressions and appearances" (L. Cerfaux, *The Christian in the Theology of St Paul* [New York: Herder & Herder, 1967], 170).

did not meet it through deliberate efforts of in- or en-culturation but simply by making use of his situation of "cross-cultural" belonging.

Yet the fact remains that, unlike Philo and the other Alexandrian Jewish writers, Paul did not attempt systematically to bridge his way to the surrounding Greco-Roman world. He spoke and wrote as a citizen of that world. He made use of the rhetorical and intellectual resources from its background. But he did it spontaneously without trying to rationalize what he did. Indeed any rationalization would have gone against his main theological thrust. His is a case of spontaneous cross-fertilization of cultures and of their spiritual values. This case presents striking linguistic, anthropological, theological, and missiological aspects. There is a certain tension between his explicit and his implicit language. The implications of his language go beyond his explicit declarations. What he is trying to say is lofty doctrine indeed. But what he does say still exceeds what he is trying to say.

PAUL AND LUKE

A comparison with Luke may help to situate the position of Paul in relation to the Hellenistic culture. A disciple and companion of Paul,[22] Luke differs very much from his master. For him, the time before Christ is represented not by the "law of sin and death" (Rom. 8:2) but by such holy and godly figures as Zechariah, Elizabeth, Mary, Simeon, and Anna. The Mediterranean world is not the brood of vipers evoked in Romans 1. It can display such noble figures as the deserving centurion of Capernaum (Luke 7:4-10) and the upright officials who represent the empire in their stand for justice (Acts 18:14-16; 19:35-40; 23:18-35; 24:10-23). Even the Roman Caesar, unconsciously but quite effectively, prepares the Bethlehem cradle for the messianic child in the beginning of the Gospel (Luke 2:1-5) while, at the end of the whole story, he provides the apostle with a tribune from where, in Rome, he can "proclaim the reign of God and teach about the Lord Jesus Christ with all boldness and without hindrance" (Acts 28:31).

In the Acts of the Apostles, echoes of Artapanus can be found in Acts 15:21, where James presumes that the law of Moses is sufficiently well known among the nations to explain common basic ethical requirements to be imposed on all. But it is the Areopagus speech in Acts 17:22-31 that shows the greatest sophistication in dealing with the Greek culture and religion.

It is commonly accepted that the discourse is not a word-for-word report of Paul's address to the Areopagites. Following conventional techniques of Greco-Roman historiography, Luke puts on the lips of the apostle his reflec-

---

[22] At least if we identify the author of Luke-Acts with Luke the physician mentioned in Colossians 4:14; Philemon 24; and 2 Timothy 4:11, and if we take it that the "we passages" in the Acts of the Apostles indicate a presence of the author at those stages of the journey.

tions on the significance of the momentous encounter of the gospel with Hellas, at its historical cultural center.

Neither is the Lukan account to be taken as the report of a failure as it is too often presented in the popular lives of St. Paul.[23] The Areopagus speech meets with the same mixed response as any proclamation of the good news. It is a sign of contradiction, for the fall and rise of many (cf. Luke 2:34). Such had been already the outcome of Jesus' first preaching in Nazareth, presented by Luke as the paradigm of the contents and process of evangelization (Luke 4:16-30). The Areopagus pericope in Acts 17 runs along the same lines as the Nazareth episode in Luke 4. For Paul (Acts 17:33) as for Jesus (Luke 4:29), the call for conversion is not heeded by the crowd. Yet in Athens quite a few people accept the message of the gospel (Acts 17:34) as the first hearers of Jesus' message had done in Luke 4:13f., 31f., 37. In between many are impressed but remain undecided and postpone their decision, in Athens (Acts 17:32) as in Nazareth (Luke 4:22). In the end, like Jesus "going through the midst of them" (Luke 4:30), Paul "goes away from their midst" (Acts 17:33). The Athenian speech does not report a mishap. It is "a symbolic encounter . . . , a symbol of Christian theology in the environment of Greek culture."[24]

Obviously the terms of this encounter have nothing to do with the Maccabean diatribe against Hellenism. Neither are they consonant with the Pauline indictment of the Greco-Roman world in Romans 1. The Athenian speech presents a positive appreciation of Greek religious longings, exemplified by the altar to the "Unknown God." It quotes Aratus and possibly Epimenides in highly laudatory terms, attributing to these "poets" the role given to the Hebrew prophets in the kerygma to the Jews. W. Nauck, B. Gärtner, and others have shown that the Areopagus discourse belongs to the Judeo-Hellenistic tradition.[25] At least it belongs to the elements of that tradition represented by Aristobulus, Philo, and others who took a "liberal" view, more open to the surrounding Greek culture than the "orthodox" tradition of the *Sibylline Oracles*.[26]

---

[23] An interpretation that is still retained in the *NJB*, 1829: "Paul's failure in Athens was all but complete." This comment is resumed from the first edition of the *Bible de Jérusalem, Les Actes des Apôtres* (Paris: Cerf, 1953), 157. But since then, J. Dupont, the original author of the translation of Acts in the *BJ*, has changed his mind (see J. Dupont, "La Rencontre entre Christianisme et Hellénisme dans le Discours à l'Aéropage," in *Fede e Cultura alla Luce della Bibbia: Acts of the 1979 Session of the Pontifical Biblical Commission* [Turin: Elle Di Ci, 1981], 264-268).

[24] M. Dibelius, "Paul on the Areopagus," in *Studies in the Acts of the Apostles* (London: SCM Press, 1956), 77; cf. L. Legrand, "The Areopagus Speech: Its Theological Kerygma and Its Missionary Significance" in *La Notion Biblique de Dieu,* ed. J. Coppens, BETL 41 (Leuven: University Press, 1976), 337-346.

[25] See the summary of the reaction to Dibelius and Norden in V. Gatti, *Il discorso di Paolo ad Atene,* Studi Biblici 60 (Brescia: Paideia Editrice, 1982), 34-46.

[26] See W. Nauck, "Die Tradition und Komposition der Areopagerede: Eine motivgeschichtliche Untersuchung," *ZTK* 53 (1956): 51-52.

For those who are inclined to consider the letter to the Romans as the epitome of Christian doctrine, constituting the canon within the canon, the Athenian discourse sounds hardly Christian. Dibelius considered it "foreign to the New Testament."[27] For him, the concluding verse on the resurrection was "the *only Christian sentence* in the Areopagus speech."[28] E. Norden went even to the point of suggesting, against all documentary evidence of the manuscripts, that the discourse could have been a massive gloss added in the second century.[29]

As a matter of fact, Acts 17 is by no means an isolated case. As Dibelius himself noted, the Athenian discourse is typical of Luke's theological perspective.[30] As a "theologian of redemptive history,"[31] Luke, in his double work, emphasizes the continuity of the successive periods of salvation history. The continuity between the old and the new dispensation is firmly indicated at the outset of his Gospel by having Jesus' cradle surrounded by a choice array of representatives of the Jewish pietistic circles. An equal emphasis is placed on the continuity between the times of the nations and the new economy. In the Lukan double work, in addition to the God-fearing and worthy government officials mentioned above, the nations are represented by well-disposed wealthy women such as Lydia (16:14), good-natured simple folk like the jailer of Philippi (16:27-34), and the "uncommonly kind" "barbarian" population of Malta (28:1-2). The Areopagus speech is not an isolated meteorite that would have fallen from some alien sky. Part and parcel of the Lukan work, it fits perfectly with the Lukan attitude toward the world, its history and cultures. If we were to eliminate the Athenian speech as un-Christian, it is the entire work of Luke that would have to be set aside.

How to account for the tension between the Pauline and the Lukan viewpoints? The personal element cannot be overlooked. Paul was a passionate enthusiast; Luke, as Dante puts it, was the *scriba mansuetudinis Christi,* the scribe of the meekness of Christ. But the setting also was different. Paul belonged to the first Christian generation, which, dazzled by the newness of Christ, wanted to make a clean break with the past. Luke's was the third Christian generation, living in the postapostolic age of the eighties. Time had elapsed since the Christ-event. This time had to be accounted for. A theology of history had to be developed. The course of time had its significance and its value. The present period was the time of the church and of the mis-

---

[27] Dibelius, "Paul on the Areopagus," 58, 64.

[28] Ibid., 56 (italics in the text). Dibelius speaks also of the "strangeness of the Areopagus speech in relation to the piety of the Bible . . . not one sentence of which accords with what we are accustomed to find elsewhere in the Old and New Testament" (p. 52).

[29] E. Norden, *Agnostos Theos: Untersuchungen zur Formgeschichte religiöser Rede* (Leipzig: Teubner, 1913), 37-55.

[30] Dibelius, "Paul on the Areopagus," 71-77.

[31] According to the title of the book of H. Flender, *St Luke: Theologian of Redemptive History* (London: SPCK, 1967).

sion to the Gentiles. Through this mission, the nations had been encountered directly and integrated in the people of God. They were no longer a cipher either of evil or of eschatological plenitude. They were a concrete reality of flesh and blood that could not be reduced to clear-cut doctrinal antitheses. For all the "ungodliness and wickedness" of a world that "suppresses the truth" (Rom. 1:18), it does have honest and kindly people, philosophers and poets whose lofty thoughts verge on mysticism. Paul himself, following the prophets, had mentioned the existence of a circumcision of the heart (Rom. 2:29), and Luke was happy to provide examples of it.

There might also have been a political element in Luke's attitude toward the Gentiles. His were difficult times for the Christian community the very extension of which disturbed both Roman and Jewish surroundings. The farewell speech of Paul to the elders of Ephesus evokes this atmosphere of persecution. "Savage wolves will come in who will not spare the flock" (Acts 20:29). In this context, Luke's aim is to show that the new "sect" is no public danger, that it is an amiable fellowship at one with all the honesty and philanthropy of the world. Therefore it deserves to be considered as *religio licita,* even though it does not identify with the official religion of the empire.

Whatever might have been the factors that prompted it, the Lukan approach to the surrounding world was positive. The call to conversion was not muted, but Luke likes to point out that it often fell on willing ears. Stress was laid on homogeneous continuity between the Christ-event and the history not only of Israel but also of the nations. The Lukan outlook preferred to emphasize convergence and predisposition rather than contrast and disruption. Significantly, the words "idolater" and "idolatry" are absent from the Lukan vocabulary, though they occur respectively five and three times in Paul. The word "idol" occurs only twice and that, once with reference to Israel's worship of the golden calf in Acts 7:41.[32] Luke does not look at the surrounding milieu as a "heathen" world. It is rather a world "groping" (Acts 17:27) for the "unknown God."

Yet the argument attributed to the apostle does not follow the apologetics of Artapanus or Aristobulus by attributing the lofty thoughts of the Greek poets to Moses. Neither does it go into the Philonic speculations on a universal *logos* that would subsume and assume any religious thinking, expression or representation. The Areopagus speech does not endorse Hellenism by giving it a Mosaic origin or an equivalent inspiration. The attitude it adopts is not of harmonization or of integration but of critical dialogue. The starting point of the discourse is no named god of Hellenism but the confession of ignorance implied in the recourse to "the unknown god" (17:23). The fact that we belong to the race of God does not mean that Zeus and God are

---

[32] By contrast, the Pauline corpus has a significantly higher frequency of the vocabulary concerning idols: the word idol occurs seven times, idolater five times, idolatry three times, idol place once.

to be put on an equal footing. The call to conversion is not omitted (v. 30), nor the castigation of human-made temples (v. 24), of material cult (v. 25), or of idols (v. 29). J. Dupont has noted the basic negative structure of the discourse. For all its positive attitude toward the audience, the Athenian discourse emphasizes their acknowledged "ignorance" of the true God and denies repeatedly the value of their common religious practices.[33] Luke's stance is based not on an ideology of integration but on the evangelical call to conversion. Standing before God and his "appointed" (17:31) legate, Jesus Christ, the Athenians, like all other human beings, are called to conversion: "he commands all people everywhere to repent" (17:30). This basic evangelical challenge to conversion rescues the Athenian speech from any Judeo-Hellenistic facile syncretism. Between the Maccabean rejection and the Alexandrian harmonization, the discourse of Athens proposes critical dialogue. As dialogue, this stance reflects the Lukan sympathetic approach to the surrounding world; as critical, it maintains the call to conversion that cannot be dissociated from the Christ-event.

CONCLUSION

Judaism presents a wide range of attitudes toward the surrounding world. One extreme is the radicalism of total rejection as found in the resistance movement of the Maccabees. The opposite extreme would be the position of Artapanos and of the Alexandrian Jewish apologists claiming identity between the teachings of Moses and the Egyptian cultural achievements. In this large range of options, Paul and Luke find themselves on both sides of the middle ground, Paul leaning toward a stand of opposition, Luke adopting a more sympathetic approach.

Paul does not show the intransigent attitude of the Maccabees. Yet his apocalyptic outlook leads him to attitudes of confrontation, at least ideologically. However, in praxis, he belongs to the world he denounces. His language, rhetoric, and thought patterns borrow abundantly from the surrounding Mediterranean culture.

Luke's emphasis on the continuity of salvation history makes him more consciously attuned to that ethos. However, along with Paul, he knows that Jesus' resurrection constitutes the great divide in the structure of time. For all his sympathies toward the Greco-Roman world, he relays the message that now the time has come for repentance, a time to break away from the past (Acts 17:30-31).

---

[33] J. Dupont, "Le Discours à l'Aréopage (Ac 17,22-31): Lieu de Rencontre entre Christianisme et Hellénisme," in *Nouvelles Études sur les Actes des Apôtres,* LD 1198 (Paris: Cerf, 1984), 380-396 (= *Bib* 60 [1979]: 530-546): "the syntactic construction of the main part of the discourse shows clearly that the stress should be put on the three main negative clauses . . . The main emphasis of the discourse is that God does *not* dwell in man made temples, that he is *not* served by human hands, that he is *not* like god, silver or stone images" (p. 396).

Paul and Luke may have different theological perceptions as regards the value of surrounding cultures. Nevertheless, for both, the newness brought about by the paschal event breaks the course of history. Faith in the resurrection keeps Luke as well as Paul away from the assimilating tendencies of Alexandrian Judaism. Philo's recourse to a universal *nous* or Artapanus's monopolizing apologetics tended to smooth over the prophetic impact of their Jewish faith. Luke also sympathized with Aratos and "Epimenides." Paul himself drew from Stoicism and the philosophical currents of his times. Yet for both Paul and Luke, the surrounding world is called to judgment by the "man" whom God "has raised from the dead" (Acts 17:31).

10

Beyond Paul

In Opposite Directions

Paul showed great boldness and creativity in taking the gospel out of his original Palestinian cradle. Yet the point he reached was not to be the end of the road. Launched by Paul, the process of cultural interrelation was to be further pursued in the apostolic and postapostolic communities. In the letters to the Colossians and to the Ephesians, the cross-cultural interaction between the gospel and the Mediterranean culture would go a step further than in the first Pauline letters. In the opposite direction, the spirit of the Maccabees was to revive in persecuted communities. This reaction found a particularly vehement expression in the book of Revelation and its radical condemnation of a doomed world. The contrast between the Captivity Letters and the Johannine Apocalypse is interesting. Their attitudes are poles apart. Yet these writings come from the same geographical area, the region of Ephesus, and they belong to the same post-Pauline period. The Lukan double work belongs also to the same period and can provide a third element of comparison. As in the case of Paul, the comparison with the Lukan position can help better to delineate the different currents that ran through the early churches.

THE COLOSSIAN CRISIS

Though traditionally attributed to Paul, the letters to the Colossians and to the Ephesians evoke cultural vistas different from those of the major epistles. Added to specific literary and theological characteristics, this difference of cultural background has led many commentators to question the Pauline authenticity of these writings. Others argue that the differences can be accounted for either by the intervention of a secretary or precisely by the new cultural situation which put new questions in the mind of a more mature apostle.[1] At any rate, these later Pauline or post-Pauline letters bear a different stamp. Even if the author of Colossians were Paul himself, it would be a different Paul, using a new style and a new phraseology, developing his thought in new directions. In terms of our line of inquiry, it would be a Paul exercising his ministry in a changed cultural setting, facing new aspects of the multiform cultural web he met with in his missionary task. Indeed, for our study, the question of authorship remains secondary. We can leave it open. What concerns us is the new cultural horizon that seems to form the background of this captivity correspondence, the new question these letters had to address, the new influences the author underwent.

THE COLOSSIAN PROBLEM

The letter to the Colossians is a response to a crisis, but it is not easy to pinpoint the exact nature of this crisis. The question of the "opponents" in Colossae is beset with still more obscurity than that of the identity of the author. The debate of the "Colossian heresy" is as old as Pauline scholarship. It is far from being concluded. Research on this point is obscured by a double level of opacity:

1. The letter is not a theological dissertation. It does not proceed methodically first with a description of the opponents' position, then with a systematic refutation point by point. It is an occasional writing, a letter addressed to people who knew what their problem was. The author wanted only to remind them of their faith in the primacy of Christ. Adverse opinions are referred to by way of allusion. Occasionally an unusual word or phrase

---

[1] The pendulum of opinion for or against authenticity swings to and fro. Compare the assessments of J. A. Grassi in the first edition of the *Jerome Biblical Commentary* (1968) ("very strong argument for authenticity," p. 335) and of M. P. Horgan in the new edition of the same *JBC* (1990), ("Col is deutero-Pauline," p. 877). The same difference of assessment is to be found for Eph according to *JBC* ("it could be attributed to Paul," p. 342) and in the *NJBC* (it is definitely "deutero-Pauline," p. 884). The case for the authenticity of Col is stronger than for Eph. See the long list of authors quoted by C. E. Arnold, *The Colossian Syncretism*, WUNT 77 (Tübingen: Mohr, 1995), 7 n. 10, himself in favor of the authenticity. But another recent commentary by M. Wolter (*Der Brief an die Kolosser. Der Brief an Philemon*, ÖTKNT 12 [Würzburg: Echter; Gütersloh: Mohn, 1993]) concludes that "Col belongs to post-Pauline times" (p. 31). The letter to the Colossians keeps closer to the Pauline mind and concerns. As for Eph, there is a large—though far from unanimous—measure of agreement that "in certain passages, *Ephesians* reads like the first commentary on *Colossians*" (E. Lohse, *Colossians and Philemon*, Hermeneia [Philadelphia: Fortress Press, 1978], 4). See a few dissenting voices in P. T. O'Brien, *Colossians Philemon*, WBC 44 (Waco: Word Books, 1982), xlif. Working on the hypothesis that *Colossians* "provided *Ephesians* with two decisive elements: an epistolary framework in the Pauline vein and the elaboration of a cosmic christology responding to the challenge met by the communities of Asia" (M. Bouttier, *L'Épître de Saint Paul aux Éphésiens*, CNT 9b [Geneva: Labor et Fides, 1995], 35), we shall base our study on Colossians without neglecting the occasional input of the other letter.

refers to the alien Colossian "philosophy." The inquiry has to manage with those indirect and fragmentary allusions.

2. Insofar as those allusions can evoke the vague contours of the Colossian errors, they give us only the image that the author of the letter had in mind. As noted by J. N. Aletti, what the letter sets forth is its reaction to the heresy, the way in which the author responds to his opponents. The Colossians themselves might have given another version. As in the case of many ideological discussions, the argument of the letter says: "You may not be aware of it but your position is fraught with dangerous distortions."[2]

Such being the case, it may not be a surprise to find commentators rambling about in a vast field of speculation. The range of hypotheses goes from Judaism (variously supposed to be mystical, apocalyptic, Essene, or Gnostic) to paganism (influenced by philosophy, mystery cults, or popular religiosity), passing through Gnosticism or an ill-defined "syncretism" mixing in various proportions Pythagorism or Middle Platonism with Jewish or Christian elements.[3]

THE SETTING

Amidst such a wide variety of opinions, it is impossible to trace a consensus and it would be presumptuous to suggest a solution or even a preference. Nevertheless, a few obvious points should not be overlooked. Particularly the geographical setting of the late Captivity Letters is to be noted. It is the neighboring cities of Colossae, Ephesus, and possibly Laodicea (Col. 4:16), cities that form also the locale of the seven churches of Revelation.

On the one hand, they were situated in the far west of Asia, facing Greece. From the most ancient times, even before the Trojan wars, this area had been associated with Greek prehistory and history. More Greek than Greece itself, it was the land of the Presocratic philosophers. Thales, Anaximander, Anaximenes, and Anaxagoras represented the school of Miletus; Xeno-

---

[2] "The author of Col insists on the christological and soteriological consequences of the Colossian errors; but the 'heretics' themselves—and even the Christians of Colossae—might not have perceived these christological and soteriological implications of the importance attributed to heavenly higher powers and to the ascetic practices they advocated. The emphasis of Col does not necessarily reflect that of the 'doctors'" (J. N. Aletti, *Epître aux Colossiens,* EBib 20 [Paris: Gabalda, 1993], 19). F. O. Francis compares the position of the present-day reader to that of an observer "listening to a friend engaged in heated argument by telephone: one can hardly make sense of what he is saying unless one can guess what the party at the other hand is saying" (F. O. Francis and W. A. Meeks, *Conflict at Colossae: A Problem in the Interpretation of Early Christianity Illustrated by Selected Modern Studies,* SBS 4 [Missoula, Mont.: Scholars Press, 1975], 1).

[3] See R. E. DeMaris, *The Colossian Controversy,* JSNTSup 96 (Sheffield: JSOT Press, 1994); or the sampling of some of the most representative opinions given in Francis and Meeks, *Conflict at Colossae.*

phanes was from Colophon near Ephesus; Heraclitus was from Ephesus itself. This Ionian coast continued to be a lively center of Greek culture during the Hellenistic period.

On the other hand, Colossae and Ephesus were situated along the valleys of the Meander and Lycus rivers, which linked the Mediterranean Sea with the Anatolian plateau, the heartland of what is now Turkey. Beyond it lay Upper Mesopotamia, Armenia, Persia, and the rest of Asia. The harbor town of Ephesus owed its prosperity to its position near the mouth of the Meander. But it was not only the goods of the east which traveled down the valley toward the Ionian harbors and the west. The river channeled also intellectual and religious currents coming from the Orient. The underground influence of the oriental cults remained vigorous. Oriental esoteric mysticism flourished. The campaigns of Alexander and the subsequent rule of the Diadochoi, his successors, had further opened the gates of the Orient. Alexander had even reached India, and the Syrian empire of the Seleucids initially extended as far as the Indus Valley. India had been influenced by these Hellenistic contacts, as witnessed by the Greco-Buddhist art of Gandhara. Reciprocally, Indian influence had been felt in the west. Asoka sent Buddhist missionaries to the west, and Philo mentions his encounter with the Indian "gymnosophists" (Jain monks?).[4] It is not without significance that Democritus, a disciple of Anaxagoras and of Leucippus of Miletus, was also reported to have "gone to Egypt to study geometry from the priests, to Persia to learn from the Chaldeans and down to the Red Sea. According to some, he associated with the gymnosophists of India."[5] Whether historical or not, the notice shows that the vast Asian background was very much part of the mental horizon of Asia Minor and that "Hellenism" did not develop in isolation in the midst of a cultural vacuum. In short, Asia Minor, the land of the Captivity Letters and of the seven letters of Revelation 2-3, had become the melting pot of a peculiar intercultural amalgam that would eventually crystallize in the different forms of Gnosticism.

Living in this world, the Christian communities could not escape the influence of this effervescent background. The "Colossian heresy" as well as the letters to the seven churches of Revelation leave an impression of intellectual restlessness. The Meander and Lycus Valleys were the epicenter of the earliest Christian heresies, usually vaguely qualified as varieties of Gnosticism or pre-Gnosticism. Faith in Jesus Christ was in serious danger of being obfuscated by mystico-philosophical speculations on angels and cosmic powers (see Col. 2:8, 16-19). The Christian communities ran the risk of turning into one of the numberless theosophical conventicles that flourished in this febrile world.

---

[4] *Quod omnis probus liber sit,* 11.

[5] Diogenes Laertius, *Philosophers' Lives and Opinions* 35; cf. Philostratus, *Lives of Sophists* 10; Strabo, *Geography* 15; Suidas, *Lexicon.*

THE RESPONSE

Whatever may have been the "philosophical" hash brewing in this cal-dron, it evoked a new mental world and put new questions to the Pauline Gospel.

Cosmic Powers

The themes of inheritance (Col. 3:24), liberation (1:23), redemption (1:14), and the opposition between the kingdoms of darkness and light (1:13) were part of the well established Judeo-Christian patrimony. With questions of Gentiles "made worthy to share the lot of the saints" (1:12, 26f.), through a "spiritual circumcision" (2:11, 13), problems of licit or illicit food, feasts, and Sabbaths (2:16), we are still on familiar Pauline ground. Parallels with other letters of the apostle are not lacking. But new terms appear suggesting a new range of issues and concerns. Interest now devel-ops in heavenly domains: thrones, dominions, principalities, powers (Col. 1:16; 2:15; Eph. 1:21; 3:10; 6:12). The latter two terms appear already in the earlier letters (Rom. 5:38; 1 Cor. 15:24). The addition of "thrones and prin-cipalities" is new. A complacent or ironic emphasis can be perceived in this lengthy listing.

Those heavenly powers are to be set in parallel, if not equated, with the "elements of the world" twice mentioned in Colossians (2:8, 20). Interest-ingly, the only Pauline parallel occurs in Galatians 4:3, 9, in the similar geo-graphical context of Asia Minor and with reference to opponents whose tenets might have had much in common with the "philosophy" of Colossae.

The Captivity Letters are wary of such an excessive interest in angelic powers, which can amount to "angel worship" (Col. 2:18). But it does not suffice to utter condemnations. Those angels represent cosmic forces, and the misguided speculations do raise the legitimate question of integrating the cosmos in the perspectives of Christian faith.

Plērōma

Is the term *plērōma* the answer to that question? When the hymn of Colossians 1 proclaims that "in Christ dwells all the *plērōma*" (v. 19), does it refer to the totality of being, divine, human, and cosmic with a possible Stoic background? Such is the opinion of a number of commentators.[6] Whether it came from a Stoic or a Gnostic background, it seems to have

---

[6] Already J. B. Lightfoot, *Saint Paul's Epistles to the Colossians and to Philemon*, 3rd ed. (London: Macmillan, 1879), 255-271; and, among many others, P. Benoit, "Corps, Tête et Plérôme dans les Épîtres de la Captivité," in *Exégèse et Théologie* (Paris: Cerf, 1961), 2:107-153; J. Dupont *Gnosis La Connaissance Religieuse dans les Épîtres de Saint Paul* (Louvain: Nauwelaerts, 1949), 419-427, 453-476; G. Delling, *TWNT* 6:300; Lohse, *Colossians and Philemon*, pp. 57f.

been a catchword of the Colossian heretics which the author of the letter christianized by subordinating it to the primacy of Christ. He did not want to enter into an argument concerning the concept itself. He just wanted to assert that, whatever *plērōma* might mean and refer to, it could be found only in Christ. The supremacy of Christ was proclaimed in the context of the Colossians' interest in cosmic powers and in light of the danger of a renewed enslavement to the "elements of the world." The term could be all the more easily christianized since it had also a rich biblical background (Jer. 8:16; 29:2; Ezek 12:19; 19:7; 30:12; 33:15; Ps. 23:1). According to this interpretation, Christ embodies

> the plenitude of being, not only the plenitude of divinity . . . but also that of the cosmos . . . He is God and by his redeeming work, he assumes in himself as a new Creation, not only the regenerated humanity . . . but also the entire new world that forms this body . . .
>
> In this way, Paul faces more clearly than before the problem of a new cosmos and gives a better definition of the universal sovereignty of Christ.[7]

This cosmic implication does not find favor with all the commentators.[8] They argue that, in 2:9, the *plērōma* is stated explicitly to be the "fullness of the divinity." For them, this seems to clinch the issue: the "plenitude" is divine and not cosmic or/and anthropological. Moreover, they add that the idea of a theo-cosmic fullness would smack of a pantheism totally alien to the biblical mentality. Yet, in 1:19, the word *plērōma* is used absolutely without any qualification, so as to keep the meaning open to wider perspectives. Should therefore the first text be understood in the light of the second or vice versa? Since, in 2:9, the "fullness" is said to be fullness of divinity, should we presume that this precision is to be understood in 1:19 also? Or, on the contrary, since *plērōma* has a greater extension in 1:19, are we to take it that the "plenitude of divinity" in 2:9 is only meant to bring further precision, to constitute an explanation that would not be a restriction? The meaning would be that, in Christ, the cosmic and human plenitude abides (1:19) because he has first of all the plenitude of divinity (2:9). This plenitude of divinity does not exclude the fullness of being given to humanity and to the world; rather it lays the foundation for this cosmic fullness. As to the suspicion of pantheism affecting the cosmic interpretation,[9] it prejudges the whole issue. Is biblical monotheism a rigidly closed concept or a living insight that could assimilate further dimensions in its encounter with other cultures? The Old Testament background of the word *plērōma* suggests this

---

[7] Benoit, "Corps, Tête et Plérôme," 145, 138.

[8] Among the recent commentators, see Aletti, *Colossiens*, 109f. Arnold, *Colossian Syncretism*, 262f.

[9] This is the objection of Aletti, *Colossiens*, 110, and of A. Feuillet, "Plérôme," *DBSup* 8:27.

open dynamism. The *plērōma* has strong cosmic connotations: it is what fills the sea (Ps. 96:11; 98:7), the earth (Ps. 24:1, quoted in 1 Cor. 10:26; Jer. 8:16; 47:2; Ezek. 12:19; 19:7; 30:12)—in short the entire world (Pss. 50:12; 89:11). More specifically and without any suspicion of pantheism, the Old Testament proclaims that God "fills heaven and earth" (Jer. 23:24), that his glory fills the earth (Isa. 6:3; Ezek. 43:5; 44:4). In Wisdom 1:7, it is the Spirit of the Lord that "fills the universe." And so, leaving aside speculations on the identity of the Colossian heresy, both the Old Testament background and the immediate context of the letter suggest a clear cosmic and anthropological connotation to the word *plērōma*.

"All Things"

Other cosmic overtones can be perceived in the frequency of the phrase *ta panta* (literally, "all the things") with reference to cosmic totality. The phrase was very common in Greek. There was even a god *Pan*, a god of unbridled sexuality and fecundity, symbolizing the "totality" of cosmic ebullience. Uncommon in the proto-Pauline writings (possibly but doubtfully in Gal. 3:22), *ta panta* occurs with unusual frequency in the hymns that form the beginning of Colossians (1:16 [twice], 17 [twice],18, 20) and Ephesians (1:10, 11, 23; cf. 3:9; 4:10). Those hymns are most likely to be "a quotation from a primitive Christian song,"[10] or possibly rather a revised formulation of a song used in the Colossian community.[11] This frequency suggests that the milieu addressed by the letters to the Colossians and Ephesians was keenly concerned with the cosmic implications of their Christian faith.

Interestingly, apart from the Captivity Letters, the best parallel occurs in Romans 11:36: "*All* is from him, through him and for him," which is also a hymnic insertion. There it is addressed to God and not to Christ. Already Hellenistic Judaism had responded to the ambient pantheism, affirming the superiority of the Creator over the cosmic *panta* while taking into account the cosmic awareness of the Greek world vision and of any nature worship.[12] The hymn quoted in Romans 11:36 follows the same line. The new factor in the Captivity Letters consists in extending this perception to the specific Christian faith in Jesus the Lord.

To conclude: in Colossians and Ephesians, there is a convergence of indications that Paul or whoever wrote in his name met with a culture in which the cosmic perspective was a matter of consequence. This concern had even seeped into the prayer forms and debates of the Christian community and found heterodox formulations. We can leave it to further specialized research to debate whether these notions stemmed from philosophical trends like

---

[10] Lohse, *Colossians and Philemon,* 42.

[11] Aletti, *Colossiens,* 88.

[12] See U. Wilckens, *Der Brief an die Römer (Röm 6-11),* EKKNT 6/2 (Zurich: Benzinger; Neukirchen: Neukirchener Verlag, 1980), 273.

Stoicism or Middle Platonism or from more esoteric Gnostic currents or from popular conceptions deriving from the old stock of Asian nature worship. However, the cosmic interest cannot be denied. It was not a totally new phenomenon. Not only was it already evident in Hellenistic Judaism; it was as old as wisdom thinking (see Job 28) and indeed as old as Genesis 1. What was relatively new, or at least became the matter of a new emphasis, was the need to relate this cosmic outlook to the Christ-event. As is often the case, the Colossian errors gave a wrong answer to a good question. It is to the credit of the Captivity Letters that they did not only refute falsehood. They addressed themselves to the underlying questions.

The resurrection had transformed the discipleship of the Galilean carpenter into a faith in the New Adam, the starting point of a new humanity. This had already been a momentous step. This new perception had been the focus of the major epistles and of the Pauline message to the nations. Now came the further step of situating Jesus Christ in the midst of the universe and speaking of a Lordship, not only over all the people but over the entire universe, with the glorious cross as the instrument of reconciliation not only for sinful humanity but for a disintegrated cosmos (Col. 1:20).

COLOSSIANS AND THE AREOPAGUS SPEECH

A similar concern for the cosmic significance of Christian faith can be found in the Areopagus speech in Acts 17:22-34, discussed in the previous chapter. The two quotations from the Greek poets in v. 28 deserve special attention. "In him, we have life, movement and our very being . . ." and "We belong to his race."

The first quotation was attributed to Epimenides by Isho'dad, a Nestorian Bishop of Merv[13] around 850. This attribution is often taken for granted in modern commentaries.[14] Epimenides was a semimythological figure of Presocratic times, philosopher, author of many books, and wonder-worker.[15] Lost as it is in this nebulous past, the very existence of Epimenides can hardly provide a solid reference for the Lukan quotation. The verse is rather a typical expression of Stoic pan-entheism: everything is in God and God is in everything.

The second quotation is taken from Aratus of Soles, with whom we stand on more solid historical ground. He was born between 315 and 305 at Soles

---

[13] Presently Mary in eastern Turkmenistan.

[14] See again the note of the *Jerusalem Bible* on this verse, p. 1829.

[15] He was reported to have lived from 155 to 299 years, fifty of which he spent asleep in a cave. Among his many miracles was the cleansing of Athens at the time of a plague. See F. Kiechle, "Epimenides," in *Der Kleine Pauly: Lexicon der Antike* (Munich: Druckenmüller, 1967), 2:319; K. Lake, "Your Own Poets," in F. J. Foakes Jackson and Kirsopp Lake, *Beginnings of Christianity: The Acts of the Apostles,* vol. 5, *Additional Notes* (London: Macmillan, 1932), 247.

of Cilicia, a town close to Tarsus. The verse quoted in Acts belongs to the prologue of the *Phaenomena,* a long poem on astronomy and the influence of heavenly bodies on earth. In this context, the lofty saying of Aratus is simply meant to account for the agricultural calendar that the book will describe. Aratus's viewpoint is not mystical but pragmatic: the divine kinship with the universe ensures that proper times and signs are determined for the various agricultural labors.

Closer to the spirit of Paul's Athenian speech is the use of the same hemistich in Cleanthes' *Hymn to Zeus:*[16]

> Unto thee may all flesh speak; *for we (or they) are thy offspring,* all those who partake of this image of things which is the sound (= the *logos*) . . . Save people from their nefarious ignorance and enable us to share in this wisdom with which you govern everything in righteousness. (*Hymn to Zeus* 4.33-35)

In addition to Aratus or Cleanthes, an Armenian *catena* attributed the hemistich to a certain Timagenes, of whom nothing is known.[17] Finally, are the quotations to be attributed to Epimenides, Timagenes, Aratus, or Cleanthes? It is more likely that those poetical fragments were freely floating fragments of anthology, Stoic slogans circulating out of context as expressions of the *Zeitgeist.* Luke was not working in a library. His dialogue was not an intellectual exchange with an elite of specific authors. It was an immersion in the culture of the day. In the catchphrases circulating in this culture, Luke found lofty expressions of Hellenistic thought and religiosity and was happy to note their convergence with the Christian message.[18]

A dialogue takes place. Kerygma and Gnosis meet on Mars Hill. "The Areopagus speech is the first witness in Christianity to an encounter between the biblical faith in the creation and the cosmic piety of the Greeks."[19]

> By integrating expressions redolent of pantheism within the monotheistic kerygma, the Areopagus speech anticipated the future. A one-sided stress on divine transcendence might isolate God from humanity and the world. The formulas borrowed from Hellenism strike a balance by recalling that the pole of transcendence is only one aspect of the divine mystery. There is the opposite pole of immanence . . . The transcendent God . . . is also present in the world and in the inmost core of the human

---

[16] Cleanthes from Assos near Troas lived from 312 to 232 and was the successor of Zeno at the head of the Stoic school.

[17] See M. Dibelius, "Paul on the Areopagus," in *Studies in the Acts of the Apostles* (London: SCM Press, 1956), 52 n. 78.

[18] See L. Legrand, "Aratos est-il aussi parmi les prophètes?" in *La Vie de la Parole: Études offertes à Pierre Grelot* (Paris: Desclée, 1987), 246-249.

[19] W. Eltester, "Zur Areopagerede," in *Neutestamentliche Studien für R. Bultmann,* BZNW 21 (Berlin: Töpelmann, 1954), 226.

soul since "in him we live, we move and have our being." Here theology turns to mysticism.[20]

Yet, in this dialogue with the ambient culture, the Athenian speech did not go as far as the Captivity Letters. It did not extend the cosmological perspectives to Christ. The viewpoint remained the same as it was in Jewish wisdom literature. The cosmos was viewed in its relationship with God, not with Christ. Insofar as Christ is concerned, the Christology of Acts 17 remains that of the early kerygma: Christ is the judge to come; his resurrection is the pledge of his return; meanwhile all are called to conversion (17:30-31). The conclusion of the Areopagus discourse recalls the terms of one of the earliest summaries of Christian faith reproduced by Paul in 1 Thessalonians 1:9-10. The formulation of the early Pauline letter was negative: it followed the Judaic polemic against the idols ("turning to God from idols"). Without muffling the biblical call to conversion, Luke takes a positive stance toward Greek thought, heeding its sense of immanence and its cosmic awareness.

THE EMERGENCE OF A COSMIC THEOLOGY

In its encounter with Greek thought and Asian esoteric speculations, the Christian gospel met with an important problem. In the wild speculations of the "doctors" of Colossae, as well as the then prevalent Stoic philosophy, human thought extended to the dimensions of the cosmos and reached the depths of the ontological substratum of world, humanity, and deity. So far, the Christian message had been expressed in terms of messianic expectations. Jesus was the Messiah announced by the prophets of old; in him the salvation promised for the last days had dawned on earth. This was an effective language for the Jews, who, through their familiarity with the Bible, had embraced a historical vision of human destiny. But the Hellenistic mental horizon—and that of the Iranian and of the Indian worlds which had begun to enter the scene—embraced wider vistas. It integrated the cosmos. It meant to account for the order and disorder of things. Beyond the fleeting character of sensible phenomena, it tried to reach the underlying reality, the true Being. It did not scrutinize history only, but also the universe and the principles underlying the realm of Being. It did not turn toward the future in expectation of a divine intervention. Its purpose was rather to perceive the pulse of the timeless divine presence abiding in the cyclic vicissitudes of life.

The early Christian kerygma, as it is found in the first speeches of Acts and the early confessions of faith, did not respond to those concerns. It left too many genuine ontological questions unanswered to satisfy the Greek and the Asian mind. It is true that there is no absolute beginning. The down-to-

---

[20] Dupont, "La Rencontre," 286.

earth language of Jesus' parables did imply a privileged relationship with nature. Occasional flashes of Pauline thought evoked the cosmic impact of the Christ-event (Rom. 8:19-23; 1 Cor. 15:37-41).[21] But it will be only at a later stage that the Greek cosmological concern will be given systematic consideration. What characterizes the Captivity Letters and the Athenian discourse in Acts 17 is that in them the Christian message resonates in another mental world. This may be the reason why Indian theology finds itself at home in those texts, as well as in the Gospel of John. In these writings, it finds a harmony with the Upanishadic quest for the authenticity of Truth and the plenitude of Life.[22] Going beyond the context of the *parousia* and of the tragedy of sinful humanity, they situate the Christ-event in the context of the tensions between cosmic forces at work in the universe.

We need not emphasize the ecological significance of this late-Pauline or post-Pauline development. The fact that we are still grappling with these ecological implications of Christian faith shows how far-reaching was the step taken by the post-Pauline churches in their encounter with the cultural currents of Asia.

AN OPPOSITE ATTITUDE: THE BOOK OF REVELATION

At the same time and in the same geographical area, the book of Revelation vented quite different feelings toward the surrounding world. To Luke's befriending approach to the Greco-Roman world and to the profound dialogue engaged in the Captivity Letters, the Johannine Apocalypse opposes a radical rejection of what it deems to be a doomed civilization. This negative attitude, combined with the esoteric apocalyptic style, disconcerts the reader. The outcome is that "the apocalypse is probably the least read book of the whole Bible . . . , the most neglected book of the New Testament."[23] Yet the book does belong to the Bible. It expresses also a response of the early church to the cultural environment. Even if we find it unpleasant, it has to be taken into account.

LUKE AND REVELATION

The previous section sampled Luke's version of the Areopagus Speech in Acts 17 as a typical case of intercultural openness. The Johannine Apocalypse proffers a totally antithetic picture of the surrounding world. Still more

---

[21] See K. J. Gabriel, "The Integral View of Humans and Nature: An Aspect in Pauline Eschatology," *Bible Bhashyam* 25 (1999): 40-46.

[22] See the papers of the Pune Conference of February 1974 published by C. Duraisingh and C. Hardgreaves (eds.), *India's Search for Reality and the Relevance of the Gospel of John* (Delhi: ISPCK, 1975).

[23] H. Richards, *What the Spirit Says to the Churches* (London: Chapman, 1966), 9. Exception could now be made of the various fundamentalist sects that find in Revelation the justification of their imminent eschatology.

than Romans 1, the book of Revelation represents the perfect antithesis to Acts 17 and to Luke's irenic world vision. Reading the two works successively, one would hardly believe that they come from the same background. Luke-Acts and Revelation both belong to the later years of New Testament times.[24] The geographical setting of the seven churches of Asia Minor, with Ephesus as its center, corresponds to that of Acts. Similar issues agitate the minds: the questions of food offered to idols and of the "prostitution" of idolatry (Rev. 2:14, 20-21; cf. Acts 15:20, 29; 21:25), the problem of the relations with fellow Jews (Rev. 2:9; 3:9; cf. Acts 28:26-28), internal strife (Rev. 2:6, 14, 20; cf. Acts 20:30), and particularly persecutions (Rev. 2:3; 3:4, 8; cf. Acts 14:5; 16:20-24; 17:6-7; 20:29).

Yet the interpretations given to this common tumultuous setting are diametrically opposed. Still more than with Paul, the vision of Revelation is sharply contrasted in black and white. The Jews are not typified by pious priests, earnest prophets, and holy women. For the Johannine seer, the most representative figures of the Old Testament seem to be Balak and Balaam (2:14), Jezebel (2:20), the great prostitute (17:1-18), and Babylon (18:1-24). Those who claim to be Jews are not true Israelites; they are the "synagogue of Satan" (2:9). This is no early Christian anti-Semitism. It is just one side of the radical indictment of the whole world. The Gentiles come under still more severe criticism. The Roman empire is a stooge of Satan, a monster coming from the abyss (13:1-10), the malice of which is compounded by the hypocrisy of its religious establishment and its spurious godliness (13:11-17). For Luke, persecutions had turned into opportunities to proclaim the gospel (Acts 6:7; 7:17; 8:2, 5-25) and had been received with joy (5:41), praise, and thanksgiving (4:24-30). In Revelation, the increasing number of martyrs does not contribute to the progress of the gospel but brings to completion the assigned number of those who are to be killed (6:11); the prayer it raises is the anguished cry: "How long, O Lord?" (6:10). Rome, the persecuting power, is Babylon wallowing in filth and drunk with the blood of the saints (17:4-6; 18:13). Its woes will carry grief to the whole world (18:9-19). In this context, the lines of communication of the empire do not constitute the apostolic highways which Paul had followed; they are the channels of the Roman colonial exploitation and of international profiteering (18:11-18). In fact, the entire course of world history is a record of wars (6:4), famines (6:5-6), and calamities (6:8). It is nothing but the plagues of Egypt in mythic proportions and stretching over the whole span of time and space (16:1-21). If Luke sang "Peace on Earth" (2:14), the chant of Revelation is "Joy in heaven and woe to you, earth and sea" (12:12).

---

[24] The date of Revelation is debated. A late date has been traditionally ascribed and seems to be the more likely hypothesis: "It seems . . . that there is no compelling reason to doubt the traditional dating of Rev attested by Irenaeus and other early Christian writers, *viz.*, the end of the reign of Domitian (AD 95-96)" (A. Yarbro Collins, "The Apocalypse (Revelation)," *NJBC*, 998).

COLOSSIANS AND REVELATION

A similar contrast can be noted between Revelation and the letter to Colossae. The two writings are so different that they seem to elude any possible comparison. Yet they have more in common than meets the eye of a casual reader. It is not only that they originate from a common geographical background. This common environment finds expression in a common church setting and identical theological viewpoints. The churches they address are disturbed by spurious doctrines taught by false doctors (Rev. 2:6, 15, 20-23; Col. 2:4, 18, 22-23). They claim "visions" and access to "depths" of knowledge (Rev. 2:24; Col. 2:18). The debate extends to questions of food (Rev. 2:14, 20; Col. 2:16). By contrast, the communities are invited to live in faith (Rev. 2:19; 13:10; Col. 1:4, 23; 2:7), love (Rev 2:19; Col 2:14) and endurance (Rev 1:9; 2:2f., 19; 3:10; 13:10; Col. 1:11; 3:12). Colossians "sing psalms, hymns, and spiritual songs" (Col. 3:16), which is what angels and believers do continuously almost in every chapter of Revelation. Cosmic powers form the base of God's throne in Revelation 4:6-9, while angels fly all over the skies of the book of Revelation; "thrones, dominions, principalities and powers" loom equally large on the horizon of Colossians (1:16; 2:15, 18). Mostly Revelation and Colossians show strikingly similar christological features. In both, by his resurrection Christ is the firstborn (Rev. 1:17-18; 2:8; Col. 1:15), the principle of creation (Rev. 3:14; Col. 1:15-18); his lordship extends to the cosmos.[25]

However, this common Christology hides a basic difference. In Colossians, the "firstborn of all creation," the One "through whom and for whom all things came to be" is the principle of cosmic cohesion (Col. 1:17) and the source of universal peace and reconciliation (1:18-20); the world shares in the plenitude that dwells in him (1:19; 2:2). In Revelation, on the contrary, the "principle of God's creation" threatens the tepid (3:14-16); those who join with him take part in his victorious battles (3:21; 17:14). In Revelation the power of the "lord of lords and king of kings" exercises itself over against the enemies (17:14-18; 19:11-21), whereas in Colossians it was a matter of gathering heaven and earth in "the inheritance of the saints in light" (1:12). Both look for a world reconciled on earth as in heaven, but the author of Colossians views it as already initially given in the church (1:12-18), whereas for Revelation it can only come down from heaven at the end of time (Rev. 21-22). In Colossians, the primacy of Christ is a matter of

---

[25] This point was already noted by W. Bousset, *Die Offenbarung Johannis*, MeyerK 16 (Göttingen: Vandenhoeck & Ruprecht, 1906; reprint, 1966), 241. It is further developed by P. Prigent, *L'Apocalypse de Saint Jean*, CNT 14 (Neuchâtel: Delachaux & Niestlé, 1981), 76. Prigent notes the geographical and chronological proximity, the possible background of "gnostic speculations strongly tinted with Judaism," and quotes the opinion of R. H. Mounce, (*The Book of Revelation* [Grand Rapids: Eerdmans, 1977], 124-125) that the book of Revelation could have derived from Colossians.

shared plenitude; it flows into cosmic peace. In Revelation the same primacy stands over against the world; it ends in annihilating victory.

CONTRAST OR CONTINUITY?

One might be inclined to qualify the outlook of the Johannine Apocalypse as the product of a jaundiced vision of the world and of history, born of a sickly pessimism. That would be unfair. We must sympathize with the distress of a persecuted community threatened with extinction. The literary form of apocalypse is also to be taken into account. Yet there is no doubt that the last book of the Bible is not on the same wave length as *Gaudium et Spes* (the Pastoral Contitution on the Church in the Modern World of Vatican II) or *Populorum Progressio* (encyclical of Pope Paul VI).

Well-minded readers have often been suspicious of the orthodoxy of so stringent a condemnation of the world. In Christian antiquity, the canonicity of Revelation was often doubted, especially in the Eastern and Syrian churches. Modern scholarship has suggested that the book could be a compilation of Jewish apocalypses, artificially linked together by a Judeo-Christian disciple of John the Baptist.[26] It is interesting to note that two works so diametrically opposed as those of Luke and John the Seer come under the same suspicion of failing the test of true Christian spirit. The very fact of their canonicity would rather be an invitation to enlarge our idea of what Christian authenticity means.

In fact, Luke-Acts and Colossians on the one side and Revelation on the other represent the opposite poles of the Christian stand toward the world, its history and cultures. R. Bultmann has summarized the issue in the dilemma between continuity and opposition.[27]

The New Testament theology of continuity pursues the Judeo-Hellenistic attempt to come to terms with the impressive richness of Greco-Roman culture. It does not go so far as Aristobulus, who, in his eagerness to recover the "treasures of Egypt," identified Greek culture and Yahwistic faith. Luke and the Captivity Letters are guided not by abstract apologetic considerations but by their mission experience. They had no mind to condone sin; they knew that the gospel message was basically one of conversion. But they knew also that human beings ought not to be demonized and that the world created by God was not pure darkness.

The Revelation of John would rather be in line with the attitude of the Maccabees and in general with the prophetic condemnation of sin in all its

---

[26] See J. Massyngberde Ford, *Revelation,* AB 38 (New York: Doubleday, 1975), 22-37.

[27] R. Bultmann, "Anknüpfung und Widerspruch: Zur Frage nach den Anknüpfung der neutestamentlichen Verkündigung an die Theologie der Stoa, die hellenistische Mysterienreligionen und die Gnosis," in *Glauben und Verstehen: Gesammelte Aufsätze* (Tübingen: Mohr, 1952), 2:401-416.

forms—personal, societal, and political. It is the merit of the Johannine Apocalypse to have echoed in the New Testament the vigorous accents of Amos, Isaiah, and Jeremiah, castigating hypocrisy, tepidity, injustice, and oppression. Of all the books of the New Testament, it is the Johannine Apocalypse that confronts the most explicitly political situations of tyranny and imperial absolutism. It does not hesitate to put momentous questions to society and its cultures. Like any human realities, cultures are ambiguous. Their remarkable achievements can conceal wretched misery and even be their product. The glory that was Egypt was also the "iron furnace" (Deut. 4:20), the "slavery of Egypt" (Deut. 15:15; 16:12; 24:22). Babylon is both Hammurabi, the law maker, and Nebuchadnezzar, the vandal. The ruins of Angkor witness to both the glory of the ancient Hindu Indo-Chinese kingdoms and to the extravagant megalomania that caused their ruin. The medieval Crusades can be perceived and presented as a magnificent upsurge of popular enthusiasm or as a dreadful display of Western arrogance and fanatic intolerance.

Examples could be multiplied endlessly. They all illustrate the biblical paradigm of the human paradox set forth in the first pages of the Bible. Genesis 1 describes a radiant world and the joy of its Creator seeing that "it was good," "very good" indeed when it comes to man and woman, reproducing the divine "image and likeness." But the third chapter reports the curse brought on the earth by human sin (Gen. 3:17). The biblical attitude to the world hangs between those two poles of rapture and distrust. The psalmist sings the harmony of a world peacefully set under the dominion of a human race crowned with glory and honor (Ps. 8:5f.). But the Psalter says also that "every one has gone astray; they are all alike corrupt; there is none that does good, no, not one" (Ps. 14:3; cf. 53:4f.). One side of the picture is the divine blessing on the world, on history and on the human achievements. The other side is of the prophetic indictment of the evil that snakes its way in mortal flesh and its evanescent feats. One aspect cannot be chosen at the expense of the other. Both correspond to the double aspect of the God of the Bible: transcendence and immanence. The immanence of the God, who is close to his people, animates their life and history and gives value to all their thoughts and deeds. The transcendence of the God who is thrice holy, totally Other, stands in sharp contrast to and in abiding judgment of human mediocrity, vanity, and meanness.

In practice, depending on circumstances, on personal temperament and charisms, one or the other aspect will be predominant. But neither should be totally exclusive. At the end of the Athenian speech, Greek culture is called to conversion, acknowledging its "ignorance" and coming under divine judgment (Acts 17:30). On the other side, in the beginning of the book of Revelation, the letters to the seven churches bring the too sharply contrasted apocalyptic vision within the field of complex human situations where good and evil, heroism and mediocrity coexist. Black and white merge into the gray dullness of humble daily life. One-sided hostility to the world would renege the Creator and his blessings. Total absorption in world values would ignore the thrice holy One. "Inculturation" must remember that, in the light of the Bible, human cultures have all the nobility of the image of God and all the frailty of created flesh.

Conclusion

Christian faith is the same everywhere: it is faith in Jesus Christ, Son of God. Yet, at the same time, it is as diverse as the multiplicity of world cultures in which it is lived. The African villager cannot apprehend, express, and live his faith in the same manner as the European or American city dweller. For that matter, the faith perspective of the European or American city dweller on the threshold of the third millennium differs widely from that of his ancestor in the Middle Ages. "Inculturation" is the term that theologians have coined to denote this grounding of Christian faith and life in the various cultural environments. The term expresses the responsibility of each local church to give shape to the faith it has received and by which it stands. "Inculturation" is another expression of the law of incarnation. God manifests himself and communicates his word, his love, and his life through a process of involvement in creation, in human history, and finally in the enfleshment of the Word in Jesus of Nazareth. All along this history, God's revelation has been intermingled with the various vicissitudes of people's life. In the paradigmatic case of the Israelites, their history has continuously passed through peaceful or violent encounters with the neighboring countries, Egypt, Canaan, Transjordan, Syria, Assyria, Mesopotamia, Persia, Greece, and Rome, in constant interaction with them. This makes the Bible itself the outcome of an ongoing process of cultural exchange with surrounding nations.

The theology of "inculturation" has been an attempt to formulate this law of incarnation and the responsibility thereby incumbent on the local church. It implies also the recognition that the history of any human group is also salvation history, that "the Spirit's presence and activity affect not only individuals but also society and history, peoples, cultures and religions."[1] Human beings cannot grow outside their bodies; similarly no faith can be authentically lived and produce fruits in an alien context. Embodying these basic insights, the theology of "inculturation" represents a considerable theological and missiological development.

---

[1] *Redemptoris Missio* (encyclical of Pope John Paul II) 28.

ENLARGING THE PERSPECTIVES

Yet, like any human formulation, this theology has its shortcomings.

A SEMANTIC FLAW

A first flaw of the term "inculturation" is that it is not scientific. It does not belong to the terminology of anthropological sciences which have a wider range of terms to express the various forms of interrelationship between cultures. The term "inculturation" seems to be restricted to the field of theological speculation. In an area where faith investigates its borders with anthropological realities, it does not bode well for theology if it cannot share a common idiom with anthropology. It is a poorly "inculturated theology" that cannot use the language of its partner in dialogue! This deficiency betrays a flawed analysis of cultural realities. Granting that any discipline, and theology as well, is entitled to its own jargon, the question remains of its adequacy. The present biblical survey has shown that the interaction with the variety of human cultures at various times and in different circumstances presents many faces. The word "inculturation" falls short of expressing this complex variety. Its validity is limited to one aspect of the question. Other aspects have also to be considered.

A ONE-SIDED "MISSIOLOGICAL" PERSPECTIVE

Another shortcoming of the concept of "inculturation" is its one-sided dependence on "missionary" situations. It continues to refer to the problems encountered when exporting a faith package to another cultural zone. In the protracted course of its human history, the Word of God met with a great variety of cultural situations. The term "inculturation" proper, in the sense used presently, would apply only to the situation that prevailed in Alexandria in Egypt in the last centuries B.C.E., when Jewish apologetic strove to present its Yahwistic faith to the Hellenistic world. In other contexts, the relationship with surrounding cultures is rather to be expressed in terms of emergence, immersion, acculturation, intercultural exchange, subcultures, counter-cultures, cross-fertilization, *métissage,* and so on. Our biblical survey has illustrated this variety of contexts. It could easily be paralleled and complemented by an anthropological study of the various forms of cultural interactions outside the Bible.

This is no mere exegetical pettifogging. In terms of concrete ecclesiology, it means that the problem of culture has to be viewed in a *deeper* and *wider* perspective than that of the "mission" to the "field afar."

A *deeper* perspective: if the encounter with culture is the responsibility of the local Church, it has to surge from inside the local church. It must be the expression of an inner appropriation and not of a disguised invasion. A *wider* perspective: it is to be a concern not only of "young churches" but of any church. It is not a problem of Asia or Africa only, of their church leaders and of Third World theologians. The task is laid upon any church in this fast-moving world of ours. To a good extent, the present "faith crisis" in the West may be due to the inability of the churches to come to terms with the deep cultural convulsions of the postmodern times. At least Third World churches have the advantage of being alert to their cultural problem and of giving it priority in their reflections. Other churches could take a leaf from this "missiological" agenda. It deserves to be shifted from the field of missiology to that of ecclesiology. It concerns the inmost nature of the church in its relationship to the world.

PROPHETIC CHALLENGE

THE SIGNIFICANCE OF COUNTERCULTURES

Another flaw of the term "inculturation" is the naive implication that cultures have necessarily positive values. Our survey has noted another biblical attitude toward cultures, that of revolt against oppressive dominating cultures. This trend of counterculture, of challenge toward the alienating aspects of dominating cultures, is a persistent and basic feature of the biblical stand. It was already epitomized by Abraham, leaving Mesopotamia, and Moses, leading Israel out of Egypt. It constitutes the underlying thrust of the message of the prophets. It is also the attitude of Jesus, the "marginal Jew," unfettered by any conventional opinion, always free to denounce any prevailing routine and latent hypocrisy. It is brought to a climax in the Johannine Apocalypse. This critical freedom represents the fundamental prophetic protest against the falsehood and injustice lurking in the most brilliant and most solid civilizations. This cultural confrontation is as fundamental as the holiness of God, whose transcendence shames human meanness. So does the glory of God expose the failings of the greatest accomplishments. So does the love of God for the lowly stand as a condemnation of arrogant achievements built on contempt of the poor and oppression of the downtrodden.

From the days of Elijah, this prophetic protest has always been raised against the risk of assimilation, of an in- or ac-culturation that would have resulted in the loss of identity of Israel as the people *of God*. Rooted as it is in the prophetic voice of a people "set apart," the countercultural challenge is a witness to the God who is thrice holy, totally Other, transcending all human baseness. It is a constant reminder of the distance that separates the finite from the Infinite, the poor human meanness from the One who says:

> As the heavens are higher than the earth,
> so are my ways higher than your ways,
> and my thoughts than your thoughts. (Isa. 55:9)

A faith perception without cultural appropriation would mean contempt of the God of the incarnation. But a cultural immersion that would lose the sense of prophetic defiance would betray the God who "is God and no human creature" (Hos. 11:9; Num. 23:19).

Like God, like Christ, the biblical character is marked by a certain estrangement. It remains typified by Abraham the migrant. This is not justifying an attitude of alienation from the world. Jesus remains the model. He was totally Jewish and Galilean, yet never a prisoner of his Galilean Jewishness. He came to the world (John 3:16-17), yet he was not of the world (8:23). He sent his own to the world (17:18) but not to be swallowed up by the world (17:14-18). The Gospel of John weaves repeatedly this dialectic of belonging and challenging, which is the very dialectic of the God immanent and transcendent. This Gospel insight works both ways: "Jesus means Freedom,"[2] but this freedom was exercised in the radical identification of an incarnation. "The Word was made flesh." Flesh it was in all the authenticity of a human birth, life, and death. Word it remained, bringing light and life but also judgment and crisis.

In concrete terms, this means that any judgmental attitude issuing from outside is mere arrogance, violent imposition of foreign cultural values. Reciprocally, an immersion that would drown the voice of God would be a betrayal. A cultural assimilation that would condone sin and sinful structures would be a breach of faith: there can be "negative values of culture."[3] "I have seen the affliction of my people who are in Egypt and have heard their cry . . . I know their sufferings," says God to Moses (Exod. 3:7). Cultural identification would play false to the God of the Bible if it remained deaf to the cry of the poor, blind to all the modern forms of Pharaoh's oppression that continue to weigh on the downtrodden, whether it be social inequality, economic injustice, bonded labor, casteism, sexism, racism, illiteracy, exploitation of children, destructive exploitation of nature, and so on. The list is unfortunately endless.

THE SIGNIFICANCE OF SUBCULTURES

In this connection, attention must be paid to the subcultures of the lowly. They are often the present-day equivalent of the ancient biblical situations, of the subcultures of the Israelites in the Canaanite context, of Jesus the

---

[2] According to the title of the book of E. Käsemann (London: SCM Press, 1969).

[3] Statement of the Federation of Asian Bishops' Conferences (FABC) Colloquium on the Social Doctrine of the Church in the Context of Asia, (Pattaya, Thailand, January 20-25, 1992), *FABC Papers* No. 65, p. 32. "In the living heritage of cultures and religious traditions of Asia we discern values and their expressions in symbols, stories and art forms that embody a vision of life; while we are critically aware of the distortions that have entered into these traditions" (Final Statement of the Plenary Assembly of the Federation of Asian Bishops' Conferences, Manila, Philippines, January 10-19, 1995, *FABC Papers* No 74, p. 85).

Galilean peasant in the Jewish world. A similar cultural option for the sub-cultures of the marginalized is called for if the "option for the poor" is to be effective. This was the call, for instance of the Asian bishops at the end of their Plenary Assembly of 1995:

> Like Jesus, we have to "pitch our tents" in the midst of all humanity, building a better world, but especially among the suffering and the poor, the marginalized and the downtrodden of Asia. In profound solidarity with suffering humanity and led by the Spirit of life, we need to *immerse ourselves in Asia's cultures of poverty and deprivation,* from whose depths the aspirations for love and life are most poignant and compelling.[4]

OPENNESS TO THE "OTHER"

The biblical types of Abraham the migrant, of Israel forging its identity in exodus and exile, of *Paul the Traveller*[5] bring to mind another biblical aspect of the cultural problem, that of intercultural openness. To the vertical openness to the transcendence of God's challenge, corresponds also the horizontal attention to the alterity of other cultures. The land of Israel was never an island. Never was it God's purpose to insulate his people from external influences. Another name of *agapē,* charity, is *koinōnia,* fellowship, openness to others. It belongs to basic Christian identity. The local church will not be Christian if it is not open to other churches and to the world in sharing and communion. The cultural appropriation of the local church would be un-Christian if it were to be closed upon itself, unmindful of the multicultural richness in which it develops. Aware or unaware, Israel expressed its identity in the context of the various cultures it encountered. The Galilee in which Jesus lived was quite a lively cultural crossroads. The gospel he proclaimed was carried on the highways and byways of the multiethnic Roman empire.

This openness is called for by the present context of increasing globalization. Nowadays through media and traveling, local cultures meet each other and are exposed to their mutual influences. At the same time, migrations for economic and political reasons bring the foreigner to the heart of most human communities. What is to be the local church and its cultural authenticity in Tokyo and Hong Kong, where, on any Sunday, more Filipinos attend church services than local Christians,[6] in French suburbs, where the

---

[4] Ibid., *No. 74,* p. 88 (italics added).

[5] According to the title of the book of W. M. Ramsay, *Paul the Traveller and the Roman Citizen* (London: Hodder & Stoughton, 1895; reprint, Grand Rapids: Baker, 1949).

[6] According to the statistics released by the Catholic Bishops' Conference of Japan, out of a total of 825,000 Catholics in Japan, 390,000 are of foreign extraction, representing therefore

church attendance is largely made of a multiracial blend of Portuguese, Africans, Vietnamese, and Tamilians, with a sparse sprinkling of autochthons? Abraham the migrant is no longer a paradigm lost in a distant past. He is present everywhere in the midst of our modern societies and faces their cultures.

In the cosmopolitan civilizations of today, the expatriate stands as a reminder of the world beyond. Like the wandering patriarchs of old, today's migrants constitute also an eschatological sign, making local cultures aware that they do not embrace the totality of human plenitude and still less of divine fullness.

Bearing today the sign of Abraham and of Israel in Egypt (Deut. 5:15; 10:19; 15:15; 16:1, 3, 12; 23:8; 24:17-22), foreigners in our midst constantly reminds the local community to transcend its boundaries. They invite the local church to cast the eyes beyond and upwards. They urge it to look beyond its cultural boundaries and to heed both the human richness and the distress of the vast surrounding world. Thereby they remind it to look above its cultural achievements at the eschatological fullness of life.

> By faith, Abraham . . . went out, not knowing where he was to go . . . He sojourned in the land of promise, as in a foreign land . . . for he looked forward to the city which has foundations whose builder and maker is God . . . His descendants . . . died in faith, not having received what was promised but having seen it and greeted it from afar, having acknowledged that they were strangers and exiles on the earth. (Heb. 11:8-10, 13)

In *The Outsider,* Albert Camus describes the character of Meursault, who remains like an outsider among the people with whom he lives, wandering about on the fringe of the surrounding society. As Camus himself explained in the preface to the American edition of his work, his hero or anti-hero refuses to lie, to play the game of conventional rules. Because he refuses to mask his feelings, society feels threatened. In conclusion, says Camus, *The Outsider* is the only Christ whom we deserve.[7] Actually, since Meursault is a murderer and not a martyr and since he is a paradigm of *ennui,* of "bore-

---

47 percent of the Catholic population of Japan. In the diocese of Nagoya, they constitute 72 percent of the 85,000 diocesans; a similar proportion is found in the diocese of Urawa, with a majority of Brazilians, followed by Filipinos and Peruvians. In Kyôtô, the proportion is 57 precent (*Église d'Asie* 246 [July 1997]: 16). See Nakagawa Akira, "Influence of Migrants upon the Japanese Church," *The Japan Mission Journal* (Autumn 1998): 152-160: What the author says of Japan has universal validity: "Inculturation or contextualization is not the process of adapting the gospel to the culture; rather it is the practice of using the Gospel to challenge the culture. Acceptance of otherness is the direction necessary for this inculturation to take place in Japan. The goal of this direction is to break down the limitations of our botanical minds and the social system that has formed them" (p. 160).

[7] A. Camus, *Selected Essays and Notebooks* (Harmondsworth, Penguin Books, 1970), 207f.

dom" and not of love, he is rather a kind of negative christic image. Nevertheless, this negative image illustrates the role of the marginal character in society and of Christ, the marginal Jew, as a figure of the divine otherness. Cultures will always tend to turn into conformist conventionality. They need the shock of foreignness to recover their human authenticity and ongoing creative dynamism. Jesus gave the culture of his days the shock of divine otherness and of eschatological newness. This is why he died, but his resurrection means, for those who follow him, the ever renewed thrust toward others and toward the Other One.

There is no going back on the theology of the local church and its consequences. Against ongoing centralizing tendencies, the nature, rights, and duties of the local church have to be upheld and defended. But a local church cannot mean a church closed on itself, bogged down in its localism. Like any other Christian reality, a church finds its identity as church *of God* only if it remains open to God's call and to the world. Attentive to God's word, it will also reach out to others, to other churches in *koinōnia*, and to the world at large in *agapē*. The theology of the local church has to open up into a theology of communion and to accept the challenge of prophetic confrontation. A church's efforts at cultural authenticity must be responsive to the alterity of other people and to the otherness of the Most Holy.

Cultures are plural and they must relate together accepting their complementarity: this is the challenge of *communion*. They are ambivalent and they must accept being confronted by the holiness of God: this is the challenge of *prophetism*. They are subject to human limitations and they have to look beyond at the fullness of times, facing the *eschatological* challenge.

INCARNATION IN THE POWER OF THE SPIRIT

These provisos being expressed, "the last word when all is said" remains that cultures are the most precious treasure of humanity. Like the heavens in the psalm, they proclaim the glory of God and the greatness of the human being. Not only are they great; they are indispensable. They are not just a garb for faith: they are the necessary means of its incarnation. There can be no truly lived faith apart from its actualization in a culture. There has never been any time when the pure Word of God was heard in the world without being embodied in a cultural background. When God reveals himself to Moses, he says: "I am the ʾelohim of your fathers, the God of Abraham, Isaac, and Jacob" (Exod. 3:6). Thereby he makes a double cultural connection. First by qualifying himself as ʾelohim, he refers to the Western Semites' belief in the divine principle ʾEl and he assumes it. Second, by evoking the "fathers," he situates his revelation in the context of a long history of peregrinations in the various lands of the Fertile Crescent and of partaking in their cultures. And in Jesus, the Word took the flesh of the Galilean Jewish subculture of an eastern Mediterranean peasant.

In this world there is no disincarnated word or Word, and culture is the incarnation of the word. We often hear the complaint that Christianity has been too much westernized. The blame is laid on Greek rationalism, Latin legalism, medieval feudalism, monarchical absolutism, or imperial triumphalism for all the present evils of institutionalism, hierarchical clericalism, abstract notionalism, and so on, in today's churches. Salvation would consist in a return to the early church, to the purity of biblical origins, to the simplicity of the Gospel and the pristine authenticity of the Jesus movement. It is true that one has always to return to the sources the better to perceive deviations and detect losses of vitality. But the clock cannot be set back. Only novels know of time machines reversing the tide of the centuries. The myth of a return to the golden age is more pagan than Christian. Christ did not leave his disciples with a promise to lead them back to the Garden of Eden. He sent them to Galilee (Mark 16:7), to the world of humble tasks, trials, sickness, sorrows, which he had encountered in his ministry, and to the hopes, struggles, and expectations of common folk. He promised them his Spirit, the Spirit that makes all things new. The way of the disciple is not that of a return to green pastures. The disciple looks ahead "with the eyes fixed on the One who, from the beginning, has been our leader in faith and will bring it to plenitude" (Heb. 12:2).

Up to now, the Christian movement has taken shape in a Latin, Greek, or Syrian environment and has found expression through their cultures. These cultures, like any culture, were not immune from ambivalence and negative aspects. They had also their values. Anyway, the solution does not consist in an impossible return to a pure virginal past that never existed. If the Christian movement has been overly westernized, the remedy to this outcome of history will not be found in a return to Semitic origins but in a greater fidelity to the power of the Spirit. The Spirit opens the Christian faith more and more to the widening world of the five continents and to their old and newly emerging cultures, subcultures, and countercultures. The Spirit inspires the churches to listen more attentively to the many voices, so far unheeded of the south and of the east. They may be voices telling the glory of world-famous cultures. They may also be voices shouting the revolt of the poor and denouncing the oppressive aspects of dominating cultures. This encounter of the gospel message with old and new cultures is a meeting of the Spirit with the Spirit, of the Spirit "that speaks to the churches" (Rev. 2:29; 3:6, 13, 22) with the Spirit that fills the universe (Wis. 1:7). Thus is the Word called to continue to grow as it did in the early church (Acts 6:7; 12:24; 19:20) and indeed from the very first day when it came into the world.

General Bibliography of Essential Sources on Inculturation

Amalorpavadass, D. S. (ed.). *Research Seminar on Non-Biblical Scriptures.* Bangalore: National Biblical Catechetical and Liturgical Centre, 1975.

Beauchamp, P., et al. *Bible and Inculturation.* Inculturation Series 3. Rome: Gregorian University, 1983.

Biblical Commission. *Foi et Culture à la Lumière de la Bible.* Turin: LDC, 1981.

Ceresko, A. R. *The Old Testament: A Liberation Perspective.* Maryknoll, N.Y.: Orbis Books, 1992.

————. *Psalmists and Sages: Studies in Old Testament Poetry and Religion.* Indian Theological Studies Supplements 2. Bangalore: St Peter's Pontifical Institute Publications, 1994.

Cox, M. A. "Inculturation and the Bible." *East Asian Pastoral Review* 30 (1993): 202-217.

Crollius, A. A. R. (ed.). The Series Inculturation. Working Papers on Living Faith and Cultures. Rome: Gregorian University.

Deissmann, A. *Light from the Ancient East.* 1927. Reprint, Grand Rapids: Baker Book House, 1965.

Dumais, R. "La Rencontre de la Foi et des Cultures." *Lumière et Vie* 153 (1981): 72-86.

Gottwald, N. K. *The Hebrew Bible.* Philadelphia: Fortress Press, 1987.

Hillman, E. "Inculturation." In *The New Dictionary of Theology,* ed. J. A. Komonchak, M. Collins, and D. A. Lane, 510-513. New York: M. Glazier, 1987.

Indian Missiological Review. "Inculturation: Celebrating a-God-with-us." 19, no. 1 (1997).

Luzbetak, L. J. *The Church and Cultures—New Perspectives in Missiological Anthropology.* Maryknoll, N.Y.: Orbis Books, 1988.

Menamparampil, T. *The Challenge of Cultures: Cross-cultural Relationships, Conflicts, Inculturation.* Bombay: St Pauls, 1996.

Mulder, M. J. *Miqra.* Amsterdam: Van Gorcum, 1989.

Schürer, E. *The History of the Jewish People in the Age of Jesus Christ (175 B.C.–A.D. 135).* Revised and edited by G. Vermes, F. Millar, and M. Goodman. Edinburgh: T & T Clark, 1986.

Shorter, A. *Towards a Theology of Inculturation.* London: Chapman, 1988.

Soares-Prabhu, G. "The New Testament as a Model of Inculturation." *Jeevadhara* 33 (1976): 268-282.

Stuhlmuller, C. *Biblical Foundations for the Mission.* Maryknoll, N.Y.: Orbis Books, 1983. [Especially pp. 36-54, 114-135, and *passim;* see index on "acculturation," p. 366.]

Tanner, K. *Theories of Culture: A New Agenda for Theology.* Minneapolis: Fortress Press, 1997.

Index of Ancient Sources

General Index

Abraham: as archetype of faith response, 61, 64; call of, 62-63, 65; migration of, 64-65; as paradigmatic figure, 61-65; promise of land to, 65

acculturation: as distinct from assimilation, 58n. 74; Paul and, 145. *See also* enculturation; inculturation

African Synod of 1994, xii

Albertz, R., 47

Albright, W. F., 42

Aletti, J. N., 154

Alexander Janneus, 93

Alexander Polyhistor, 52

allegory: distinguished from parable, 108-9

Alt, Albrecht, 19-20

Amarna Letters, 5, 20

ʿam ha-ʾarets, 100, 103, 111. *See also* "People of the Land"

Amos, book of, 28-32, 46

angels: belief of Pharisees in, 93

anti-Semitism, Christian, 75-76

apocalyptic expectations, 71

Aramaic, Palestinian: as language of Jesus, 77-79

archaeology: and Canaanite monarchs, 22; and city of Jerusalem, 20; and Dead Sea Scrolls, 76; in Egypt, 128-29; and first-century Judaism, 76; and Galilee, 98; and Jerusalem temple, 12; and law codes, 9-10; and Pauline writings, 128-29; and settlement of Israel, 7

Areopagus speech: and letter to the Colossians, 159-61

Aristeas, 52, 56, 57

Aristobulus, 52, 56, 57

Ark of the Covenant, 12

Artapanus, 52, 57

Asian Synod of 1998, xii

Assyrian laws, 9-10

Barclay, J. M. G., 57-58

Betz, H. D., 130

Bible: attitude of, toward surrounding cultures, 1; kingship in, 23-24

Bonsirven, J., 115-16

Book of the Covenant, 10

Bultmann, R., 130, 165

Canaan: Israel and, 3-17; monarchs of, 21-23

Canaanites, 4

Cazelles, H., 44

Ceresko, A. R., 6n. 11

Christ of faith, 74

Code of Hammurapi, 9, 10

Colossae: setting of, 155

Colossians, letter to, 152-62; and Areopagus speech, 159-61; authorship of, 152-53; cosmic overtones in, 158-59; cosmic powers in, 156; crisis or heresy of, 153-55; Gnosticism and, 159; Middle Platonism and, 158-59; "opponents" in, 153; *plērōma* in, 156-58; setting of, 154-55; Stoicism and, 158-59

conquest: of Canaan, 4, 7

contextualization, xv, 11, 111

cosmic theology, 161-62

countercultures: significance of, 170-71

Crossan, John Dominic, 105

"crowd," 94-95

cult: of ancient Israel, 12; Jewish, in time of Jesus, 79-80

culture: anthropology and, xiii-xiv; biblical attitude toward, 69-70; consecrated value of, 69; intercultural openness and, 172-74; law and, 118-20; meaning of the term, xiii-xv, 73; relativity of, 70

Cynics, 105

Dalit (outcastes), xv n. 15

David: and history of Jerusalem, 20-21

Davidic dynasty, 44

Davies, W. D., 83, 118

Dead Sea Scrolls, 76, 85, 116